PLOTINUS

ENNEAD IV.4.30–45 and IV.5

THE *ENNEADS* OF PLOTINUS
With Philosophical Commentaries

Series Editors: John M. Dillon, Trinity College, Dublin and Andrew Smith, University College, Dublin

Also Available in the Series:

Ennead IV.3–4.29: Problems Concerning the Soul
by John M. Dillon and J. H. Blumenthal

Ennead IV.8: On the Descent of the Soul Into Bodies
by Barrie Fleet

Ennead V.5: That the Intelligibles are not External to Intellect, and on the Good
by Lloyd P. Gerson

Ennead VI.4 & VI.5: On the Presence of Being, One and the Same, Everywhere as a Whole
by Eyjólfur Emilsson and Steven Strange

Forthcoming Titles in the Series include:

Ennead I.2: On Virtues by Suzanne Stern-Gillet

Ennead I.6: On Beauty by Andrew Smith

Ennead II.4: On Matter by Anthony A. Long

Ennead II.5: On What Exists Potentially and What Actually
by Cinzia Arruzza

Ennead II.9: Against the Gnostics
by Sebastian Ramon Philipp Gertz

Ennead III.8: On Nature and Contemplation
by George Karamanolis

Ennead IV.7: On the Immortality of the Soul
by Barrie Fleet

Ennead V.1: On the Three Primary Levels of Reality
by Eric D. Perl

Ennead V.8: On Intelligible Beauty
by Andrew Smith

Ennead VI.8: On Free Will and the Will of the One
by Kevin Corrigan and John D. Turner

PLOTINUS

ENNEAD IV.4.30–45 and IV.5

Problems concerning the Soul

Translation with an Introduction and Commentary

GARY M. GURTLER, SJ

PARMENIDES PUBLISHING

Las Vegas | Zurich | Athens

PARMENIDES PUBLISHING
Las Vegas | Zurich | Athens

This edition published in 2015 by Parmenides Publishing
in the United States of America

ISBN soft cover: 978-1-930972-69-8
ISBN e-Book: 978-1-930972-72-8

Library of Congress Cataloging-in-Publication Data

Plotinus.
[Ennead. Selections. English]
Ennead IV.4.30-45 and IV.5 : problems concerning the soul / Plotinus ; translation with an introduction and commentary Gary M. Gurtler, SJ.
pages cm. -- (The Enneads of Plotinus with philosophical commentaries)
Includes bibliographical references and index.
ISBN 978-1-930972-69-8 (pbk. : alk. paper) -- ISBN 978-1-930972-72-8 (ebook)
1. Plotinus. Enneads IV, 4.30-45. 2. Plotinus. Ennead. V, 5. 3. Soul--Early works to 1800. 4. One (The One in philosophy)--Early works to 1800. I. Gurtler, Gary M., 1947- II. Plotinus. Enneads. IV, 4.30-45. English. III. Plotinus. Ennead. V, 5. English. IV. Title.
B693.E52E5 2015b
186'.4--dc23

2015004026

Photo credit for Gary M. Gurtler, SJ: John Siberski, SJ

Typeset in Janson Text & Frutiger by Parmenides Publishing
Printed and lay-flat bound by Edwards Brothers Malloy
www.edwardsbrothersmalloy.com

www.parmenides.com

In memoriam

W. Norris Clarke, SJ

1915–2008

Ζακχαῖε, σπεύσας κατάβηθι,

σήμερον γὰρ ἐν τῷ οἴκῳ σου δεῖ με μεῖναι.

—*Luke, 19: 5*

Contents

Introduction to the Series With a Brief Outline of the Life and Thought of Plotinus (205–270 AD)

Plotinus was born in 205 ad in Egypt of Greek-speaking parents. He attended the philosophical schools in Alexandria where he would have studied Plato (427–347 BC), Aristotle (384–322 BC), the Stoics and Epicureans as well as other Greek philosophical traditions. He began his serious philosophical education, however, relatively late in life, at the age of twenty-seven and was deeply impressed by the Platonist Ammonius Saccas about whom we, unfortunately, know very little, but with whom Plotinus studied for some eleven years. Even our knowledge of Plotinus' life is limited to what we can glean from Porphyry's introduction to his edition of his philosophical treatises, an account colored by Porphyry's own concerns. After completing his studies in Alexandria Plotinus attempted, by joining a military expedition of the Roman emperor Gordian III, to make contact with the Brahmins in order to learn something of Indian thought. Unfortunately Gordian was defeated and killed (244). Plotinus somehow managed to extract himself and we next hear of him in Rome where he was able to set up a school of philosophy in the house of a high-ranking Roman lady by the name of Gemina. It is, perhaps, surprising that he had no formal contacts with the Platonic Academy in Athens, which was headed at the time by Longinus, but Longinus was familiar with his work, partly at least through Porphyry who had studied in Athens. The fact that it was Rome where Plotinus set up his school may be due to the originality of his philosophical activity and to his patrons. He clearly had some influential contacts, not least with the philhellenic emperor Gallienus (253–268), who may also have encouraged his later failed attempt to set up a civic community based on Platonic principles in a ruined city in Campania.

Plotinus' school was, like most ancient schools of philosophy, relatively small in scale, but did attract distinguished students from abroad and from the Roman upper classes. It included not only philosophers but also politicians and members of the medical profession who wished to lead the philosophical life. His most famous student was Porphyry (233–305) who, as a relative latecomer to the school, persuaded him to put into writing the results of his seminars. It is almost certain that we possess most, if not all, of his written output, which represents his mature thought, since he didn't commence writing until the age of forty-eight. The school seemingly had inner and outer circles, and Plotinus himself was clearly an inspiring and sympathetic teacher who took a deep interest in the philosophical and spiritual progress of his students. Porphyry tells us that when he was suffering from severe depression Plotinus straight away visited him in his lodgings to help him. His concern for others is also illustrated by the fact that he was entrusted with the personal education of many orphans and the care of their property and careers. The reconciliation of this worldly involvement with the encouragement to lead a life of contemplation is encapsulated in Porphyry's comment that "he was present to himself and others at the same time."

The *Enneads* of Plotinus is the edition of his treatises arranged by his pupil Porphyry who tried to put shape to the collection he had inherited by organizing it into six sets of nine treatises (hence the name "*Enneads*") that led the reader through the levels of Plotinus' universe, from the physical world to Soul, Intellect and, finally, to the highest principle, the One. Although Plotinus undoubtedly had a clearly structured metaphysical system by the time he began committing himself to expressing his thought in written form, the treatises themselves are not systematic expositions, but rather explorations of particular themes and issues raised in interpreting Plato and other philosophical texts read in the School. In fact, to achieve his neat arrangement Porphyry was sometimes driven even to dividing certain treatises (e.g., II.2–3; IV.3–5, and VI.4–5).

Although Plotinus' writings are not transcripts of his seminars, but are directed to the reader, they do, nevertheless, convey the sort of lively debate that he encouraged in his school. Frequently he takes for granted that a particular set of ideas is already familiar as having been treated in an earlier seminar that may or may not be found in the written text. For this reason it is useful for the reader to have some idea of the main philosophical principles of his system as they can be extracted from the *Enneads* as a whole.

Plotinus regarded himself as a faithful interpreter of Plato whose thought lies at the core of his entire project. But Plato's thought, whilst definitive, does according to Plotinus require careful exposition and clarification, often in the light of other thinkers such as Aristotle and the Stoics. It is because of this creative application of different traditions of ancient thought to the interpretation of Plato that Plotinus' version of Platonism became, partly through the medium of later Platonists such as Porphyry, Iamblichus (245–325), and Proclus (412–485), an influential source and way of reading both Plato and Aristotle in the Middle Ages, the Renaissance, and up to the early 19th century, when scholars first began to differentiate Plato and "Neoplatonism." His thought, too, provided early Christian theologians of the Latin and particularly of the Byzantine tradition, with a rich variety of metaphysical concepts with which to explore and express difficult doctrinal ideas. His fashioning of Plato's ideas into a consistent metaphysical structure, though no longer accepted as a uniquely valid way of approaching Plato, was influential in promoting the notion of metaphysical systems in early modern philosophy. More recently increasing interest has centered on his exploration of the self, levels of consciousness, and his expansion of discourse beyond the levels of normal ontology to the examination of what lies both above and beneath being. His thought continues to challenge us when confronted with the issue of man's nature and role in the universe and of the extent and limitations of human knowledge.

Whilst much of Plotinus' metaphysical structure is recognizably an interpretation of Plato it is an interpretation that is not always immediately obvious just because it is filtered through several centuries of developing Platonic thought, itself already overlaid with important concepts drawn from other schools. It is, nevertheless, useful as a starting point to see how Plotinus attempts to bring coherence to what he believed to be a comprehensive worldview expressed in the Platonic dialogues. The Platonic Forms are central. They become for him an intelligible universe that is the source and model of the physical universe. But aware of Aristotle's criticism of the Platonic Forms as lifeless causes he takes on board Aristotle's concept of god as a self-thinker to enable him to identify this intelligible universe as a divine Intellect that thinks itself as the Forms or Intelligibles. The doctrine of the Forms as the thoughts of god had already entered Platonism, but not as the rigorously argued identity that Plotinus proposed. Moreover the Intelligibles, since they are identical with Intellect, are themselves actively intellectual; they are intellects. Thus Plato's world of Forms has become a complex and dynamic intelligible universe in which unity and plurality, stability, and activity are reconciled.

Now although the divine Intellect is one it also embraces plurality, both because its thoughts, the Intelligibles, are many and because it may itself be analyzed into thinker and thought. Its unity demands a further principle, which is the cause of its unity. This principle, which is the cause of all unity and being but does not possess unity or being in itself, he calls the One, an interpretation of the Idea of the Good in Plato's *Republic* that is "beyond being" and that may be seen as the simple (hence "one") source of all reality. We thus have the first two of what subsequently became known as the three Hypostases, the One, Intellect, and Soul, the last of which acts as an intermediary between the intelligible and physical universes. This last Hypostasis takes on all the functions of transmitting form and life that may be found in Plato, although Plato himself does not always make such a clear distinction between soul and intellect. Thus the One is the ultimate source of all, including this universe, which is then prefigured in Intellect and transmitted through Soul to become manifest as our physical universe. Matter, which receives imperfectly this expression, is conceived not as an independently existing counter-principle, a dangerously dualist notion, but is in a sense itself a product of the One, a kind of non-being that, while being nothing specific in itself, nevertheless is not simply not there.

But this procession from an ultimate principle is balanced by a return movement at each level of reality that fully constitutes itself only when it turns back in contemplation of its producer. And so the whole of reality is a dynamic movement of procession and return, except for matter, which has no life of its own to make this return; it is inert. This movement of return, which may be traced back to the force of "love" in Plato or Aristotle's final cause, is characterized by Plotinus as a cognitive activity, a form of contemplation, weaker at each successive level, from Intellect through discursive reasoning to the merest image of rational order as expressed in the objects of the physical universe.

The human individual mirrors this structure to which we are all related at each level. For each of us has a body and soul, an intellect, and even something within us that relates to the One. While it is the nature of soul to give life to body, the higher aspect of our soul also has aspirations toward intellect, the true self, and even beyond. This urge to return corresponds to the cosmic movement of return.

But the tension between soul's natural duty to body and its origins in the intelligible can be, for the individual, a source of fracture and alienation in which the soul becomes over-involved and overwhelmed by the body and so estranged from its true self. Plotinus encourages us to make the return or ascent, but at the same time attempts to resolve the conflict of duties by reconciling the two-fold nature of soul as life-giving and contemplative.

This is the general framework within which important traditional philosophical issues are encountered, discussed and resolved, but always in a spirit of inquiry and ongoing debate. Issues are frequently encountered in several different contexts, each angle providing a different insight. The nature of the soul and its relationship to the body is examined at length (IV) using the Aristotelian distinctions of levels of soul (vegetative, growth, sensitive, rational) whilst maintaining the immortal nature of the transcendent soul in Platonic terms. The active nature of the soul in sense-perception is maintained to preserve the principle that incorporeals cannot be affected by corporeal reality. A vigorous discussion (VI.4 and 5) on the general nature of the relationship of incorporeals to body explores in every detail and in great depth the way in which incorporeals act on body. A universe that is the product of design is reconciled with the freedom of the individual. And, not least, the time-bound nature of the physical universe and human reason is grounded in the life of Intellect, which subsists in eternity. Sometimes, however, Plotinus seems to break outside the framework of traditional metaphysics: the nature of matter and the One, each as non-being, though in a different sense, strains the terminology and structure of traditional ontology; and the attempt to reconcile the role of the individual soul within the traditional Platonic distinction of transcendent and immanent reality leads to a novel exploration of the nature of the self, the "I."

It is this restless urge for exploration and inquiry that lends to the treatises of Plotinus their philosophical vitality. Whilst presenting us with a rich and complexly coherent system, he constantly engages us in philosophical inquiry. In this way each treatise presents us with new ideas and fresh challenges. And, for Plotinus, every philosophical engagement is not just a mental exercise but also contributes to the rediscovery of the self and our reintegration with the source of all being, the Platonic aim of "becoming like god."

While Plotinus, like Plato, always wishes to engage his audience to reflect for themselves, his treatises are not easy reading, partly no doubt because his own audience was already familiar with many of his basic ideas and, more importantly, had been exposed in his seminars to critical readings of philosophical texts that have not survived to our day. Another problem is that the treatises do not lay out his thought in a systematic way but take up specific issues, although always the whole system may be discerned in the background. Sometimes, too, the exact flow of thought is difficult to follow because of an often condensed mode of expression.

Because we are convinced that Plotinus has something to say to us today, we have launched this series of translations and commentaries as a means of opening up the text to readers with an interest in grappling with the philosophical issues revealed by an encounter with Plotinus' own words and arguments. Each volume will contain a new translation, careful summaries of the arguments and structure of the treatise, and a philosophical commentary that will aim to throw light on the philosophical meaning and import of the text.

John M. Dillon
Andrew Smith

Abbreviations

DK	1951–1952. *Die Fragmente der Vorsokratiker.* Edited by H. Diels and W. Kranz. Berlin: Weidmann.
Dox Gr	1965. *Doxographi Graeci.* Edited by H. Diels, 4th edition. Berlin: De Gruyter.
HS_2	1964–1982. *Plotini Opera.* Edited by P. Henry, SJ and H.-R. Schwyzer, Vol. 1–3. Oxford: Clarendon Press (*Editio Minor*).
L-S	1958. *A Greek-English Lexicon.* H. Liddell & R. Scott, 9th edition revised by H. Jones. Oxford: Clarendon Press.
SVF	1905–1924. *Stoicorum Veterum Fragmenta.* Edited by H. von Arnim. Leipzig: Teubner.

Acknowledgments

I am grateful to John Dillon and Andrew Smith for their invitation to be part of this important series translating the *Enneads* of Plotinus. They have been most generous with encouragement and advice about all the facets of the project, but especially the translation and commentary. I am grateful as well to Gale Carr and the editorial staff at Parmenides Press for their excellent work in bringing the final version to production. I also want to acknowledge the support of Boston College in awarding me a sabbatical for the academic year 2012–2013, providing the leisure needed to sink into the intricacies of Plotinus' Greek and emerge with a modicum of clarity about his meaning.

Introduction to the Treatise

THE THIRD AND LAST PART OF "Problems concerning the Soul" takes up the final three problems or *aporiai* of this remarkable treatise, in which the insights of the first two parts are applied to specific issues, the influence of the planets and the attendant problems of their memory and cooperation with evil in IV.4.30–39, the possible benefits and harms to different souls in IV.4.40–45, and then the nature of vision and light in IV.5.1–8.

In the first part, IV.3.1–IV.4.5, Plotinus dealt with the nature of the soul, its unity and multiplicity, and human souls' entrance into, presence in, and departure from the body. The departure of soul from body raises the question of memory in the soul, which Plotinus analyzes in terms of a double imagination and memory that are restricted to the human soul while in the body. In the second part, IV.4.6–29, Plotinus argues that other souls, of the stars, the Demiurge and the cosmos, do not have memory, and turns back to the human soul to examine its affections, pleasures and pains, appetites and angers, with brief mention of the presence of soul in the earth and the presence of vegetative, sensitive and intellective souls in living things. Finally, in the third part, Plotinus addresses two specific questions raised in the middle part but left for later analysis: whether the planets have memory, since their answers to prayers often seem delayed (from IV.4.6–8 and 25–26), and whether a medium is needed for sight (from IV.4.23). While these issues indicate the structural connections of these last two sections to the previous part, they occlude the thematic unity of this last part in terms of sympathy, which these particular issues only serve to occasion.

Emphasizing these structural connections has, however, affected the appreciation of the unity and coherence of the argument in these final sections. In particular, IV.4.30–45 has suffered from a neglect of the astronomical and astrological background as setting the stage for Plotinus' elucidation of the cosmos as a living thing of great complexity, while IV.5.1–8 has been generally taken as a series of doxographical fragments and unrelated problems gathered and appended to the treatise as a whole. Careful study and more exact translation reveal an argument in both sections that is more rigorous and coherent, with the sympathy of the cosmos as the major idea that joins the two sections together and explains their relation to the earlier parts of the treatise. In addition, the role of sympathy depends on Plotinus' principle of two acts as the means by which one part of the cosmos can influence another, whether it be the benefits of the planets and stars toward things on earth or the possibility of sensing at a distance.

Plotinus also relies on extra-philosophical sources, the astronomical and astrological works of Ptolemy (c. AD 90–168) as well as the medical treatises of Galen (AD 131–201/216). Scholars may not be interested in the intricacies of Hellenistic astrology, but in a way neither is Plotinus. His goal is not to give philosophical support to such practices, but to render them harmless by reducing their esoteric claims to the ordinary operation of human skill taking advantage of powers ready to hand in Nature. Similarly, Plotinus uses the advances in understanding the senses and nervous system contained in the writings of Galen to clarify more carefully the operation of the senses, though he does not hesitate to emend Galen's account when he feels philosophically justified.

Several factors may assist the reader's access to the issues underlying this section of the treatise on the soul. First, the edifice of his account is built on the nature of the cosmos as a single living thing. Second, his principle of two acts is at the center of his explanation for action at a distance. Third, the operation of sympathy allows this action to explain planetary influence as well as sight and hearing. Fourth, some familiarity with ancient astronomy and astrology helps situate the context of his discussion and its implications for moral responsibility. Fifth, sensitivity to his analogies and metaphors can clarify a proper translation and indicate elements of Plotinus' method for philosophizing.

A Single Living Thing

IV.4.30–39 presents the **Sixth Problem: The Influence of Planets, Their Memory and Cooperation in Evil**. Plotinus' argument rests on the assumption that the cosmos is a single living thing, which we can trace back to Plato's *Timaeus* 30d–31a1. The unity of the cosmos as a living thing explains how the different parts can relate to one another and to the whole, both parts on earth and parts in heaven. To make this work, however, Plotinus employs several supplementary ideas. From Plato's *Laws* 889a–d, he borrows the different ways in which Nature and craft operate—Nature generating the four elements and their qualities with their mixtures producing the rich variety of corporeal things in the heavens and on earth, while crafts produce articles that by comparison are little more than toys, or merely cooperate with Nature. This distinction specifies the activities characteristic of agents in the cosmos, highlighting the perfection of the cosmic soul and those stellar souls most like it. Human souls, by contrast, share in this capacity to produce in a much more limited way, a key element in Plotinus' account.

The sympathy of the Stoics adds to the agency of these cosmic beings their further interaction with one another, especially as one affects another. For the Stoics, of course, sympathy functions within a materialistic understanding of the cosmos, so Plotinus transforms sympathy into a manifestation of the power of soul to care for and unite the cosmos affectively. Sympathy sets up a relationship between parts of the cosmos in which the action of one part has influence on another part that is in some way similar to it. This move to affection (*pathos*) allows Plotinus to distinguish this influence from doing or making and to introduce the asymmetry of affections that may be harmful as well as beneficial. It is also essential for explaining action at a distance, since the influence or affection produced by an agent is received by the recipient even when separated by cosmic distances, as long as what is in between does not block the affection and is not itself affected. Plotinus, having set out the principles of the self-sympathetic single living thing and its reliance on the two acts and sympathy, ends by listing the ways they resolve the problem of stellar complicity in evil by appealing to the complexity of the cosmos. In particular, the planets can give signs of things on earth but do not actually cause them and what they do cause is always beneficial, but the recipient may be affected adversely because of the resistance of its matter and additions attributable to its choices.

The Principle of Two Acts

IV.4.40–45 in turn presents the **Seventh Problem: The Susceptibility of Souls to Benefit and Harm.**

Plotinus uses in this context, and indeed throughout this part of the treatise, the principle of two acts, which also traces back to Plato, especially passages like *Timaeus* 29e1–3, where the goodness of the Demiurge is free of jealousy and is shared as fully as possible with its products, or the *Symposium*, where the jealousy of the gods in Aristophanes' myth (190b–c) is contrasted with their generosity in Diotima's account of beauty (211a–b). Plotinus' application of this principle in the present treatise involves a number of complex permutations. In IV.4.30–45, the sun serves as the prime example of a being with two acts. The first act is that by which the sun is itself, the fire that constitutes the very essence of the sun as a fiery body (as defined in IV.5.7, 33). The second act that flows out from this primal act appears, in fact, as three different acts, its light, life, and heat (IV.4.29, 1–55). Light and life are second acts that flow out incorporeally and go directly to their objects, while heat seems to move corporeally from its source to the object. The recipients of these acts, moreover, receive them in diverse ways. Light washes over the surface of a body and departs from that surface as soon as the source of light moves on. Warmth, by contrast, penetrates a body and may remain for some length of time after the source of warmth is gone. Life, as the presence of soul, remains independent like light, but its effect on the body penetrates more deeply than warmth, giving the body the motions of a living thing and occasionally lingering briefly after the soul as source of life departs.

It is Plotinus' claim that these second acts of the heavenly bodies are constant and beneficial, rooted in their perfect and divine nature. Any harmful effects, therefore, must be on the side of the recipients in terms of their material substrate or the additions they make, especially in the case of human beings by their choices. Some of these harmful effects derive from human crafts, using these beneficial powers in the operations of Nature in evil ways. Plotinus argues that the harm of these effects is limited in scope. In the case of the heavenly bodies, they are immune from harm in soul and in body, since their bodies have a perfection that minimizes any harm and their souls have a concentration on the intelligible that is immune to distraction. The human body is not so fortunate, since its composition is susceptible to harm by Nature and by craft. The soul, however, if properly directed to the intelligible, remains immune and free of the effects of magic and other evils. Since the cosmos, moreover, is a single living thing, any evil done will be pursued with the force of justice, and the evil effects will be purified with relentless care. This section then applies the results of the previous problem to the different ways in which souls, as present in the cosmos to planets, daemons, and humans, are susceptible to this sympathetic interaction, whether for good or for ill, with a discussion of the activities of the human soul that introduce the way in which sages can keep their souls immune from both harmful influence and evil action in contrast to the dominance of external influences on the souls of evildoers. Magic is here identified with the work of Nature in turning a soul, specifically human souls and daemons, toward sensible things rather than keeping them focused on the intelligible world where their origin and identity are found.

Sympathy and Vision

In IV.4.32, 13–22, Plotinus assumes that similar parts of a living thing can be affected even when separated by parts in between that are unaffected and discontinuous, but in IV.5.1–8 this lack of affection becomes the crucial issue, indicating the **Eighth Problem: The Nature of Vision and Light**. In the context of sensation, he argues against both the Aristotelian notion that the transparent body needs to be actualized by the illumination of light in order to see as well as the Platonic theory that the visual ray coming from the eye needs to join daylight to arrive at the object of sight. Curiously, Plotinus appeals to the obvious fact that we can see at night to question the hypotheses of his predecessors. Plato's *Timaeus* actually states that when the sun sets, human beings are no longer able to see and thus are induced to sleep, a consequence that Socrates and his companions in several dialogues seem quite capable of resisting. In the case of Aristotle, however, he argues that the transparent body is essentially dark, with the activity of light, any light, more or less able to overcome it. Both theories require transmission through the intervening body for the visual object to be seen by the eye, but Plotinus counters, on the basis of the principle of two acts, that the activity of the visual object allows it to be seen at a distance without the necessity of affecting the intervening body at all. The principle of two acts, moreover, has one of its clearest and most complete articulations in IV.5.6–7, which is also explicitly related to his assumption that the cosmos is a single living thing in sympathy with itself.

Astronomy and Astrology

For a proper understanding of IV.4.30–45, some familiarity with ancient astronomy and astrology are important. Plotinus relies on the writings of Ptolemy, which include the mathematical calculations that explain the apparent motions of the planets and which then present the astrological theory detailing how the different positions of the planets influence human events. Ptolemy is concerned with the seven planets, Sun, Moon, Mercury, Venus, Mars, Jupiter and Saturn, that are at the center of astrological theory. Plotinus accepts the accuracy of Ptolemy's astronomical calculations and focuses his attack on the astrological application which follows in his text. This attack has several facets. Plotinus disputes the association of certain planets with one rather than another of the four humors, hot, cold, wet, and dry. His reason is that the heavenly bodies are in fact composed of a single element, fire, which precludes them from having qualities like wet and cold associated with the other elements that compose things in the sub-lunar world. He also indicates that the elements and their associated qualities cannot directly influence living things and their characters, building on Aristotle's account that the soul moves the elements within living things contrary to their natural motions (*De Anima* 2.4.416a6–9).

In addition, the more distant one's character or the events of fortune are from direct corporeal contact, the more unlikely is the kind of elemental influence at the center of astrological theory. While this attack on astrology no doubt seems reasonable, Plotinus' acceptance of Ptolemy's astronomy may still seem unwarranted to modern readers. It is important to note, however, that Ptolemy's calculations, as the synthesis of ancient astronomical observation and theory, have a high degree of accuracy in describing the apparent motions of the heavenly bodies, especially the planets. The earth, for example, is not quite at the center of this ancient cosmology, but at a slight distance from it, explainable in modern theory as due to its elliptical orbit around the sun. The system of cycles and epicycles, moreover, continues to serve for the construction of the gears controlling the movements of modern telescopes in following objects in the sky. Plotinus thus rightly accepts

Ptolemaic astronomy as a genuine science different from any astrological application as completely unscientific, even in terms of the scientific assumptions of his day.

Translation and Method

I will discuss here a few observations on translating the text, with perhaps the occasion to note some aspects of Plotinus' philosophical method. First, the current translations all take *astra* in IV.4.30–45 as referring to stars in general, the fixed sphere of stars in their constellations as well as the planets. In writing the commentary, however, it became clear that Plotinus is more exclusively concerned with the planets. This becomes obvious in this part of the treatise when he talks of the influence of the sun and planets in IV.4.31, 10–15, the discussion of those stars that move at irregular speeds in 34, 6, the denial that the sun or other planets hear prayers at 41, 1, and the conclusion mentioning the motions of sun, moon, and planets in their changing positions at 45, 39, which serves as an *inclusio* with the opening chapter, IV.4.30. It is also explicitly the case in the two other treatises where Plotinus attacks the claims of the astrologers, III.1.5–6 and II.3.2–6. Translating *astra* as planets in most instances thus makes Plotinus' purpose more accessible and the unity of this section more obvious.

There are more serious problems in the translation and analysis of IV.5. Translators and commentators have taken IV.5.2, 1–15 as a series of disconnected fragments, similar to the doxographical texts of other authors in late antiquity that they take as the source for this chapter. This overlooks, however, the rather complete report these opening lines give of the Platonic theory of vision from *Timaeus* 45b–d and 67c–68d, which Archer-Hind, 1888, 156–157, analyzes rather fully in terms of three lights that are also central here (and later in IV.5.4): the visual ray (*opsis*) going out from the eye, the daylight between that allows the visual ray to move to the object, and the light or color emitted by the object that alters the visual ray so it can report back to the eye. With this textual evidence in mind, Plotinus' project in the first chapters of IV.5 takes on a deeper clarity and unity. He is attempting to remove the role both of Aristotle's transparent body and Plato's intermediate daylight from a proper account of the nature of vision.

The Stoic and Epicurean allusions at IV.5.2, 11–15 can then be seen as different ways in which the Platonic visual ray will be interpreted in later chapters, with the Stoic impact assimilating sight to touch at IV.5.4, 39–49 and the Epicurean void capturing the hypothesis of Plotinus that light from the object can jump over the intervening space and affect the eye directly at IV.5.3, 14–15 and 6, 14–17. Both Plato and Aristotle, for different reasons, make vision dependent on sunlight, as joining with the visual ray or as activating the transparent medium, and Plotinus argues instead that vision depends on the nature of light as an activity that can function day or night as long as this light from a luminous body is not blocked or hindered in reaching the eye. Air is thus essentially dark and luminous bodies can be seen even when the intervening air or space is not itself illuminated, giving evidence of Plotinus' keen eye and rigorous logic in analyzing the phenomenon of sight.

The Stoic theory, where light is like a cane reaching to the object, is in turn used to overcome his other problem with the Platonic theory, that the visual ray goes out to the object. Plotinus indicates that this makes sight a form of touch, which has two difficulties. First, Plato makes the eye the active element in sight. It is Plotinus' conviction, however, that light is the activity coming from an object and affecting the eye directly with its form or with the forms of objects it illuminates, so that vision is passive or receptive and takes place at a distance. Second, the elimination of distance in the Platonic theory makes vision like touch, especially as analyzed in Archer-Hind, 1888, 156 and 237, where the visual ray is actually ensouled and reaches out to the object like an appendage of the eye itself. Plotinus argues, however, that touch does not convey forms directly to the knower, but the form of what is touched is known by memory and inference. This clarifies the meaning of IV.5.4, 39–49, where the touches (*hai haphai*) have invariably been rendered in the singular and the strange locution that touch depends on a prior moment of direct contact that is subsequently used by memory and reason is mangled at best. It seems fundamental, however, that images and metaphors should be simpler than the more difficult ideas they are meant to illustrate. The task thus becomes imaginatively reconstructing the image or metaphor that Plotinus has in mind. For this passage, imagining how someone blind would use a cane makes sense of the text as it is, without emendation or fanciful translation. It also reveals something intriguing about Plotinus' account of touch, that it is, oddly enough, a mediated form of sensing, unlike seeing or hearing where the form is conveyed to the organ immediately and as a whole.

The unity of IV.5.1–8, furthermore, is confirmed by a proper understanding of the problems that Plotinus sees in current accounts of seeing and hearing in IV.5.1–5, and by his own account of these two cases of sensing at a distance, which he develops in two ways. First, in IV.5.6–7, he explains light as a second activity that always remains dependent on the source of light as its first activity. In a counterintuitive move, Plotinus holds that light is only superficially related to the illuminated object and its color. His observation is acutely accurate, that light from the sun, or another source, never becomes part of the object illuminated but always accompanies its source. He is thus able to separate the pigment or color that belongs to the object from the light that illuminates it but remains totally separate from it. This is accomplished through the principle of two acts, which receives one of its most explicit articulations in IV.5.7. Second, in IV.5.8, Plotinus returns to the cosmos as a single living thing, an *inclusio* both of this whole third part of the treatise, "Problems concerning the Soul," and of this particular section, where he repeats the account of sensation in IV.5.1 as the way in which the soul and the object can come to a common affection on the basis of organs that establish a likeness between them. This likeness is now firmly grounded in the nature of the cosmos as a single living thing, such that any similarity between sense organs and their proper sensible objects is due to the one cosmic soul that has made all things within the cosmos and suited them for one another through its self-sympathy.

Note on the Text

LINE NUMBERS IN THE TRANSLATION are approximate and do not always match the original Greek text. Since the commentary follows the sequence of the English translation, there may sometimes be a slight discrepancy in the ordering.

The Greek text adopted is that of the Oxford edition (taking into account the Addenda ad Textum in vol. 3, 304–325). Deviations from the text are noted in the commentary. Each *Ennead* is referred to by Roman numerals, followed by the number of the treatise, the chapter of the treatise, and, finally, separated by a comma, the line number or numbers, e.g, V.1.3, 24–27.

It is customary to add the chronological number given by Porphyry in his *Life of Plotinus* (*Vita Plotini*), so that, for example, V.1 is designated V.1 [10]. In this series the chronological number is given only where it is of significance for Plotinus' philosophical stance. The following chart indicates the chronological order.

Chronological Order of the *Enneads*

Enn.		*Enn.*		*Enn.*		*Enn.*		*Enn.*		*Enn.*	
I.1	**53**	II.1	**40**	III.1	**3**	IV.1	**21**	V.1	**10**	VI.1	**42**
I.2	**19**	II.2	**14**	III.2	**47**	IV.2	**4**	V.2	**11**	VI.2	**43**
I.3	**20**	II.3	**52**	III.3	**48**	IV.3	**27**	V.3	**49**	VI.3	**44**
I.4	**46**	II.4	**12**	III.4	**15**	IV.4	**28**	V.4	**7**	VI.4	**22**
I.5	**36**	II.5	**25**	III.5	**50**	IV.5	**29**	V.5	**32**	VI.5	**23**
I.6	**1**	II.6	**17**	III.6	**26**	IV.6	**41**	V.6	**24**	VI.6	**34**
I.7	**54**	II.7	**37**	III.7	**45**	IV.7	**2**	V.7	**18**	VI.7	**38**
I.8	**51**	II.8	**35**	III.8	**30**	IV.8	**6**	V.8	**31**	VI.8	**39**
I.9	**16**	II.9	**33**	III.9	**13**	IV.9	**8**	V.9	**5**	VI.9	**9**

	Enn.		*Enn.*		*Enn.*		*Enn.*		*Enn.*		*Enn.*
1	I.6	**10**	V.1	**19**	I.2	**28**	IV.4	**37**	II.7	**46**	I.4
2	IV.7	**11**	V.2	**20**	I.3	**29**	IV.5	**38**	VI.7	**47**	III.2
3	III.1	**12**	II.4	**21**	IV.1	**30**	III.8	**39**	VI.8	**48**	III.3
4	IV.2	**13**	III.9	**22**	VI.4	**31**	V.8	**40**	II.1	**49**	V.3
5	V.9	**14**	II.2	**23**	VI.5	**32**	V.5	**41**	IV.6	**50**	III.5
6	IV.8	**15**	III.4	**24**	V.6	**33**	II.9	**42**	VI.1	**51**	I.8
7	V.4	**16**	I.9	**25**	II.5	**34**	VI.6	**43**	VI.2	**52**	II.3
8	IV.9	**17**	II.6	**26**	III.6	**35**	II.8	**44**	VI.3	**53**	I.1
9	VI.9	**18**	V.7	**27**	IV.3	**36**	I.5	**45**	III.7	**54**	I.7

Synopsis

IV.4.30–39 Sixth Problem: The Influence of Planets, Their Memory and Cooperation in Evil

Chapter 30

1–13 Problems to investigate: memory and sensing in the planets, and their complicity in evil.

14–20 Evidence for memory and sense: prayers are answered, often later; evidence for memory in Demeter and Hestia for their benefits to human affairs.

21–32 Four tasks:

(1) Apparent fact of memory as a problem peculiar to our theory.

(2) A properly philosophical defense of the gods against complicity with evil.

(3) Extension of this defense to the whole cosmos, especially against human spells.

(4) Daemons as subject to spells and involved in evil.

Chapter 31

1–3 Scope: all actions and affections in the whole cosmos, whether by Nature or by craft.

3–8 Natural actions or affections are from the All to the parts, from parts to the All or parts to parts. Those by craft are completed in the product or cooperate with natural processes.

8–15 The whole cosmos exercises influence by its celestial circuit, affecting itself and its parts, both in the heavens and on earth. For parts, the actions and affections of the sun and planets on earth and the elements are well known.

15–24 Some crafts terminate in the product, others contribute to natural processes, and others make souls better or worse. Questions: How many? What power do they have and why?

25–30 The heavenly circuit affects its celestial parts and terrestrial things, both in body and soul.

30–48 We grant common opinions if they are reasonable and need to explain how this influence works. Bodily causes cannot explained it, as based on the primary qualities of the elements, warm, cold, wet and dry, since the planets are all fiery bodies; also the characteristics of living things cannot be reduced to the qualities of their bodily components.

48–58 Choice, knowledge, or calculations of the planets or the whole cosmos are also excluded as explanations.

Chapter 32

1–4 If not bodily causes or planetary choices, then what explains the influence moving from the heavens to the earth?

4–13 (1) The world is one living thing with all living things within it. The soul of the All extends to all its parts, though some parts have souls of their own. Parts then can be completely under the soul of the All, or have some independence in terms of their own soul.

13–22 (2) The world as one living thing is sympathetic, like an animal. Similar parts can affect one another even when separated by discontinuous parts that are not affected. The unity of the whole keeps spatial distance from blocking the nearness of similar parts.

23–32 When a part and an agent are alike, they share an affection, but when they are unlike, the affection is unpleasant, and can even bring harm.

32–44 The cosmos is not only one living thing but many. As one, the parts are preserved, but as many, the self-interest of one part can harm or destroy another. Unity is seen even in this harm, since a part takes what is akin to it for its own survival.

44–52 Generation and corruption, alteration for better or worse, are all part of the unity of the whole working toward a single end. Parts are not the end and so do not exist forever nor can they remain the same; only the whole exists forever and is always the same, as its motion shows.

Chapter 33

1–7 (3) The heavenly circuit has the rationality of a living thing, producing harmony of agent toward recipient and putting its parts in array toward one another. Every position of the planets produces corresponding dispositions on earth, like the choreography of a dance.

7–25 A dance has external elements, instruments, songs, and staging. The dancer's limbs in their movements express each figure, but the dancer looks beyond these to the whole, with each part contributing to it, as a critic observes.

25–41 This is what the planets and stars do, occasionally only giving signs. The whole cosmos configures its parts, but the parts have their own positions relative to the whole and one another that produce effects accompanying that of the whole. All these occur within the whole cosmos, since it does not make anything outside itself. The figures in the heavens have affections accompanying them in living things on earth, with their own nature and internal necessity.

Chapter 34

1–7 Human beings are affected as physical parts of the cosmos, but since they do not belong to it completely, these affections are within limits, like skilled workers receiving instructions that do not remove personal initiative.

7–17 The planets run at unequal speeds, but do so rationally. Their different positions are accompanied by different affections among us, so the question arises whether the planets cause the affections, or the figures alone or with the planets. Different portents or actions seem to come from different figures and the same planet seems to have different effects in different figures.

17–26 The dispositions resulting on earth seem influenced both by the configurations and the planets, and these dispositions are at times both actions and portents, and at times only portents.

26–33 They are parallel to the dance: the configuration is like the movement of the whole dance, the planets like the limbs of the dancer, and the dispositions on earth like the tendons and veins of the hands and fingers.

Chapter 35

1–19 Astrological theory comes under closer scrutiny in the angles of the planets and the precise nature of their influence. This cannot be from their bodies or their choices, so it must come from the sympathy of the cosmos, especially in its rational nature as manifest in the fixed degrees of planetary orbits. The activity comes from the All in its figures, with the particular contribution of the planets configured into the equation and contributing to the unity of the All.

19–37 The figures are like the proportions and dimensions of the All as a living thing, while the planets are set at intervals like the limbs of the animal, with other powers lacking choice corresponding to the tendons and veins of an animal. The choice of the All is dominant but other choices are operative within it. Examples include the way that appetite, anger, growth, and generation occur in animals. The parts, like skilled workers, make their own contribution but look to the same good as the master.

37–61 The sun and planets do good for things on earth while looking to what is above them. Effects come from the sun, some are corporeal like warming, but others are transmitted by soul, especially the vegetative soul. The planets give illumination, each figure accompanied by a corresponding disposition, as is evident. Someone is frightened by a particular figure, without prior experience and without that figure frightening others; this is due to a natural relation between them, as the beauty in a face is seen by one individual but not another, or as colors are seen. If bodies or their qualities can have certain effects, why cannot the planets?

61–69 General principle: beings act or are acted upon by Nature; some just act, while others can both act and be acted upon. Human beings function like substrates, acted on but also able to act; for example, crafts use reason to make artifacts from stones, or share in natural powers to make medicines from herbs.

Chapter 36

1–15 The diversity of the All is exceptional, with rational natures and diverse powers. We are unaware of it, unless it is pointed out by experts. As medicine reveals the complexity of human anatomy, so astronomy reveals the even greater complexity of stellar motion. The cosmos is not like a lifeless house, composed from just a few things, but is everywhere awake and alive.

15–27 This solves the puzzle of how something inanimate can be alive; language restricts life to things perceptibly self-moving. If even the parts of the human body can be considered alive, the parts of the All are even more alive. They are not produced by choice, since the action of the All is more primordial than choice.

Chapter 37

1–11 Consequences: nothing of the All is disposable. The activity of any part can be explained only in terms of the All. We do not usually investigate ordinary things, but an expert's knowledge shows how amazing they are.

11–25 Ordinary things: each has an irrational power forged in the All, each somehow shares in soul, and each is surrounded by the All and is part of it. Some parts are more powerful than others, especially the clearer beings in the heavens. These powers do not need choice or awareness of their effects, since they, like the All, look to what is above them.

Chapter 38

1–7 Effects: come from the All in its different life when nothing sets it moving, but when it is set in motion, for instance, by prayers, the effects need to be examined first before attributing them to the All or planets. Beneficial effects indicate influence flowing from the better to the lesser parts of the cosmos.

7–16 Unpleasant effects, especially at the births of living things, come from the substrate's inability to receive the good. Mixtures of effects from different planets are beneficial in themselves, but may have more diverse effects in the mix. The cosmic order does not give to each what it wants, and the recipients make their own additions.

17–23 All things are woven into one and have a harmony, even things coming from opposites. If a generated thing lacks something this is due to its matter. In sum, good effects are traceable to the planets, unpleasant effects to matter or the recipient's additions.

Chapter 39

1–17 The interconnection of all things toward a single end implies all things are indicated by signs. Virtue oversees the cosmic order, as things here depend on those above and this cosmos on still higher Beings. This excludes spermatic reasons as causes, since they cause nothing beyond themselves. Higher comprehensive reasons have the power to generate things, to bring them to completion from matter and to make them active toward one another. This reason is like lawgivers in a city, who know how individuals will act and interweave them by incentives and penalties to produce a common harmony.

17–23 Signs are not predictive by design, but by the causal generation of things as one and as part of one cosmos: cause from effect, consequence from premise, composite from its parts. All things together come from the one source.

23–32 Problems resolved:

(1) The gods do not cooperate in evil: not by choice nor by activity, but by natural necessities in the parts generated within one living thing.

(2) Generated beings add things on their own.

(3) None of the planets produce evil, but in the mix something else comes about.

(4) Life is not for each part but for the whole.

(5) Underlying matter receives one thing, but is unable to master it.

IV.4.40–45 Seventh Problem: The Susceptibility of Souls to Benefit and Harm

Chapter 40

1–4 Applications:

(1) How do magic spells work?

(i) by sympathy,

(ii) by the harmony among similar things and opposition among dissimilar things,

(iii) by the diversity of the many powers contributing to the perfection of the whole.

4–9 (2) Magic works with or without contrivance:

(i) Love and Strife as the work of Nature, which human magicians only imitate.

9–27 (ii) Love's magic is a natural tendency aided by a craft, using several methods:

(a) traces of substances that bring individuals together;

(b) figures in the heavens have powers that can be induced in individuals here, as the magician brings these powers into play by spells and incantations;

(c) music and gesture attract powers, affecting the irrational parts of the soul.

27–32 (3) Prayer's efficacy is not by choice:

(i) those of us cast under spells or mesmerized by an object are affected not in the rational part of the soul, but only the lower parts;

(ii) so a planet is not affected by a spell, but an influence comes from it.

Chapter 41

1–9 (4) Prayer is not heard by the sun or a planet, but the prayer establishes a sympathy of one part with another:

(i) like a single string plucked at one end and vibrating at the other end;

(ii) like strings on separate lyres tuned together, so plucking one affects the other;

(iii) things in the All are even more completely tuned to one another.

9–15 (5) Harm can occur without the intention of the cause:

(i) anger drawn along with bile changes the liver;

(ii) like a relay race where the first player passes fire to a second, who in passing it to a third causes him injury.

Chapter 42

1–10 (6) Prayer does not need:

(i) memory and sensations transmitted from here;

(ii) assent from deliberate choice there.

This is the case since the influence comes with or without prayer, on the natural sympathy of things within a single living thing. Powers without choice are many and work by Nature or by craft. Benefit and harm come from how things are disposed to one another. Some things can be compelled to share their power by crafts, such as medicine or magic.

10–19 The All is more fundamentally available to all its parts, since none of them are alien, even if they are evil. That the All is available to evil is no cause for surprise, since it is common and follows from the nature of giving as unstinting and indiscriminate. Everything given is coordinated by justice, so those taking what they ought not are pursued relentlessly.

19–23 The parts of the All are affected differently.

(1) The All itself is unaffected. Its ruling principle is completely impassible and any affection reaching its parts does not need to reach the All since nothing in the All is counter to its nature.

23–30 (2) The planets as parts are affected, but they are unaffected in their choice and unharmed in their proper nature, so influence from their souls does not diminish them nor are their bodies harmed so there is no perception or notice of these affections.

Chapter 43

1–12 (3) The sage is unaffected in the rational part of the soul by magic or spells, so they cannot change his opinion. The sage's irrational parts can be affected. If love means assent to the affection of another, the sage is immune to drugs. If a spell is cast on the sage, the irrational part can be affected, but the sage can use counter spells. This may not ward off bodily disease or death as effects of those incantations, or another part or the All itself. Delays in effects are not a departure from nature's operation.

12–24 (4) Daemons are also not impassible in their irrational parts; memory and sensation are also not absurdly attributed to them, so being enchanted or under a spell is not impossible and is due to their own drawing too close to things here.

General Principle: one is enchanted by or subject to what one is turned to; to be free of spells is to be turned only to oneself.

(1) The practical life is inherently under a spell to the things of this life. Nature, thus, is the real magician, bringing deceit and linking one thing to another completely without any help from magicians. Contemplation alone is immune to spells.

Chapter 44

1–6 (2) Comparison of the sage and the practical man.

The sage: (i) is one,

(ii) his object of contemplation is the self,

(iii) his reason is not deceived,

(iv) his own life is his task, doing what he ought.

The practical man:

(i) his task is not There,

(ii) reason is not his impulse,

(iii) his principle is irrational and his premises are the passions.

6–16 (3) Nature's natural inclination or magical deceit:

(i) children and marriage vs. pleasures,

(ii) anger vs. political action and office,

(iii) proper fear vs. excessive greed

(iv) filling in Nature's gaps and the inclination to preserve life.

16–24 (4) Objection:

(i) beautiful actions are immune from spells,

(ii) contemplation is subject to spells.

Reply: (1) If beautiful actions are done only as necessary, they are immune to spells. One is not looking to the effect nor turned to anything other than oneself, but is moved by the force of human nature and the natural inclination to preserve one's own life or another's. Suicide in fact is to be under a spell.

25–37 (2) If beautiful actions are themselves the source of delight, their traces of beauty cast a spell. This is to be deceived by Nature's magic: seeking as good what is not good and following irrational impulses.

(3) Only someone who denies that what his other parts say is good and keeps to what he knows and has already grasped as good is not drawn anywhere else.

Chapter 45

1–10 Conclusion: each thing contributes to the All, in the same way that parts of an animal contribute to its perfection, render service, and consent to their positions. Parts have a kind of consciousness toward the whole and if each were an animal it would have its own function.

10–26 The human situation includes not only our presence as bodies but also our other nature, the soul, with innate powers and connections. On the one hand, we cannot share what we do not have, the good, but, on the other hand, we could not receive any good without a capacity for it. This ambiguity explains how some can be evil, and are dragged to their fate, while others are good, give like higher beings, to which they remain connected as if by strings, like puppets.

27–52 The order of the All is wonderful, the silent work of justice. Those who pay no attention to justice are led unknowingly to their fate, but the good recognize justice and depart with hope for divine companionship. Reversing the image that begins the chapter, parts in small animals have little consciousness and remain alive only briefly, if at all, but in the vastness of the All, the parts have a life of their own, not only heavenly bodies but human beings. As these heavenly bodies change their positions and character, so our experience orders us differently. Some souls, choosing nothing here, are rewarded, while punishments are applied to diseased parts restoring the All to health.

IV.5.1–8 Eighth Problem: The Nature of Vision and Light

Chapter 1

1–13 Problem deferred: Does sight need a transparent body between the eye and the object? Sensing in general must come through a body, since the soul has to be in contact somehow with sensible objects through organs that resemble them, fashioning a common affection with them.

13–17 If contact with objects is needed, it can be either by direct touch or at a distance, as in seeing or hearing.

Question 1: Does sight need a body between eye and color, as Aristotle claims?

17–19 Reply: No, such a body may impinge, but contributes nothing.

19–22 Question 2: If dense bodies hinder and finer ones do not, do the latter cooperate?

23 Reply: No, all bodies hinder.

23–27 Question 3: If the body between receives the affection first, if it were not affected, would the affection not reach the eye?

27–34 Reply: No, the body between does not need to be affected if the eye is by nature affected. The body could be affected differently, as a fishing rod is not affected in the same way as the hand receiving the shock.

34–40 This involves the sympathies spoken about previously. The organ is affected sympathetically by the object because of the similarity between them, but the body between is not affected as different. It would be better if there were nothing between.

Chapter 2

1–11 Platonic account of sight: the visual ray coming from the eye joins daylight and goes straight to the object. The colored body changes the visual ray, so it should be able to affect the eye immediately. Since light goes straight, the visual ray does not need a body between to support it.

11–12 Stoic account: an impact causes sight, so a body between is necessary.

12–15 Epicurean account: images pass through a void, so having no body between supports the theory.

15–21 Plotinian account: if sight is by sympathy, it would be lessened by having a body between, and if that body were affected it would interfere completely with sight, as surface fire does not affect the interior of a body.

21–33 Sympathy in an animal: parts related sympathetically are affected less by having a part in between, but as determined by Nature. Some parts prevent excess, which implies they are not affected in the same way or at all as the two parts in sympathy. Does not the sympathy of the All depend on the continuity of all the parts and so the sympathy of sensation implies continuity? The parts of the All, including the body between, are essentially continuous, but sensation as an affection is continuous accidentally.

33–48 The visual ray can pass through air without affecting it, as is also the case with natural motions of stones downward or fire upward. Reciprocal replacement by the air pushing behind them is not needed. The motions of living things, trees growing and humans walking, also do not need reciprocal replacement to aid their movement. If bodies can move through air this easily, bodiless forms in the visual ray can do so even more.

48–61 If these forms can so pass through the air, it does not need to be affected. If affecting the air were necessary, seeing would be of the air nearby, as with warming. This would be an instance of touch, but touch prevents sight and air is essentially dark.

Chapter 3

1–15 Stars and fires at night do not illuminate the air, but the fiery form is seen at a distance. If the transparent air were activated, sight would be caused by the dim air and not the bright object.

15–26 The absence of a body between is not about whether or not it is affected, but about the absence of the sympathetic connection between the two as parts of a single living thing. Test case: an object or world outside this one.

26–38 If the air needs to be affected, this implies touch so that only a part of the object is seen, corresponding to the size of the pupil in direct line with that part. But the whole object is seen, which is not corporeal but based on the nature of soul as sympathetic.

Chapter 4

1–10 The Platonic theory examined.

(1) The visual ray and daylight go to the sensed object:

(i) air between, not needed and only accidentally affected;

(ii) daylight between, not affected.

As already argued, no affection is needed and, since light is not a body, no body between is needed. A light other than the visual ray is needed only to see at a distance.

10–17 (2) The visual ray is ensouled, with the soul moving through it to the object:

(i) no light between is needed;

(ii) seeing is like touch, the visual ray moves to the object.

17–22 (3) This visual ray travels through an interval:

(i) if the interval is a body, removing it allows for sight;

(ii) if it is just a space, the visible object does nothing, which is impossible.

22–38 (4) Touch and sight compared:

(i) with air between, eye and nearby air receive the activity of light from a fire immediately, while warmth is delayed;

(ii) with a solid body between, touch reports the fire indirectly, but sight is blind.

(5) Consequences:

(i) If an object can act on an organ, and the visual ray can be acted on at any distance, there is no need for anything in between, including sunlight.

(ii) The Platonic theory also does not explain seeing stars and fires at night.

38–49 (6) In the Stoic version, the soul remains inside:

(i) Light is like a cane joining the eye and the object;

(ii) like a cane, light is striking the object and its color is pushing back;

(iv) for a cane to work, it needs to know the terrain ahead of time and up close, and the touches are reminders that are used to infer the object's presence;

(v) but seeing is immediate.

(7) If the external light needs to be affected, this is the same as needing the air to be affected, already refuted.

Chapter 5

1–4 (A) Questions about hearing.

(1) Does the first motion making the sound affect the adjoining air, coming to the ear?

5–8 (2) Is the air between affected accidentally as in the middle, so removing it allows the sound to meet us directly?

8–10 (3) Is the first motion only necessary at the start, but after it the struck air is the cause?

10–18 (B) Examination and response.

(1) This last theory makes air responsible for sound:

(i): The air needs to be struck by two bodies clashing together and the next portion of air by its prior;

(ii) this does not explain differences other than loud and soft.

18–27 (2) These differences:

(i) not due to air or the strike, which are one;

(ii) due to two bodies clashing, which are many and diverse;

(iii) air causes sound when it acts like a solid against which something strikes;

(iv) internal sounds of animals: parts clashing together produce sound.

28–31 (C) Conclusion: hearing is like sight, an affection that is a kind of consciousness in a living thing.

Chapter 6

1–4 (A) Question: Is light possible without air?

(1) Theory in favor: sunlight shines on the surface of bodies, but the void between is only accidently affected.

4–7 (2) Theory in contra: affections like warmth exist because of air, so light as an affection cannot be present without air.

7–11 (3) Evidence, pro and con:

(i) Light is not an affection of air at all, but belongs to fiery bodies, even gemstones.

(ii) Light passing from one luminous body to another cannot do so without air.

11–22 (B) Reply:

(1) Presumes light is a quality, but a quality is in a substrate, which needs to be specified.

(2) But light is an activity from one body that goes to the other by jumping over the void.

(3) Supporting reasons:

(i) light goes straight and does not need a supporting body;

(ii) light goes down, by moving itself, not as forced or drawn out by the object;

(iii) thus light is not accidental, possessed by or a quality of the recipient, but depends on the source and is present only as long as the source is.

23–31 (C) Conclusions:

(1) Light is not a body or in a body, but in a place. If it were a body, as the sun shines it would lose the activity coming from it; similarly the light would be independent. Activity is from one substrate but not into another, only affecting it by its presence. It is like the relation of body and soul: the presence of soul enlivens the body, but the soul remains the same whether present or not to the body.

31–40 (2) The nature of air as corporeal does not produce light but dims it. If light is a modification of air, then the air needs to be changed from its essential darkness. But air remains unchanged, so the color in the object illuminated depends on the light and not the air.

Chapter 7

1–2 (A) Question: Does light perish or return to its source?

2–13 (1) If light were in and possessed by the participant, then it perishes.

(2) If light is an activity not flowing away from its source, then it does not perish:

(i) as long as the source remains;

(ii) when the source shifts, light changes place, not as flowing back or changing course, but as belonging to the source.

(iii) distance is irrelevant, only a body blocking its path.

13–23 (B) Principle of two activities:

(1) First activity: within a body, like its life and source of its second, external activity.

(2) Second activity: beyond the source, reflection of its internal activity, and not separate from its prior.

(i) Every real being: has a second activity, a likeness existing as long as it does.

(ii) Its being remains within, but its activity projects out, strongly or weakly.

(iii) A strong activity projects far out, present at the source and the object at once.

23–33 Examples of weak activities:

(i) Animals with shining eyes: see as their light moves from them to objects.

(ii) Animals with light shining from them: bodily parts block or allow the light to be seen outside.

33–41 (3) Light is the activity of a luminous body toward the outside.

(i) The internal light of such a body is its essential substance.

(ii) When a luminous body as an activity is in contact with matter, a body that can receive its activity, it produces color.

(iii) The activity from the body only colors over, not making the body colored, since the color remains dependent on the activity and its source.

41–49 (4) Light is incorporeal, but belongs to a body.

(i) "Absent" or "present" have a different meaning, referring to the source.

(ii) Reflection in a mirror is also an activity depending on the body reflected and the nature of a mirror to receive that activity without being changed.

49–63 (5) Soul present in a body is like light, the activity of a prior activity.

(i) It is present as long as the prior soul is present.

(ii) Soul is present like the activity of light, as independent, and not like the color as a quality inherent in a body.

(iii) When the body perishes, that prior soul and its activity, or presence as soul, is no longer there.

Chapter 8

1–4 (1) Final Question: Can a body outside the heavens be seen?

5–7 Reply: If sensing, sense organ and sense object all depend on the sympathy of a single living thing, then this body as outside this living thing cannot be seen.

7–9 (2) Objection: What if they had qualities corresponding to their proper organs?

9–19 Reply: If the hypothesis is correct, no.

(i) The source of this illogical claim needs to be determined.

(ii) The claim of the objection fits the sympathy in a single animal.

(iii) If the cosmos is a living thing, sensation is grounded in the sympathy of its parts.

19–26 (3) Objection refined: sensation is due to similarities, not sympathies.

(i) Perception and sensation relate animal and object because the organs establish a similarity between them.

(ii) This cosmos can sense things not in itself because they are similar to things in it.

26–34 Reply: Things are similar here because the single living thing made them so.

(i) A different soul would be the maker of a different cosmos, having nothing in relation to this soul, and so also the qualities assumed to be alike will have no relation to it.

(ii) This absurdity reveals the inconsistencies in the hypothesis:

(a) the other soul is soul and not soul, akin and not akin;

(b) the things it makes are alike and unlike.

(iii) The hypothesis is impossible because of these contradictions:

(a) the soul of this cosmos is all and not all, other and not other, nothing and not nothing, complete and not complete;

(b) the hypothesis must be dismissed, as examining its consequences is self defeating.

Translation of *Plotinus* Ennead *IV.4.30–45 and IV.5*

IV.4.30–39 Sixth Problem: The Influence of Planets, Their Memory and Cooperation in Evil

30. But now since we settled that memories in the planets are superfluous, but gave them sensing, hearing as well as sight, and said they listen to the prayers that we make to the sun and some people even to planets, | and since it is believed that through them much is accomplished for men and they do this so carelessly that not only are they partners in right actions, but also in the many actions of evildoers, we need to investigate these incidental topics that have arisen. For there are difficulties concerning the greatest matters themselves and much confused chatter among | those who cannot endure that the gods have become cooperative causes of unnatural deeds, particularly those concerning intemperate desires and relations, and so [we inquire] for these reasons also about what has especially been a topic from the beginning, their memory.

It seems obvious, moreover, that if when we pray they act, and | do not do so at once, but later and often after a long time, they remember what men have prayed to them. But the account we gave earlier did not allow for this. But [the memory], as it were, of Demeter and Hestia, insofar as they represent earth, would also [demand] some such account for their benefits to men, | unless someone were to claim that benefiting human affairs is due to the earth alone.

We must try to explain overall: (1) how we deal with this fact of memory in them, which is a problem proper to us and not to what others suppose who have no hesitation giving them memory, (2) if it is in any way possible to give a defense of the gods in the heavens against the charges about those undesirable effects reputed to come about [through them], which is the | work of philosophy to investigate, (3) also about the whole cosmos itself, as the same charge is brought against it, if they are to be believed who say that the whole heaven itself may come under spells from the reckless | skill of men, (4) and finally the account will inquire about daemons, whether they are said to render such services, unless by the solution of the prior problems we might solve that of the daemons as well.

31. We need to undertake generally, therefore, [the study of] all actions and affections, which happen in the whole cosmos, those called natural and those that happen by craft.

We need to say that among those that are natural some happen from the All to the parts and | from the parts to the All or of parts to parts, but those happening by craft either some are completed, as they began, in the products, or others use the help of natural powers for the actions and affections of natural operations.

I claim, first, that the actions and affections of the whole are whatever the whole circuit does to itself or to | the parts, since as it moves it influences both itself and its parts, both the things in the heavenly circuit and whatever it provides to things on earth. The affections and actions of parts on parts are certainly well known to everyone, the positions of the sun toward the other planets and toward things on the earth's surface as well as the [qualities] in the other elements. We need to inquire carefully about each one of these, the [sun], the other planets, and things on the earth's surface and [the qualities] in its | other [elements].

The crafts, that make a house and other artifacts, terminate in these products, but medicine and farming and other such crafts are subordinate and contribute help to natural [processes], insofar as they are directed naturally; but | rhetoric and music and all arts of persuasion lead changed souls either to better or worse. In investigating these crafts, we need to say how many crafts there are, and what power they have, and, if possible, for all of those [crafts] relevant to our present purpose we need to treat as far as we can the reason why. |

It is evident in many ways, therefore, that the heavenly circuit acts, first influencing itself and the things within it differently, then indisputably also terrestrial things, [acting] not only on bodies but also on the dispositions of the soul, and each of its parts acts on terrestrial things and things below it generally. But whether these things here [act] on those above, we will consider | later.

Now, however, we will allow things granted by all or by most to be the case, as much as it appears so through reason, and once we have understood, we must attempt to state the mode of this activity from the beginning. For it is not that [the heavenly circuit produces] only hot and cold and such things, which are called the primary qualities of the elements,[1] nor can it be said to produce sufficiently from the mixture | of these, nor that the sun [produces] everything by its heat, but some other [planet] by its cold—for what cold could there be in a heavenly and fiery body?—nor another [the moon] by its humid fire. In this view, it is impossible to understand the difference of these [qualities], and also impossible to reduce many of the things generated to any one of them. | For if one were to attribute differences of character to them according as such temperaments predominate over bodies through cold or heat: how could one reduce anger, jealousy, or wickedness to these? But even if [one could], how then for fortunes,

1 Aristotle *Meteorology* IV 1.1378b11–13; *On Generation and Corruption* II 3.330b3ff.

worse or better, rich | or poor, the nobility of their parents or themselves, and the discovery of treasures? One could name countless cases, leading far from the bodily quality that passes from the elements into the bodies and souls of animals.

We also need to attribute what befalls each of the things under them neither to the choice of the planets, to the knowledge of the all, | nor to the calculations of these beings. For it would be strange for those beings to scheme about human affairs, how some might become *thieves*, others *slave traders, housebreakers, temple robbers*,[2] still others effeminate and feckless in their deeds and affections, | carrying on outrageously. For not only is it not [a proper activity] of the gods, but not even of men of measure nor perhaps of anyone at all, to do and scheme about such things, from which no benefit at all would accrue to them.

32. If then we are to attribute neither to bodily causes nor to their choices, whatever comes to us and other animals from outside [the earth], and generally from the heavens to the earth, what is left as a reasonable cause?

First, we must assume that this All is *one living thing surrounding* | *all the livings things existing within itself*[3] and [that it] has one soul extending to all its parts, insofar as each is part of it. Each thing in the sensible All is part, completely as bodily, but it also belongs to the All to

2 Plato *Republic* 344b3–4.
3 Plato *Timaeus* 30d3–31a1.

whatever extent it participates in the soul of the All. | Those things, then, that participate in this soul alone are parts wholly, but as many as [participate in] another [soul], keep from being entirely a part of this [soul of the All], but are affected no less by the other [parts], to the extent that they keep something of the [All Soul], owing to the [bodies] which they have.

This one All, moreover, is sympathetic, indeed as one living thing, and the far is near, just as in one of the individual animals, nail, horn, finger, and | any other of the limbs that are not contiguous, even though the part between is discontinuous and is not affected at all, the non-near part is still affected. The parts that are alike do not lie next to each other, but are separated by other parts between them, but are affected together by their similarity, and it is | necessary that what is done by one part reach to the distant part, though it does not lie beside it. Since it is a living thing having unity as its end, nothing is so distant in place as not to be near, by the nature of a single living thing to be sympathetically affected.

When a part has a likeness to the agent, its affection is not alien, but if the agent is unlike, the recipient's affection is alien and even unpleasant. | It should also not be surprising that one part inflicts harm on another in a single living thing, since in us as well one part might harm another by our activities, since bile and anger, so it seems, stifle one part or spur another on. Certainly there is something in | the All resembling anger and bile as well as one part [harming] another; even in plants one part can block another, so that it withers away.

This All is not only seen as a single living thing but also as many, so that insofar as it is one, each part is preserved by the whole; but insofar as it is many, when they fall upon one another they hurt one another in diverse ways | by their differences. One even hurts another for its own need, and indeed makes food of another that is similar in kind, although different at the same time; as each is naturally anxious for itself, it takes to itself whatever is akin from the other, but, whatever is alien, it destroys completely *in its self-interest*.[4] In performing its own function, | each profits what can take advantage in any way of its workings, but what cannot withstand the impact of its function is destroyed or maimed, as [plants] wither at the advance of fire or small animals are swept aside or even trampled underfoot by the rush of bigger ones.

The | generation and corruption of all these things, and their alteration for better or worse, brings the unimpeded and naturally existing life of that single living thing toward its completion, since it was not possible for each of these things to exist as solitary beings, nor being parts to be and look toward themselves as the end, but toward that [whole], of which | they are parts. Further, since

4 Plato *Gorgias* 485a2.

they are different [from the whole], all these beings are unable to keep themselves forever in a single life; it is thus impossible for any [of them] to remain wholly the same, whereas the All is able to remain [the same] because its motion keeps it the same.

33. Since the heavenly circuit is not random, but is borne along by the rationality inherent to a living thing, there must be a harmony of agent toward recipient as well as a certain order for putting the parts in array among one another and toward one another, so that according to every position | of the heavenly circuit and in turn of the parts accompanying the circuit there is one disposition after another, like one dance with the intricate choreography of its movements.

Since even in dances among us the external features, according to each of their motions as they turn quickly from side to side, contribute to the dance, | as for instance the flutes and songs and other incidental elements, do we need to mention such obvious things? But the limbs of the one performing the dance out of necessity cannot stay the same throughout each figure; as the limbs of his body follow along with the dance and bend, one limb is | pressed tight while another goes free, one works strenuously while another receives a slight relaxation with the different configuration. The purpose of the dancer looks beyond himself, and his limbs are affected consequently by the dance, promote the dance, and help to bring the whole dance to completion, so that a | dance critic would be able to say how a particular limb of the body is lifted this height for such a configuration, another is bent, another is hidden, a different one is brought low; the dancer does not choose to do this randomly, but in dancing with the whole body | each particular limb receives this necessary position in performing the dance fully.

One must indeed say that the heavenly bodies act in this manner in everything they do, although sometimes they simply act as signs. Or better the whole cosmos exercises its own whole life, moving the main parts in itself and always changing their configuration, but the positions of the | parts toward one another and toward the whole and their different dispositions, as when a single living thing moves,[5] provide for the other effects coming after, first holding in this way according to these particular positions, dispositions and configurations, but then in that way according to those. In this case, the configured [planets] are not making [the effects], but the | configuring [cosmos]. Furthermore, the configuring [cosmos] in making another is not making something else, for it does not [make] in something else, but is itself all the things that come to be. The figures are there [in the heavens], but the necessary affections accompanying the figures are here, in an animal that so moves, and further is so composed |

5 Cf. Plato *Timaeus* 30d3.

and constituted by nature, that it is both affected and acts by its own internal necessities.

34. Since we give part of ourselves to being affected, as far as part of us belongs to the body [of the cosmos], but do not think our whole self belongs to that, we are affected by it within measure. In the same way, for instance when skilled workers are hired, in part they serve the master of the work, | but in part they belong to themselves, and receive more measured orders from the master because of this, since they are not slaves nor belong totally to another.

But it is necessary that the difference in the configurations of the [planets],[6] running their courses at unequal speeds, happen as it now does. Since they are borne along rationally and take on different | positions in the living thing, and here below things among us then take on affections in sympathy with the [figures] there, it is reasonable to inquire whether we need to say that these sympathetic affections are consequences of those [planets], or the figures have the powers for producing them, and whether it is the figures simply or the [figures] with these [planets]. | For the configuration itself of the same [planet] in respect of another [figure] and in turn others does not actualize the same portent or action, since each [planet] even by itself appears to have a different nature.

6 This group of heavenly bodies includes the planets, the sun, and the moon, but for convenience "planets" will suffice.

About this, one can correctly say that the particular configuration of these [planets] is in fact a particular disposition, but that of other [planets], though the same in configuration, is | a different [disposition]. But if this is so, we shall give [these dispositions] no longer to the configurations, but to the [planets] themselves that are configured. Even better, to both: for certainly, to the same [planets] when they take a different position, but even to one and the same [planet] when it has a different place, [we give] different [dispositions]. But what [do we give them]: actions or portents? In many cases [we give] to the complex configuration belonging to these [planets] both actions and portents, but in some cases | only portents.

This account thus gives powers to the configurations but also powers to the configured [planets], since also among dancers each hand and the other limbs have some power, but the figures have | greater power, and finally the third parts accompanying [the figures] are the constituents of the very limbs employed in the dance, like the clenched fingers of the hand and the tendons and veins affected with them.

35. How then do these powers work? We need to say more clearly, what difference one triangle has from another triangle, what [difference] this planet has from that, and based on what and up to what point it works this particular effect. We gave an account of their deeds, moreover, neither in terms of their bodies nor their | choices; not

their bodies, because the effects were not merely products of a body, and not their choices, because it was unnatural for the gods to produce unnatural things by choice. If we remember that [the cosmos] is a single living thing and keeps itself sympathetic with itself, it necessarily follows | that the whole course of its life is rational and in agreement with itself, that there is nothing random in its life but rather it is a single structure and order, and that the configurations are rational and each of the parts of the living thing move in their orbits according to fixed degrees over time. Thus, it is necessary to admit that the activity of the All is both | the figures occurring within it and the parts [planets] of it that are configured, and the [effects] that also follow from these. This is the way the All lives and all the powers contribute to this [All], and the parts having these very [powers] came to be by what made them in their rational natures.

While some figures are like the proportions or dimensions | of an animal and the recurring motions and positions of an animal according to reason, other [figures] are limbs set at intervals and configured; and the living thing has other powers without choice that are like parts of an animal, where the lack of choice in these [parts] does not in fact contribute to the nature of this particular animal. The | choice, then, of the single living thing is one, even though it has many other powers directed to itself. As many choices as occur in it are directed to the same [end] to which the single choice of the whole is directed. Appetite is, for example, of one part for another among the parts within the living thing: for one part wants to take some part from the others when it is in need; anger is likewise against the other, when | it provokes it somehow; growth also receives from another part and generation ends in something other than the parts [from which it came]. The whole living thing, however, does these things in these parts, while it seeks the good, or rather looks toward it. This [good] then is what right choice seeks beyond the passions and by this it contributes to the same end. As in the case of | those skilled workers in the service of another, many of their deeds look to following the orders of the master, but their longing for the good looks to the same good to which the master is looking.

If then the sun and the other planets do some good for things here below, one needs to think that the sun itself is looking above—necessarily giving an account of just this one case—| while causing effects from itself, as in warming things on the earth, and also for any effects following after that, by passing influences downward through soul, as there is much in it of the vegetative soul. Any other planet similarly without exercising choice gives off a power from itself like an illumination. All planets, moreover, when they | come to be so configured in some unity, give in turn one disposition or another: in this way the figures have powers—for by being configured this way or that now one disposition and then another follows—and something happens because of their being so configured—for by configuring these planets and then others there follows this or that effect. For the figures themselves, further, one can see from the things here below | that they have powers. Why, for example, are some figures frightening to those who see them when these frightened individuals have suffered nothing from these figures before, while the sight of others does not provoke fear? Why indeed do some figures frighten some individuals and other figures others? The reason is that these particular figures work on someone of a certain type, but other figures on someone of another type, since the figures | are incapable of not acting on what is naturally related to them. Further, something configured this way stimulates the sight of an individual, but configured another way does not stimulate the same individual. If someone were to say, for example, that beauty is what stimulates, why does one beauty stimulate this individual and another beauty that one, if the difference according to the figure does not have this power? Why, moreover, | do we claim that colors have the power to act [on the eye], but not claim that these figures do?

So in fact it is completely absurd to say that something exists among beings, but that nonetheless it has no influence it can exercise. A being is indeed of such a kind that it can either act or be acted upon:[7] we must grant acting to some beings, but for others both acting and being acted upon. In the substrates, | there are also powers because of the figures: and at our level of existence there are many [powers], which hot and cold do not produce, but they are generated by different qualities, actively formed by reason and by sharing in the power of Nature, as for example the natures of stones and the active powers of herbs produce many wondrous results.

36. The All is exceptionally diversified, containing within it both all rational natures and infinitely diverse powers. It is as they claim about man, that the eye has one power and the bone another, this bone one and that bone another, so the fingers of the hand this power and those | of the foot that power, and there is no part that does not have a power and one that is its own. We, however, are ignorant of this unless someone has studied such things, and this is also true, and much more so, in the All; or better, these things here are a mere trace of those in the All, where there is an indescribable and amazing diversity of powers, especially so in the stars | orbiting through the sky. For it is of course [possible]—like a soulless house otherwise large and complex, [made] from a few kinds of materials, like stone and wood, and if desired other such things—that [the All] did not need to generate itself into

7 Plato *Sophist* 248c4–5.

a [living] cosmos, but in fact the All is itself everywhere awake and its parts are alive in one way or another, and nothing can be | that is not in this All.

From the above account, the difficulty is also solved of how something inanimate can be in an ensouled living thing, for the account claims that different things live differently in the whole. We do not, however, speak as if something that is not perceptibly self-moving is living; nevertheless each of these things has a hidden life, and something perceptibly alive is composed of parts | that are not perceptibly alive but they provide marvelous powers to the life of this kind of living thing. Man in fact would not have been moved to such investigations if he were moved by completely soulless powers within him. The All, in turn, would not live in the way it does if each of the living things within it did not have its own life, even if choice | is not present in the All, for its making does not need choice, since it is more primordial than choice: on this account the multitude of living things serve this All by their powers.

37. For the All, then, nothing of its own is disposable. Since in fact we call fire and any number of such things active, if someone were to investigate what this activity actually is, even among those who now reputedly understand it, he would run into difficulties, unless he were to define it by that power which is | in the All, and say much the same also for other familiar objects. We do not,

however, think investigating ordinary things worthwhile nor do we find them strange, but about things whose powers are extraordinary we find them strange, so [we investigate] how each one functions, since *we are amazed at the unusual,*[8] but we could add being amazed at | these ordinary things, if being unacquainted with them someone presented each of them and explained in full their powers.

We need to say then that each of these has a certain irrational power forged and shaped in the All, each has a share somehow in soul from this whole ensouled being, and each has been surrounded by this kind of whole and is a part of this | ensouled being, for there is nothing in it unless it is some part of it. Further, some parts are more powerful for doing than others, both those on earth and especially those in the heavens, which enjoy a clearer nature. Many things in fact happen according to these powers, but the thing done seems to flow from these beings not by choice, for these powers are in | beings that do not have choice, nor do they turn their attention to the influence of the power, even when something of soul flows from them. For living things could be generated from a living thing not by a productive choice, or even by [the living thing] lessening itself or being aware of the effect, for choice, if it had one, could be inactive or not what produced the

8 A Stoic commonplace; Cicero (106–43 BC) *On the Nature of the Gods* II.56, Seneca (ca. 4 BC–AD 65) *Naturales quaestiones* VII.1.1.

effect. If some living being | did not have choice, then even less would it be aware of the effect.

38. The effects, then, coming from the All when nothing sets it moving derive from its different life, and as many [effects] as [come] when something else sets it moving, like prayers, either simple or chanted with skill, all these [effects] should not be referred to each of those [planets], but to the nature of the | effect done. Whenever these effects are beneficial for life or correspond to some other need, these should be referred to the influence flowing from the better to the lesser part.

When something unpleasant is said to come from the [planets] at the births of living things, it should instead be attributed to the inability of the | substrate to receive the good effect; for what happens does not simply happen, but happens to this particular thing here and now, especially as the recipient both now and in the future has a certain underlying and particular nature. Mixtures [of influence] also produce many effects, with each [planet] giving something beneficial for life. It may happen, however, that | naturally useful effects do not suit this individual, and the entire cosmic order does not always give to each individual what it wants. Further, we ourselves also add many things to what has been given us.

Nevertheless, all things are woven into one and have a remarkable harmony, with some things coming from other things, even flowing from opposites, for all are part of one [living thing]. If then one | of the things generated lacks something in excellence by not being actively formed to its end because its matter has not been mastered, it lacks as it were noble birth, and robbed of this falls into ugliness. Some effects, then, are produced by the planets, some are referred to the underlying nature, and some are added by things on their own.

39. Since all things are always set in array together and they all contribute to a single end, all are indicated by signs. *But virtue has no master*;[9] its works, however, are woven together in the cosmic order, since the things here below depend on those above, the things in this All depend on | more divine beings, since this cosmos participates in those higher beings. Consequently, the things in this All are not generated according to spermatic reasons, but according to comprehensive reasons and these things are prior to those generated according to spermatic reasons. There is in fact nothing in the spermatic reasons beyond the spermatic reasons themselves: nothing of the things generated, or | of things brought to perfection from matter in the whole, or of things active toward one another among those generated. But the reason of the All is more like what establishes the order and law of a city according to a reason[10] that already knows what the citizens will do

9 Plato *Republic* 617e3.

10 Heraclitus (c. 535–c. 475 BC) Fr. 114 (*DK* 22), Plato *Laws* 904a–905a.

and why they will do it, and makes laws with a view to all these matters and | interweaves by the laws all their experiences and works, and the honors and dishonors merited by their works, with everything moving along as if spontaneously toward a common harmony.[11]

Giving a sign, however, does not occur in order to signal beforehand, but since effects are generated in this way some things are signaled from others. Because they are one [together] | and belong to one [living thing], one thing can be known from another: a cause from what is caused, the consequence from the premise, and the composite from one of its parts, because [the reason of the All] makes the one part and the other together.

If these arguments, therefore, are stated correctly, the difficulties are already solved: for example, that influence from the gods leads to evils in that | their choices are not the active causes, but whatever comes from above is generated by natural necessities, as of parts in relation to other parts and as consequences for living of one [living thing]; that many things are added to these generated things by [the recipients] themselves; that the things given by each of the planets are not evil but in the mixture something else is generated; that the life is not for the sake of | each one but for the sake of the whole; and that while the

11 Plato *Statesman* 305e.

underlying nature receives one thing it experiences another and is unable to master what is provided.

IV.4.40–45 Seventh Problem: The Susceptibility of Souls to Benefit and Harm

40. But how do magic spells work? In three ways: by sympathy, by the natural tendency of harmony among similar things and opposition among dissimilar things, and by the diversity of the many powers that contribute to the perfection of the one living thing.

Many things are, in fact, drawn under magic spells with the contrivance of nothing | else: indeed the true magic in the all is *Love*, and *Strife* as well.[12] This Love is the first *magician and alchemist*,[13] whom men observed well, using his drugs and spells on one another.

Because there is a natural tendency to fall in love and | things causing love bring about a mutual force of attraction, a magical erotic art has appeared as an aid, whose practitioners apply traces of a variety of natural substances to different individuals bringing them together and bearing love engrafted within them, and so they join one soul to the other, as if they were clinging to one another like plants in a hedge. They | use, besides, figures bearing powers within them, and configuring themselves just so they silently induce these powers into themselves, as they

12 Empedocles (c. 490–430 BC) *Fr* B17. 7–8; B26. 5–6.

13 Plato *Symposium* 203d8.

are within one [living thing] and act for one [end]. Since indeed if someone were to assume that such a magician were outside the All, he could not attract or bring down [these powers] either by *spells or incantations*.[14] But as it is, because the [magician] does not lead [individuals by these spells] as if he were somewhere else, he can lead them | knowing the very way one thing in the living All is led to another. There is a natural tendency, moreover, [for attracting these powers] with spells sung to a tune, and accompanied by the particular chanting and gesture of the one casting the spell, for such things attract, like piteous gestures and groans. For since it is not choice or reason, but the irrational soul that is captivated by music, | such magic is not surprising. People, furthermore, like being charmed by music, even if they would not themselves ask this of accomplished musicians.

One must not suppose, finally, that any of the prayers [to the planets] are answered from choice, for neither do those captivated by spells [respond] in this way, nor when a snake mesmerizes a man, has | the one mesmerized any awareness or feeling of it, but knows, after it already happened, that he had the experience, while the ruling part in him remains unaffected. So when someone prays to a planet, some influence comes toward him or toward another from that planet.

14 Plato *Republic* 364c3–4; *Laws* 933d7.

41. But the sun or another planet does not actually hear the prayer. The effect, thus, happens in accord with the prayer because one part comes into sympathy with another, just as in a single stretched string, when plucked at the lower end the higher end vibrates as well. It also often happens when one string is plucked | another has a kind of feeling by the harmony of being tuned to the same scale. But if the vibration in one lyre so passes to another, insofar as there is sympathy between them, even more in the All is there a single attunement, even if it were to come from opposites; but it is in fact from similar things, both all things of the same kind and of their opposites.

Many things harm | men without intending to harm, as when anger is drawn along with bile and enters into the nature of the liver; for example, when someone, taking a flame from a fire, injures a third party. The first had planned that the flame not go where the second who received it made it go, at least as it was passed from that individual to the next; but when it reached the third, the flame harmed him, | if he was unable to receive it.

42. There will also be no need of memory in the planets for answering prayers—the reason for discussing these issues at length—or of sensations transmitted from here. Nor is their assent to prayers in any way, as some think, some kind of deliberate choice, but with | or without prayers some influence comes from them as parts belonging to one [living thing], since powers without choice are many

and [work just as well] either on their own or by craft, as in one living thing. Indeed some things benefit and harm others by being naturally so disposed, and other things | are compelled to share some of their power with others by the crafts of physicians or of spells.

And the All in the same way gives to its parts both on its own and when another draws something from it for a part, for it is spread out at the service of its parts by its own nature, so no one who asks is alien. If however the one who asks is evil, there is no need to be surprised, | for evil people also draw water for themselves from streams, and whatever gives does not itself know to whom it gives, but only gives. But nevertheless even what is given is coordinated with the nature of the All, so that, if someone takes what he ought not to take from those things spread out for the service of all, justice pursues him with a relentless law.

We cannot assume, finally, that the All can be affected. We must instead assume that | its ruling principle is completely impassible, but when affections occur in its parts the affection has reached them, but since nothing in the All is beyond its nature, what happens [in a part] does not arouse an affection that [reaches] to the All itself.

Next, for the planets also, insofar as they are parts, affections have reached them, but they themselves, on the contrary, are unaffected because their | choices remain unaffected and their bodies unharmed in their proper natures, and because, even if they give some influence through the soul, their souls are not diminished and their bodies remain the same and, if anything flows from them, it goes imperceptibly, and if something is added to them, what is added | escapes notice.

43. How is the sage affected by magic and drugs? On the one hand, one can say that in his soul he is unaffected in the face of magic and so his rational part would not be affected nor would he change his opinion; but, on the other hand, whatever irrational part of the All is in him, he would be affected relative to that, or rather | that part would be affected. But [he would] not fall in love from drugs, if falling in love is when one soul gives assent to the affection of another. Just as the irrational part is affected by incantations, so also by counter chants and incantations he may release himself from those powers. He might, however, suffer death or diseases or any type of bodily harm from such incantations, | for his part of the All might be affected by another part or by the All, but he himself would remain unharmed. That the effect does not come immediately but later, does not, moreover, constitute a departure from Nature.

Daemons, further, are themselves not impassible in their irrational part; it is also not absurd to attribute memory and sensation to them and that they allow themselves to be enchanted with magical spells and to be | subject to those who summon them, because they themselves are akin to things here to the degree that [they turn] to those things. For everything that [turns] to another is under its spell; for that to which [it turns] casts a spell and draws it. Something only [turned] to itself is free from spells. Because of this all practical activity has been under a spell and the whole life of the practical man; for he is moved | toward those things which enchant him: whence the saying, *the citizens of great-hearted Erectheus appear fair of face.*[15] What is the reason someone turns to the other? He is drawn not by the skills of magicians but by those of Nature, which brings deceit and links one thing to another not spatially but with the magic potions it offers.

44. This leaves contemplation alone immune to being cast under a spell, because no one [turned] to himself is subject to spells. He is in fact one, his object of contemplation is the self, and his reason is not deceived, but he makes his own life his task, doing what he ought. But | when one's task is not there, then reason is not the impulse, but the principle is in fact irrational and the premises are passions.

[Nature's magic can be seen in the following]: First, the cares of children and for marriage hold an obvious force of attraction, but also any pleasures whose occurrence entice men in their passions. Then, there are actions set in motion irrationally by anger | and similarly by the passions, but political actions and desires for office have our own ambition prompting them. Next, those actions

15 Plato *Alcibiades* I 132a5; cf. Homer *Iliad* 2. 547.

taken to avoid pain have fear as their origin, but those to acquire in excess have the passions. Finally, those actions, which seek | to fill in Nature's gaps for [bodily] needs, clearly have the force of Nature inherently urging us to live.

But if, on the one hand, someone says that beautiful actions are immune from being cast under a spell or, conversely, claims that the contemplation of beautiful things is also subject to spells, [the answer is that] if one were to do these so-called beautiful actions as far as they are necessary, | holding that the beautiful itself is different, one has not been put under a spell. In this case, one recognizes the necessity and is not looking toward the effect here nor is one's life turned toward things other than oneself, but [one is moved] by the force of human nature and by the inherent urge to preserve the life of others or oneself. In fact, not removing oneself from life on account of this inherent urge seems indeed reasonable, because in the contrary case one would be under a spell.

| But if, on the other hand, one is delighted with the beauty within the activities and chooses these actions, deceived by their traces of beauty, one is already cast under a spell in running after the beauty of things here below. In general, this attention to what seems true and any attraction to it is the result of being deceived by those things that draw one to themselves. But this is the | magic Nature works, that one seeks as good something not good, drawn to that thing's form by irrational impulses;

this is being led unknowingly where one does not want to go. What else would anyone call this but magic? Thus the only one immune to spells is the one who when he is drawn by his other parts says that none of the things are good | that those parts claim are good, but only what he himself knows [as good], neither being deceived nor in hot pursuit, but already grasping it. He would certainly not be drawn anywhere else.

45. From everything we have said this is clear, that, as much as the nature and disposition of each of the things in the All allows, each brings the All to perfection, is acted on and acts, just as for each animal each of its parts, | as much as its nature and condition allows, brings the whole to perfection, renders its service, and consents to its position and purpose. It gives what comes from itself and receives those things coming from the other parts, only as much as its nature can receive. There is thus a kind of consciousness of every part toward the whole, and if each of the parts were also | an animal, it would have the functions of an animal different from those it has as a part.

This latter point indeed brings to light how it is with us, that when we do something we are also in the All, not only so far as body acts against body and receives repercussions in return, but also we ourselves introduce our other nature, since we are connected by the innate powers that are within us to | the innate powers of those [beings] outside us. Since we indeed have become connected by our souls and dispositions, or rather we are connected, to things in the next daemonic realm and to things beyond them, there is no way we can overlook what sort of people we are. It is certainly not the case that we all give the same things or receive the same thing, for how could we share with another | what we do not have, such as the good? Conversely, we could not receive any good without a capacity for the good. Someone therefore who is connected to evil is recognized for who he is and according to his own nature is thrust into that which holds him here and is removed from there to another such place by the pulls of his own nature. | But for the good man, his acts of taking, giving, and exchanging are different, since these exchanges take place as if by certain pulls of Nature on strings.[16]

How wonderfully is this All possessed of power and order. All things happen *in their silent way according to justice*,[17] which no one can flee. The bad man pays no attention to justice and | is led unknowing to that place in the All where his fate necessarily takes him, but the good man, in contrast, recognizes justice and departs when he must, and discerns before departing where necessity is taking him to dwell, in the firm hope that he will be with the gods.[18] In a small animal, on the one hand, the changes in the parts and their consciousness [of one

16 Cf. Plato *Laws* 644e2–3.

17 Euripides (c. 480–406 BC) *Trojan Women* 887–888.

18 Cf. Plato *Phaedo* 63b–c.

another] are slight and | the parts in it cannot be living, except perhaps briefly in some cases,[19] but in that Living Thing, on the other hand, in which the distances are so vast that each of the things in it has free play and many are living things, their motions and interactions must be equally vast. We see, for example, that the sun, the moon, and the other planets change their positions and their motions in order. | It is therefore not unreasonable that souls change their positions, since they do not always keep the same character, and also not unreasonable that they are ordered by what they experience and what they do, some receiving the rank, as it were, of the head and others of the feet, in harmony with the All, since the All itself encompasses differences of better and worse. The soul, however, that would neither choose the | better here nor consort with the worse, exchanges those things for a different place, receiving this pure place, which it chose for itself. The punishments, by contrast, are like those for diseased parts, some you treat with drugs but others you extract or even amputate, so that the whole may be healthy when each part is disposed as it should be. | The health of the whole thus comes when one part is amputated, while another is extracted from the place where it was diseased and put where it will not be diseased.

19 Cf. Aristotle, *De Anima* 409a9, 411b19–22, 413b19–24.

IV.5[29]1–8 Eighth Problem: The Nature of Vision and Light

5.1. Since we deferred examining if it is possible to see when there is nothing between, air or any other so-called transparent body,[20] we must examine it now. We said that seeing and sensing in general must | come about through some body, for without a body the soul is entirely in the intelligible. Since sensing is the perception not of intelligible but only sensible objects, the soul has to be somehow in contact with sensible objects through things suitably resembling them, fashioning a certain association with them of knowledge or affection. | Knowledge comes through bodily organs for this reason: for through these organs, which are connatural and continuous [with sensible objects], the soul somehow comes as if to unity with sense objects themselves and so a certain common affection occurs with them.[21]

If then there must be a certain contact with these known objects, then about the kinds of things one knows by touch of some kind, | what should we investigate? And about sight, and perhaps later also about hearing, but for the moment [should we investigate] about seeing whether a body is at all necessary between the eye and the color?

20 Cf. Aristotle *De Anima* 2.7.418b4.

21 Cf. Plato *Timaeus* 45bc.

I answer that a body between might impinge[22] accidentally, but contributes nothing to the sight of those who see.

But, if when the | bodies are dense, as earthy things tend to be, seeing is hindered, but insofar as these bodies between become ever subtler, we see better, could we hold that the bodies between cooperate with seeing, or if they do not cooperate, they do not hinder?

I answer that we must say that these bodies hinder.

But, if the body between receives the affection first and as it were is imprinted [by it], a sign | of which is that, if someone in front of us is looking toward the color, he also sees it, if the affection were not present in the body between, would this affection also not reach us?

I answer that it is not necessary for the body between to be affected, if what is naturally affected, the eye, is affected. Or, if it were affected, it is affected differently, as the | rod between the torpedo fish and the hand [is not affected in the same way] that the hand is affected. And yet even there, if the rod and line were not between, the hand would not be affected. This itself could also be disputed, for, if the fish is in the net, the fisherman is said to feel the shock.

In any case, | the argument may be leading to the sympathies mentioned. If this [organ] is by its nature, thus,

22 Cf. Alexander of Aphrodisias *De an*, Suppl. Aristot II.1.130, 15; =SVF, II.864; Chrysippus in Ps.-Plutarch *De plac philos* IV.15.901de; =*Dox Gr* 406.4–6; =SVF II.866.

affected sympathetically by this [object] because it has a certain similarity to it, then the [body] between as dissimilar would not be affected, or it would not be affected in the same way. If this is so, something that is naturally affected would be much more affected if there were nothing between, | even if what was between were such as to be affected somehow itself.

2. If then seeing is such that the light of the visual ray combines[23] with the light[24] between [and reaches] as far as the sense object, this light must be between. The hypothesis itself actually requires this [light] to be between. If, moreover, the colored body[25] underlying [sight] | effects a change,[26] what hinders the change from going immediately to the eye, since there is no [body] between, especially if now from necessity, while [seeing] is active, what lies before the eyes is somehow changed? Those who stream visual rays out[27] would, therefore, not have to hold that there is any [body] at all between supporting [them], unless they feared | that the beam would fall. But it is light, and light flows straight.

23 Cf. Alexander of Aphrodisias *De an*, Suppl. Aristot II.1.130, 15; =SVF II.864.
24 Cf. Plato *Timaeus* 45b4–d3; 67c–68d; Aristotle *De Anima* 2.7.418a19–b2; *De Sensu* 438a25–b2.
25 Cf. Strato *Fr* 113; =Stobaeus *Anth* I.52.3.483, 16–17; =*Dox Gr* 403, 26–28.
26 Cf. Alexander of Aphrodisias *De an*, Suppl. Aristot II.1.142, 19.
27 Cf. Plato *Timaeus* 45bc; Alexander of Aphrodisias *De an*, Suppl. Aristot II.1.127, 28.

Those who allege an impact[28] as the cause [of sight], however, would absolutely need a body between.

The champions of images,[29] who say that they pass through the void, require space so that [sight] is not hindered; thus, if it will hinder even less when nothing at all is between, they would not | dispute the hypothesis.

Those who say, that seeing is by sympathy, will assert that seeing would be lessened if there were some body between, as it would hinder, impede, and weaken the sympathy. But it would follow even more to say that a kindred [body] completely weakens [the sympathy], insofar as it is affected itself. For example, if a body continuous in | depth were set on fire, its depth is affected less by the fire than the surface.

But if the parts of a single animal were in sympathy, would they be affected less because some part is between? I say that they would be affected less, but the affection would be commensurate with however much Nature decreed, | the part between preventing excess, unless perhaps what is granted is precisely that the part between is not affected at all. But, if sympathy belongs to the living thing by being one and we are affected because we are in [this] one and belong to it, how is continuity not needed, when there

28 Cf. SVF II.867; Ps-Plut *De plac philos* IV.13.901a; =*Dox Gr* 403, 2.
29 Cf. Epicurus Fr 319; Lucretius *De Nat* IV.29-238; Alexander of Aphrodisias *De an*, Suppl. Aristot II.1.134, 30; Ps-Plut *De plac philos* IV.13.901a; =*Dox Gr* 403, 2.

is a sensation of something at a distance? I answer that continuity and the body between are needed because the living thing is | essentially continuous, but the affection is continuous only accidentally, or we will be asserting that everything is affected by everything. But if this is affected by that, but something else by another, not the same, then one would have no need of a body in between anywhere.

If someone says that [a continuous affection] is still necessary for the visual ray, he must state why, since what goes through the air does not seem in any way to cause the air | to be affected, but only to divide it; like a stone if it falls from above, what else happens except that the air does not support it? Since the motion is according to nature, it is unreasonable to claim it is by the reciprocal replacement[30] [of the air]. In that case fire would also rise up by the reciprocal replacement of air, but this is absurd, for fire by its quick movement outstrips | the reciprocal replacement of the air. But if anyone asserts that the reciprocal replacement is speeded up by the quickness [of fire], nonetheless it would happen accidentally and would not rise upward. This is also clear in other cases: the impulse upward comes from the trees themselves and not from things pushing them; and when we move, we cut through the air, and the reciprocal replacement of the air does not | push us, but would only follow and fill the space left

30 Cf. Aristotle *Physics* 8.10.267a16–17; Alexander of Aphrodisias *De an*, Suppl. Aristot II.1.129, 1.

empty around us. If then the air is divided by these kinds of bodies and is not affected, what prevents it from making way for the forms in the visual ray to pass through it without division?

But if the forms do not pass through the air as in a stream, why does it need to be affected and for the affection to reach | us through it by being affected first? If our sensation, however, did come from the air being affected first, when looking at the color we would not see the visible object, but we would have sensation of the air nearby, just as in being warmed. In that case, not the distant fire, but the warmed air nearby seems to | warm [us], for this is by touch, but for visible objects there is no touch, which is the reason why placing the sense object on the eye does not cause seeing;[31] instead, the body between needs to be lighted up, perhaps because air is dark. If air, however, were not dark, it would perhaps not need light, for the darkness that is a block to seeing needs to be overcome by | light. But perhaps when the object is brought close to the eye, it is not seen because it brings both the shadow of the air and of itself.

3. The clearest evidence that seeing the form of the sense object is not through an affection of the air, as if by transmission,[32] is that fire and stars and their shapes are seen at night in the dark. For nobody asserts | that forms

31 Cf. Aristotle *De Anima* II.7.419a12–13.

32 Cf. Alexander of Aphrodisias *De an*, Suppl. Aristot 2.1.41, 5.

present in the dark are by that connected [to the eye], but rather that it is no longer dark where the fire illuminates its own form. For even when it is entirely dark and the stars are hidden so the light from them does not shine, the fire from beacons is still seen and | that from lighthouses gives signals to ships. But if someone claims, contrary to sensation, that the fire passes through [the air] in these cases, then the visual ray would necessarily be activated by the perception of the dimness in the air and not by the fire itself, which is bright. If darkness, however, is in between and what is beyond it is seen, then it would be | [seen] more easily with nothing in between.

But one might check out this point, that seeing without a body between is impossible, not because nothing is between, but because the sympathy of the living thing toward itself and of its parts toward one another, which depends on its being one, is destroyed. It seems, moreover, that sensing of any kind belongs essentially to this, that the living thing, this | All, is sympathetic to itself. If this were not the case, how would one thing participate in the power of another, especially at a distance? We should also consider this, if there were another cosmos, another living thing not contributing toward this one, and there was an eye on *the back of the sky*,[33] would it be able to see that cosmos at a proportionate distance or would there be

33 Plato *Phaedrus* 247b7–c1.

| nothing in this one related to that? This, however, we will discuss later.

Now, however, we might give this further evidence that seeing does not occur because the [body] between is affected in this way. For if the air between were affected, without a doubt it must be affected bodily. But this is to produce an impression, as in wax. Then, however, part of the | seen object must be impressed distributively on each portion of the air, so that the portion [of the air] connected by the visual ray is as large a portion of the seen object as the pupil could receive in relation to itself. But as it is, it is all seen, and whoever are surrounded by the air see it at the front and from the side, from afar, nearby and behind, as long as their view is not | obstructed; so that each part of the air has the whole seen thing, such as a face; this affection is not due to the body but is due to higher necessities of Soul in a single self-sympathetic living thing.

4. But how is the light of the visual ray connected to the [day]light around the visual ray and [extended] right to the sensed object? I say, first, that there is no need for air between, unless it might be claimed that the light would not be there without air.[34] In my view, however, this [air] would accidentally be between, | but the light itself would be between without being affected; generally, there

34 Stobaeus *Anth.* 1.52.7.484, 7–12, = *Dox Gr* 404, 14–21.

is no need for an affection here, but still for [something] between; since light is not a body, there is no need for a body [between]. The visual ray would therefore not need another light between simply to see, but only to see at a distance. The question whether light could occur without | air, we will consider later.

Now, however, we must consider the first question. If indeed this connecting light [the visual ray] becomes ensouled, and the soul moves through it and has come to be in it, just as with the internal light [of the eye], then surely in perceiving, which is what seeing is, there is no need at all for [day]light between, but seeing will be | akin to touch: since the seeing power perceives by light with the [body] between not affected at all, but the motion of the visual ray comes to be there [at the object].

We need to ask about this, whether the visual ray needs to be carried there because there is a certain interval or because there is a certain body in the interval. If it is because | there is a body in the interval, if this separator is removed, [the eye] will see. If, however, it is simply because there is an interval, one needs to suppose that the nature of the visible object is idle and does nothing at all. But this is impossible.

Touch, in fact, not only tells that something is near and being touched, but in being affected it reports different aspects of the object touched, and if nothing were separating it, | it would sense [the object] even at a distance. For the air between and we sense fire together, not waiting for that [air] to be warmed. A solid body is warmed even more than the air, so that [we would sense the fire] more on account of it, but not through it. If then [an object] has the power to act and the [organ], for instance | the visual ray at any range, to be acted on, why does [the object] need something else in the middle [to act] on what it already has the purpose to act on? This is indeed to need an obstacle. Thus, when the light of the sun is approaching, it does not need [to affect] first the air and then us, but both together, even before [its light] is active near the visual ray, often being elsewhere, so when the air is unaffected we | see [the object] to which the visual ray needs to be connected, although the [air] between had not been affected and [sun] light had not yet come [to the visual ray]. Thus seeing the stars, or generally any fire, at night is difficult to justify on this hypothesis.

If the soul, however, remains in itself, but needs light like a cane[35] to | reach the object, perception is necessarily violent since light is pitted against and has been stretched out [toward the object], and the sense object, the color as color, is itself pushing back, since this is how the touches [of a cane occur] through a medium. Thus, at first, [touch] occurred up close with nothing then between, but, later, touching through a medium produces | knowledge as if

35 Cf. Alexander of Aphrodisias *De an*, Suppl. Aristot 2.1.130, 17 = SVF 2.864; Diogenes Laertius 7.157 = SVF 2.867.

by memory and even more by reasoning. But as things are, [seeing] is not like this. If, then, the light near the sense object needs to be affected and then [the affection] needs to be transmitted as far as the eye, this hypothesis becomes the same as the one that first modified the [air] between by the sense object, against which a difficulty has already been raised in other places.

5. About hearing, do we need to concede that the first motion by the thing making the sound affects the adjoining air, and by this same [motion] affecting the air as far as the ear, it thus arrives at sensation? |

Or: is the [air] between affected accidentally by being present in the middle, but if the [air] between were taken away, once the sound occurs, as when two bodies have dashed together, the sensation reaches us immediately?

Or: is the first [motion] necessary when the air is struck,[36] but from that point on the | [air] between is already [struck] differently?

In this view of things, it seems that air is responsible for sound. For it would seem that no sound would occur in principle, when two bodies are clashed together, unless the air, being struck and thrust out by their rapid coming together, struck the next [portion of air] in succession, and delivered it as far as the ears and hearing. But if air is responsible for | sound and the strike for this moving [air],

36 Cf. Diogenes Laertius, 7.158 = SVF 2.872.

why would there be differences of voices and sounds? For bronze against bronze sounds different from bronze against something else, and other things also sound differently.

The air, however, is one, and also the strike [moving] in it, but the differences are more than only loud and soft. But if because the strike occurring against the air makes | a sound, one must say that it is not as air [that there is sound]. Air then sounds, whenever it takes the condition of a solid body,[37] standing fast as something solid before it flows. In effect, the things striking together are enough to explain that the clash together is the very strike that comes to sensation as the sound. The internal sounds of animals, moreover, are evidence that it is | not air, but the clashing together and striking of one thing on another, for example, the bending and grinding of joints rubbing against one another, since there is no air between.

Let us conclude the difficulty about this, as the inquiry here is already similar to the very thing said about the essence of | sight, since the affection related to hearing is also a kind of consciousness as within a living thing.

6. Could light occur if there were no air, as when the sun shines on the surface of bodies, if there is a void between which is accidentally illuminated, only because it is there?

37 Cf. Aristotle *De Anima* 2.8.419b21–22.

On the contrary, if | other things are affected because of this [air] and the substance of being light is because of air—for it is an affection of it—there will then be no affection unless what will be affected also exists.

I say, first, [light] is not primarily of air nor insofar as it is air, since it belongs to each fiery and shiny body; there are even stones of this sort with a luminous | color.

On the contrary, would the [light] passing from one thing having such a color to another exist without that [air]?

I say, if it is only a quality and a quality of something, since every quality is in a substrate,[38] it would be necessary to investigate in what body light will be. But if it is an activity from another [body], there being no adjacent body, | but a kind of void between, if that is possible, why will it not be there [in that body] and jump over to the [body] beyond [the void]? For, since [light] is straight, why does it not pass right through without riding on anything? But even if it were the kind of thing to fall, it is moving itself downward, and then indeed neither the air nor the illuminated object is in any way drawing this out of the illuminating source and | forcing it to advance. It is thus not something accidental, so that it would be completely in the other, nor is it an affection of the other, so that the affected object will need to be, nor does it have to

38 Cf. Albinus *Didasc* 11, 166, 17.

stay once it has come: but at one instant it goes away, and comes back at another.

Where then is it?

I say, it only needs a place to be in. If not, the body of the sun would lose the activity that is from itself: | but this is light. If this were so, light would not be of anything. But activity is from some substrate, but not into another substrate; although it would affect this other substrate in some way, if it were present. But just as life as the activity of soul would be the activity of something affected, such as the body, if it were present, but when not present | it still exists, what would prevent this in the case of light, if it is a kind of activity?[39]

For the illumination of the air does not as a matter of fact generate light, but being mixed with earth it makes it dark and not entirely pure. So that it would be like saying that the sweet can exist, only if mixed with the bitter. But if someone were to say light is a modification of | air, one must necessarily say that the air itself is modified by the modification and its own darkness altered to become not dark. But as a matter of fact, air remains such as it is, as in no way affected. But the affection needs to be of that of which it is the affection; [light] thus is also not the color of air, but is of itself [color]; | air is merely present. Let us then conclude this question.

39 Cf. Aristotle *De Anima* 2.7.418b9.

7. Does light, then, either perish or run back [to its source]? Perhaps we might also take something from this discussion to resolve the previous problem.

So, on the one hand, if [light] were something within the participant, as already its own, one could perhaps say that it perishes. But, on the other hand, if [light] is an activity not flowing away | —for in that case it would flow around and pour more inside [the recipient] than however much the light from the active source was casting upon [its surface],— it would not be destroyed while the source of light actually remained. But when the [source of light] shifts, the light is in another place, not as flowing back or changing course, but as the activity belonging to and arriving with that [source], | insofar as nothing prevents it. Even if the distance from the sun to us were many times greater than it now is, light would reach as far as here, provided nothing hindered it or no obstacle stood between.

First, the activity within it, as it were the life of the luminous body, is greater and as it were the principle and source | of the [outer] activity. Next, the second activity beyond the limits of the [luminous] body and reflection of its internal [activity], is inseparable from that superior [activity]. Every real being has an activity, which is its likeness, so that while it is, that will be; but while the being remains [within itself], that activity will project far out, some quite fully, | others less so. Indeed, some [activities] are so weak and dim that they are scarcely noticeable, but of those that are greater and do project far out, when one is far out, it is necessary to think that it is there, where the active and powerful body is, and also at the point to which it extends.

In the case of animals with luminous eyes, seeing with these eyes is possible, since for them light | still comes to be outside the eyes; and then in the case of animals that have fire compressed inside, with their expansions their light shines outside into the dark and in their contractions nothing of the light remains outside, nor has it perished, but either it is or is not outside. What then? Has it gone back in? I answer that | it is not outside, because the fire is not toward the outside, but has sunk back to the inside. Has the light itself sunk inside? I answer, no, but only that [the fire has sunk inside]. When it sinks, however, the rest of the body is in front of it, so that its activity is not directed outside.

Light from bodies is, thus, the activity of a luminous body toward the outside. | But the light itself entirely within such bodies is primarily that kind of substance according to the form of a primarily luminous body. When such a body has contact with matter, it produces color. The activity alone, however, does not produce [the color], but as it were colors over [the surface], inasmuch as the activity is of another [body] and | is dependent on that, as it were, so [a body] separate from that body is also separate from its activity.

It is necessary to hold that [light] is totally incorporeal, even though it belongs to a body. Therefore neither "it has gone away" nor "it is present" are proper, but these [phrases] have another mode [of signifying], since the substance of light is as an activity. For example, we need to say that the reflection in a mirror | is the activity of what is seen in it, occuring on something receptive without flowing into it. Thus when it is present, that [reflection] also appears there and is there precisely as a reflection of patterned colors, and when it goes away, [the mirror] no longer has the appearance, which it had before when it held the object seen actively in it.

But also | in the case of the soul, insofar as it is an activity of another prior activity, while the prior remains, this subsequent activity also remains. But what if someone [says] that it is not an activity, but the product of an activity, as we said that life belongs already to the body, just as light has already been in contact with bodies? I answer that in this case the color | occurs because [the light] that makes it has already been mixed [with bodies]. What then in the case of the life of the body? I answer that it has [life when] another soul is adjacent [to it]. Then, when the body perishes—for it cannot persist without some share of soul—so as the body is perishing and neither the life-giving soul, nor any adjacent soul if there is one, is able to ward it off, | how would life remain? What happens then? Has life itself perished? I answer that life itself has not. For this body is a reflection of the shining out [of the life of the soul], but the soul is simply no longer there [in that body].

8. But what if there were a body outside the heavens, and some eye from here were looking, with nothing hindering, would it see anything if it had no sympathetic link toward that body, if in fact sympathy is due to the nature of a single living thing?

I answer, if the sympathy due to belonging to a single | living thing [is necessary] for sense [organs], sense objects, and sensations, then it would not [see it] if this outside body were not part of this particular living thing; if it were a part, it would see [it] immediately.

Even if, on the contrary, it were not a part, but a body colored and having other qualities, as if it were here, [each quality] corresponding to its organ?

I answer, quite simply, no, if our | hypothesis is correct. Unless someone were trying to destroy the hypothesis by this same supposition claiming that it is illogical, that the eye does not see a color present, and the other senses are not activated toward sensible objects, when they are present to them. But we will respond: this illogical claim, from what source does it appear? As here we do and experience these things in | being one and of one, we must then examine this [other supposition], to see if our contrary [hypothesis] has been sufficiently shown; if not, it must be shown by other arguments. It is clear that an animal is sympathetic to itself. If the All is also a living thing, that is sufficient, as the parts [would be sympathetic to one another] as parts of one living thing.

On the contrary, what if someone were to say [sensation] is due to similarities [and not to sympathies]? | Perception and sensation, moreover, are related to an animal because the animal itself shares in the likeness [of the thing], given that its organ is like it, so that sensation is the perception of the soul through organs like the things perceived. If then being a living thing, [this cosmos] were sensing things not in itself, then, as a | living thing, it will perceive things like those in itself, as the things perceived will be perceived not as of itself, but as like things in itself.

I answer, the things perceived are thus perceived as things that are like, because the soul itself has made them like, lest they be incompatible. Thus, if the maker in this case were a soul completely different [from this soul], then the [qualities] assumed to be like in this case have nothing in relation to this soul. But the absurdity, moreover, demonstrates | the inconsistency in the hypothesis since it is the cause of it, for it claims at the same time [that it is] soul and not soul, and akin and not akin, and these things are alike and unlike, so that having these contradictions in itself it would make the hypothesis impossible. It even asserts that soul is in this [other cosmos], so it holds it as all and not all, | as other and not other, nothing and not nothing, and complete and not complete. In sum, one must dismiss the hypothesis, as it is not possible to investigate its consequences without destroying the hypothesis itself in the process.

Commentary

IV.4.30–39 Sixth Problem: The Influence of Planets, Their Memory and Cooperation in Evil

Chapter 30

The first problems that Plotinus returns to in this chapter are memory in the planets, from IV.4.6–8, and sensing by them, from IV.4.25, 13–26, 4. A more serious issue arises in the cooperation that these divine beings seem to provide to human evil. The chapter continues with the evidence that prayers addressed to the planets are answered and at times after a long interval, challenging Plotinus' earlier account that precludes memory from the planets. It concludes with a list of projects: reconciling this evidence for memory with his account of the planets, giving a properly philosophical defense against their complicity in evil, and extending that defense to include the cosmos as a whole as well as daemons.

While brief, this list provides the issues that are investigated in the subsequent chapters about astrology, prayer, magic, and more ordinary human affections and experiences.

30, 1–13 *But now since . . . beginning, their memory*: The chapter begins by listing consequences that seem to conflict with the basic premise of the treatise as a whole, that all souls are alike. This likeness seems to imply that living things in the cosmos have the same powers and faculties, which Plotinus wants to argue against without undermining their substantial unity. Earlier, at IV.4.6, 9–17, he held that planets do not have memory, making them different in general from living things on earth, since they do not have the needs requiring memory. They are also different from human beings, who fall into perplexity and thus need discursive reasoning and calculations to navigate their experience, whereas, at IV.4.7, 1–3, he states that the planets always see the intelligible, not needing recollection and the discursive reason based on it to remain in their orbits. In IV.4.25, 13–26, 4, on the contrary, Plotinus argued that if the planets answer prayers it seems plausible that they hear and if it is also reasonable that they are aware of their influence upon events on earth, in some fashion they see, but that earlier passage also indicates that these phenomena are based on a linking and sympathy, leaving open their exact relation to sensing. The next difficulty comes from a different perspective, that the influence of the planets makes them accomplices in human evil as well as good, a carelessness problematic in itself and in its discussion, some of which Plotinus dismisses as confused chatter. The concern about the gods cooperating in evil, moreover, merits proper philosophical attention and is thus added to the problem of memory that has been central up to this point in IV.4.6–29.

30, 1 *In the planets*: Armstrong, 1984, 225, translates the Greek *astra* as heavenly bodies and stars, but planets seem to be the focus of attention in this part of IV.4, which also lessens a bit the strangeness he picks up in Plotinus' reference to "we" who pray to the sun, while "others" pray to the stars (Armstrong, 1984, 225n2). The sun and moon are included among the planets and are the primary bodies central to ancient astrology; the five planets also have the names of the gods in the Greek or Roman pantheon, and are thus objects of cult throughout the ancient world. While the outer sphere of stars and its motion (*phora*) clearly have a role in astrology, it is not as direct as that of the planets and their relation to the specific constellations of the zodiac. In most cases, therefore, I have translated *astēr* as planet throughout these chapters.

30, 10–12 *Those who cannot . . . desires and relations*: I have toned down the translation from Armstrong, 1984, 225; it seems to me Plotinus is not specifying any particular perversions, but, as we shall see later (Chapters 43–45), any situation where one is enchanted and led by desires.

30, 14–20 *It seems obvious . . . the earth alone*: This opening section continues with two observations that set the framework for discussing memory and the scope of the benefits as coming from earth as well as heavenly bodies. First, the delayed response to prayer indicates the particular counter-evidence that Plotinus must explain, since it contradicts his earlier thesis denying memory to the planets. Second, in attributing earthly benefits to the work of Demeter and Hestia, Plotinus returns to the discussion of the earth at IV.4.26, 5–27, 17, immediately following the passage about sensing by the planets, referred to above. He had established in that context a variety of affections in earth's soul similar to the senses and concludes with a hierarchy of powers, moving from the generative, vegetative, and sensitive, to the other soul or intellect, called Demeter and Hestia at IV.4.27, 16. Plotinus indicates in the present context that in addition to, or because of, these different powers, an account of earth's bounty includes memory unless the earth acts without the involvement of an intellective soul. These issues are not presented in a manner that easily fits our preconceptions, but some ability to imagine the world from a pre-modern perspective is necessary for understanding what is at stake. For the ancients the cosmos is a living thing, which is central in Plotinus' analysis of stellar and planetary influence. His effort is to show that the cosmos as a whole, individual planets, and Nature do not operate in the way human souls do, depending on the senses, memory, and discursive reason, even though they share the same nature as souls. Both in this treatise and throughout his writings Plotinus endeavors to remove any hint that these beings could be acting anthropomorphically, identified with the way crafts work, using reason to plan and design, and calculations to carry them out. This approach can function for us as an ironic contrast to the modern image of the universe as a machine, lifeless and impersonal, an image which is indeed essentially anthropomorphic and precisely in the sense that Plotinus is seeking to combat, that some kind of discursive reason operates in it that can be subsequently replicated in propositional form by human science. The irony in the present passage, however, is most poignant in the supposed anthropocentric character of a geocentric cosmos. Nothing could be further from the attitude of the ancients, who found the earth as the least desirable and most imperfect place to be, in contrast to the order and beauty of the stars.

30, 18–20 *But [the memory] . . . the earth alone*: My translation drops the comma after *toiouton* and takes the subject of *ēn* (30, 18) as *hē mnēmē*, suggested in HS_2 as the referent of *toiouton*, for which the more likely candidate is *logos* (30, 17) and which must be construed as the subject or object of an unexpressed infinitive of obligation or necessity (cf. Smyth, 1980 [1920], #1774).

30, 19 *Demeter and Hestia:* The discussion at IV.4.26, 5–27, 17 attributes the whole range of the soul's powers to the soul of the earth, but illustrates as well that their operation does not involve the kinds of organs found in animals nor do they imply the same need. This last point is expressed in identifying the soul of the earth as precisely that other, intelligible soul, with the names Demeter and Hestia. Igal, 1985, 414–416 has helpful notes, giving Platonic and other sources and indicating some of the philosophical implications of this mythical allusion; see also Brisson, 2005, 241–264. Demeter, or Mother Earth, underlines the fecundity of the generative and vegetative powers of the soul of the earth, while Hestia, or Hearth, the earth's stability, not completely immovable, but hard to move and not movable from its place (IV.4.22, 26; 26, 8–9). As with Plotinus' discussion of nature, the soul of the earth functions neither like the gods, without senses and with their gaze fixed on intellect, nor like human and other animals, with specific organs and discursive calculation. The immobility of the earth is determined by being at the cosmological center (more or less), where the element earth is concentrated, in mixture with the other elements. Bodies on the earth are subject to locomotion and change, but, while the body of the earth is not immune to motions, dramatically in earthquakes and volcanic eruptions, these cannot dislodge it from its place nor alter it substantially. For an account of Nature, see Deck, 1967. The irony in the negative evaluation of geocentrism is amply present in the exposition of IV.3-5 in terms of the descent and ascent of the soul. Descent and ascent clearly have a metaphorical sense, but for Plotinus they also have a cosmological sense. The world soul remains above and gives life to the cosmos as a whole; the planetary souls descend only so far as the planetary bodies they are present to and have perfect motions that allow them also to be in direct contact with the intelligible; human souls descend to the earth and are present to bodies whose motions are random and incomplete, with the result that they do not have easy contact with the intelligible; finally, Nature as soul of the earth has no proper motion, is unconscious, but is manifest in vegetative and sensitive life. Despite the overwhelming evidence that the ancient geocentric view is negative, many scholars are immovable in the contrary opinion that this centrality is nothing but anthropomorphic egocentrism.

30, 21–32 *We must try . . . daemons as well*: In the conclusion to this preamble, Plotinus presents the four issues he will investigate. He makes explicit that the problem of memory is peculiar to his understanding of the nature of the souls of the planets and their memory. He then indicates that it is proper for philosophy to investigate the charge that the gods, now expanded to include the whole cosmos as well as daemons, cooperate with human evil. This investigation is properly philosophical precisely in the sense of Plato (427–347 BC) and Aristotle (384–322 BC), as about the highest objects of first philosophy or metaphysics.

Chapter 31

This chapter functions as a presupposition, indicating the nature of actions and affections in the cosmos. Some of these actions and affections are natural and others are due to craft. Those that are natural include all the actions and interactions of the cosmos as a whole and its parts, including their influence on the earth. Crafts are divided into three types, those that make particular kinds of artifacts, those that in some manner assist Nature in relation to bodies and their conditions, and those directed to changing souls through some kind of persuasion. Three questions are posed relative to these crafts, their number, power, and why they work as they do. The final section of the chapter turns to investigating the influence that the heavenly circuit and the planets have not only on bodies but also on the souls that inhabit the earth. Plotinus grants the most accepted explanations, insofar as they are reasonable, with the particular task of determining how this influence actually works. It cannot be in terms of the primary qualities, such as hot and cold, given the nature of heavenly bodies as fiery. This corporeal view of their influence, further, does not at all explain what Plotinus considers to be incorporeal, the dispositions of souls, arguing that even bodily temperaments cannot determine character, nor even less such accidents as fortune, wealth, and noble lineage. The primary qualities in the bodies of animals are far different from their characteristics as living things. While this influence cannot be reduced to corporeal changes, neither can it be explained by choice, knowledge, or calculation on the part of the planets. This would be unworthy of them, and is necessarily a part of his negative response to their complicity in human evil.

31, 1–3 *We need to . . . happen by craft*: Plotinus specifies the formality under which his investigation will continue, all the actions and affections that can occur by nature or craft. He deliberately uses more general terms, *poiēseis kai peiseis*, which can include those things that act but are not acted upon, those that act and are also acted upon, those that are acted upon, and also what is acted upon without being affected, a key addition from Plotinus' point of view. In the two previous treatises, II.5 [25] and III.6 [26], Plotinus explores this idea of acting or being acted upon. In II.5 he uses Aristotle's language of act and potency (*energeia kai dunamis*), but these Aristotelian terms are used most specifically of change horizontally, so to speak, how sensible things are generated and corrupted at the sense level. Plotinus wants to extend the concept to include a vertical dimension of action and reception among things at different levels of reality. This kind of change, unlike Aristotle's, is first of all non-reciprocal, so that the action of something at a higher level produces an effect at a lower level, but without any change or diminution in the higher being. One of the earliest discussions of this non-reciprocity occurs in I.2 [19] 2, 6–10, where Plotinus makes explicit how the otherness of the effect makes its relation to the source different from the reciprocal relation of things at the same level. This innovation is essential for Plotinus' account of the relation of intelligible forms to sensible particulars, and even more for the relation of the One to the beings overflowing from it. At the other extreme, elaborated in III.6, Plotinus seeks to describe how matter or the receptacle can be described at the same time as both affected and not affected by the action of any form as higher. It is in this context, at III.6.7, 38–40, that Plotinus employs the terms used here, *poieseis kai peiseis*, to cover kinds of change not anticipated in Aristotle's account, as well as the image of a reflection in a mirror, which will be used again at IV.5.7, 44–49 in the analysis of light.

31, 3–8 *We need to say . . . of natural operations*: The following lines distinguish the range of actions and affections happening by nature and by craft. By nature, each being in the cosmos is capable of acting and being acted upon. Action comes from the nature of a being, as Plotinus has argued in a number of early treatises, especially in VI.4 [22] 7–8, where he uses three images to illustrate how a power can be present as a whole in a body, the power of a hand present in an object it is lifting or throwing (7, 8–23), a small luminous mass illuminating an opaque sphere (7, 23–39), and the light of the sun illuminating the sky (7, 39–47). This is related to both the principle of two acts (Rutten, 1956, 100–106) and the limitation of act by potency (Clarke, 1952, 167–194). Both of these issues are relevant in the present context to explain both the action of planets and light and its reception by appropriate corporeal objects (Gurtler, 2008, 113–127). The primary action is that by which a being is what it is and the secondary action is what flows from it. Being acted upon is a consequence of having a body, since bodies divide and block the way forms can be present. Some forms are so present to a particular body as to be possessed by it, whether as the forms that constitute the body in combination with matter or forms present as qualities, not actually being bodies themselves, but qualifying bodies in multiple ways. Souls, however, are present without being possessed by the body, but as activities that more or less overcome the division of the body. Plotinus discusses these differences in VI.4.1–5, where qualities and affections have the same relation to bodies, since they are possessed by them (VI.4.1). Plotinus contrasts this possession, which is one in form but diverse in number, with the unitary presence of the soul, which is omnipresent. This contrast and its implications for distinguishing affections from the soul's activities are the topic of VI.4.2–4 and will have a major role in unraveling the difficulties examined in the present section of IV.4.30–45 and IV.5, allowing Plotinus to make precise distinctions about what can give rise to affects in other things and how those things receive affections.

31, 8–15 *I claim, first . . . its other [elements]*: This next section begins with the actions and affections in Nature, the whole circuit of the cosmos and its parts. Since the cosmic soul can only exist in relation to the Intelligible, its primary action is a desire for the Intelligible, and this first act of the whole flows out to establish the celestial circuit. This relation to the Intelligible and its manifestation in the circular motion of the heavenly sphere is also described in VI.4.2, 39–49. The cosmic soul looks toward the perfection of the Intelligible, but needs to take into account the division of matter as well. In turning toward the Intelligible, the cosmic soul constitutes the cosmos as having its own kind of perfection, most clearly seen in the heavenly sphere, the sphere of the fixed stars. The unfolding of time appears in the much later treatise, III.7 [45] 11, examined by Manchester, 1978, 101–136.

The desire of the cosmic soul, as not in the Intelligible, is thus translated into movement, both spatial and temporal, a turning toward the Intelligible that achieves an image of perfection in the circular motion that constitutes the outer fixed sphere. Its parts can then come to be within the heavenly sphere, acting in their own right and being affected by the heavenly circuit itself in terms of their relation to one another and to the whole. This primal movement establishes the basic rhythm of the day, a complete and eternal motion that is as close to perfection as possible. Within that movement, the relation of the parts to one another establish other cycles, such as moon and sun for the month and year. Planetary motions are much more complex, with cycles extending over thousands of years before commencing again. The point at issue, of course, is the influence of this circuit upon bodies on earth and the elements from which they are formed, with Plato's discussion in *Laws*, X 889a–d providing a parallel that indicates the cosmic scope of nature and the human scope of craft relative to the four elements and the corporeal mixtures formed from them.

The influence relative to earthly bodies can be easily illustrated in the change of seasons marked by different constellations, tides caused by the moon, and the effects of the sun in bringing warmth and growth, particularly at the vegetative level. The influence on the elements needs somewhat more teasing out, especially for us. While fire is the element characteristic of the heavens, all the elements, earth, water, air, and fire, can be found on the earth, but only in the mixtures that make up the variety of bodies observed on earth and their four basic qualities, hot, cold, wet, and dry. It is the claim of the astrologers that specific planets exercise their influence through these elements precisely in terms of their four primary qualities, with different planets associated with different qualities. Further, they claim that these qualities determine the character of the individual, regulated according to the theory of the four humors, with both astrological and medical sources. It is this level of influence that will be the primary target of attack in Plotinus' account of planetary and stellar influence.

Plotinus's discussion of the elements often occurs in his accounts of matter, as in II.4 and III.6; the former, II.4.6–12, deals with the quantitative and qualitative aspects of matter and the latter, III.6.6–10, discusses the presence of qualities and affections in the elements but the complete impassibility of matter itself. In V.1.2, earth, fire, water, and air only have value in the compounds that the presence of soul brings to them, ordering and adorning them to form the cosmos in all its array, as discussed in Gurtler, 2005, 197–214, and 2013, 123–130. The medical side of this theory has roots in the four elements of Empedocles (c. 490–430 BC) and receives classical articulation in Galen (AD

131–201/216). Finally, Ptolemy (c. AD 90–168), *Tetrabiblos*, Book 1, 4–8, associates the theory of humors with the planets and their influence; see http://en.wikipedia.org/wiki/Humorism (last modified March 18, 2015).

31, 15–24 *The crafts, that . . . the reason why*: Plotinus next turns to crafts and his brief comments continue to depend on Plato's discussion in *Laws*, X 889a–d, with some significant omissions. There is no mention of chance as a cause working with Nature, and some central crafts in the *Laws*, such as politics and legislation, are omitted without comment, although there is an allusion to them in Chapter 39, 11–17. Unlike Nature, crafts work by planning and calculation and use what Nature provides to make small things, artifacts as Plato calls them. Plotinus divides the crafts, following Plato, in terms of those that make an artifact and those that assist Nature. Medicine and farming cooperate with Nature in producing health in a body or in the breeding of animals and the pollinating and propagating of plants. These crafts supplement natural processes, rather than make an artifact not existing in nature but arising from some human need. Rhetoric and music, further, are classified separately. They are like crafts that produce something and they are like medicine and farming in that their influence works with Nature. These crafts, however, as directed to the soul make the individual better or worse. Perhaps the other crafts can also make things better or worse, but presumably they do not do so deliberately and their influence is not in the moral sphere. He turns finally to three questions. The first, about an exhaustive numbering of the crafts, is not addressed here, or anywhere else in the Plotinian corpus. From one point of view, it is unanswerable, but from another, his brief list of types gives the parameters for an ongoing process of listing. The power of these crafts and the reason they have this power is dealt with later in Chapters 40–44. It is in terms of the working of crafts that Plotinus will understand the power of prayer and magic. Magic and prayer work either as crafts assisting and exploiting natural processes and objects, or as crafts directed to the soul by means of some kind of persuasion, or a combination of the two.

31, 25–30 *It is evident . . . will consider later*: The heavenly motion, or *phora*, is by its nature in act and has influence on itself and its constituent parts, the fixed stars, and the planets. This motion cannot but have influence on earth as well, as is obvious at the most basic level of days, months and the seasons of the year. In extending this influence to the soul, however, Plotinus is careful to keep the soul itself from being affected, so only its conditions or states are under consideration. On the vegetative level the influence can be seen in growth; on the sense level, being awake or asleep and sensing in general come into view; and finally on the rational level, human virtue and vice are the matters in contention. He puts off until Chapters 40–42 whether this influence goes in reverse, from things on earth to the heavenly bodies, one of the central issues concerned with divine cooperation in human evil or the possibility of these heavenly beings coming under human spells. At this point, however, he grants the most accepted explanations, without naming them, but still holds them to be reasonable, as will be tested by examining this influence from its beginning or origin.

31, 30–48 *Now, however, we . . . souls of animals*: It becomes clear in this next sentence that Plotinus takes starting from the beginning very literally, the qualities of the elements and their mixtures, the bodies on earth. He denies, first, that the qualities and their mixtures are effects of the *phora*; then, that certain qualities can be traced to particular heavenly bodies, the sun for hot, a planet for cold, and the moon for wet. His reason is simple, that all heavenly bodies are by nature composed of fire. The differences in qualities and mixtures, thus, cannot be understood if all the causes are more or less the same, nor can the many things that happen beyond the elemental level of qualities and mixtures be traced to one of these corporeal qualities rather than another. Plotinus is saying, on the one hand, that the corporeal things on earth do not come about directly from the action of the *phora* but have their own innate structure in terms of the mixture of the elements that constitutes them as bodies, and, on the other hand, that many of the more complex effects produced cannot be reduced simply to one of these qualities or another, striking at the heart of the astrological account. This being the case, moral character is related to factors other than the bodily temperaments and the dominance of one or another of the four qualities or humors, as commonly described in astrological works of his time. Affections, like anger and jealousy, therefore, cannot be reduced to these bodily humors, nor can an habitual state like wickedness, which he seeks to trace to the individual's choice, as explored in the ethical treatises of the Greek philosophical tradition. His next line of attack deals with those things removed from individual choice, such as fortune, parentage, or chance events. All these things also have little to do with the balance of the elements in the particular body of an animal. Plotinus sees life as introducing something different from the merely physical interaction of the elements, even at the vegetative and sensitive levels. To reduce things back to that primordial level cannot provide a satisfactory or, as he says, reasonable explanation. Shaw, 2006, 9–10, indicates the Aristotelian background here, where the soul overcomes the natural motions of the elements in its causal role within the living thing (*De Anima* 2.4.416a6–9).

While Galen's (AD 129–c. 201/216) writings on the humors would be familiar to Plotinus, his major focus is on the astrologers. He does not deny their theory *tout court*, but makes a distinction between temperaments, habits and actions due to choice against the fatalism of the astrologers. III.1 [3] 5–6 presents an early treatment of the humors and their astrological attribution to the planets, and II.3 [52] 2–6 a later and much more detailed treatment and refutation of astrological theory. See http://en.wikipedia.org/wiki/Tetrabiblos (last modified March 4, 2015), for Ptolemy's (AD c. 90–168) association of the planets and the sphere of the fixed stars with the four humors. In Ptolemy, astronomy refers to the motions of the stars while astrology deals with their influence on earth (Riley, 1987, 243). Plotinus is interested in arguing against any malevolent influence on the part of the stars as well as any sense of fate, reserving choice to the individual in terms of the nature of the soul.

31, 33–39 *For it is . . . one of them*: For this sentence, I follow Igal, 1985, 427, in taking the *phora* as the subject that does not produce the qualities of the elements nor their mixtures, with the argument then moving to the sun, planets, such as Saturn and Mars, and finally the moon, which Igal notes also comes from Stoic sources (SVF, II, 673–674).

31, 48–58 *We also need . . . accrue to them*: This last section moves from the physical influence just excluded to various modes of human thinking that need also to be excluded, specifically choice, knowledge, and calculation (*proairesis*, *gnomē*, and *logismos*). This exclusion is a commonplace in the writings of Plotinus, but here it is specified in terms of attributing to the gods a scheming that is reprehensible even among human beings. Plotinus quotes Plato about the kinds of disreputable activities inappropriate for such scheming and will later (39, 11ff.) indicate the way in which the All interweaves things so that they contribute spontaneously to a common harmony. In conclusion, this section indicates that the influence of the *phora* is primarily in terms of soul rather than body, but it is a soul that does not operate at all like the human soul. Both of these are central for his argument in the subsequent chapters, which excludes a reductionist account of stellar and planetary influence in terms of bodies and an anthropomorphic account of souls' causality patterned on human knowing and producing. III.1.8–10 and II.3.16–17 have similar discussions of soul's causality, both the cosmic soul and individual souls. Since Plotinus traces all causality ultimately to soul, he is able to distinguish proximate from remote causality, such that one's parents are more determinant of temperament than the configuration of planets. Within the context of the cosmic soul's overall causality, Plotinus defines the precise ranges for psychic and corporeal causality, targeting philosophical determinism and astrological fatalism.

Chapter 32

The next two chapters present two complementary assumptions for Plotinus' explanation of the influence of the heavenly circuit and of individual heavenly bodies. One is of the cosmos as a single living thing, employed earlier in the treatise, but playing a central role both in this section on planetary influence and the subsequent section on light. The other is a corollary to the first, the interdependence and coordination of the parts of the cosmos. Within this single living thing, the parts have two aspects, their bodies and their share in soul. As bodies they are completely parts of the All, but as they share in souls they achieve different degrees of independence from the All. Sympathy is crucial for this single living thing, allowing parts at a distance to be affected by their similarity to one another. This likeness among some implies also an unlikeness among others. These two factors explain how harming another part can occur, without destroying the overall unity of the whole. The ends of individual parts contribute to the general end of the whole, while some are so completely parts as not to have an end of their own.

32, 1–4 *If then we . . . a reasonable cause*: The chapter begins with a brief statement of the conclusion of the previous chapter that the influence from outside, from the heavens, is not due to bodily causes or to choice, and poses the question: what then is a reasonable explanation for this influence? III.1.8, 1–2, begins with the same question about a cause, after eliminating the alternative causes of Stoics, astrologers, and others, as fatalistic and excluding choice.

32, 4–13 *First, we must . . . which they have*: Plotinus begins with a quote from the *Timaeus* that the cosmos is one living thing that surrounds all living things within it. This implies that the soul of the cosmos extends to all its parts. All bodies are parts, completely so insofar as they are bodies, but insofar as some of these bodies also participate in a soul of their own, they have an element of independence. This double presence, as body and as soul, provides the framework for understanding how each thing relates to the All and to the other parts. This relation is denoted by the term sympathy, a Stoic term that Plotinus exploits richly for his own purposes. He explains it here simply as the capacity of one part to be affected by another even when they are not physically next to one another but have instead some similarity. He uses the example of sensing in an animal, where a part can touch something that passes over intervening, dissimilar parts to a distant but similar part that can be affected. His knowledge of the nervous system grounds this in animals, but he extends it in principle to the whole cosmos, however different from sensing it functions on that grand scale.

Sympathy plays a key role in the very early treatise, III.1 [3] 5, where Plotinus accepts the evidence of the astrologers about the causal role of the stars while disagreeing with their application of this to the human soul. In the late treatise, II.3 [52] 13, Plotinus emphasizes the degrees of participation in the All by different kinds of souls, stellar and human, where sympathy, including an allusion to the analogy of the lyre, similarly plays the crucial role. See Gurtler, 1988, ch. 3, 91–137 (=2002, 241–276) for a discussion of both these treatises.

32, 13–22 *This one All . . . be sympathetically affected*: That similar things can affect one another has a long history in Greek philosophy, epitomized in the phrase that like is known by like. Plotinus' example acknowledges this origin in sensing and knowing, but the ground for the possibility that like things can affect one another is his understanding of sympathy, as he will confirm later in IV.5.8, when he discusses whether a cosmos external to this one could be seen. Sympathy is thus the new item in Plotinus' explanation for the interaction of parts of the cosmos with one another and the whole. This sympathy is further rooted in the ensouled nature of the cosmos, making it different from the materialistic understanding of the Stoics, from whom he borrows the term. He thus states here that it is the nature of a living thing to have unity as its end and consequently something distant spatially will be near because this one living thing is by nature sympathetically affected. There are thus a number of ingredients in play, the cosmos as a living thing, the unity of this living thing and all its parts, the unifying end of this whole, and the sympathy and similarity among the parts. Plotinus in the following chapters draws out the implications of the parallel between the cosmos as a whole and an individual living thing encountered on earth, noting the differences between them and yet their underlying similarity.

32, 23–32 *The part then . . . it withers away*: The following section plays with the likeness among some things and the unlikeness among others. He begins by indicating how the similarity between parts allows one part to be the agent and the other the recipient, with a common affection occurring between them; similarly, if the two parts are unlike, the recipient will undergo an alien and unpleasant experience. Thus within the single living thing, harm and injury are as possible as benefit and healing. To indicate the reality of this, he uses the example within us of things that can harm us, such as bile and anger, which can stifle some of our activities and spur on others. Bile is a bodily excretion, while anger is a state of the ensouled composite, but they both have influence over our activities. The whole is like that, and so too are simpler living things, such as plants, where one part can block the other from receiving sunlight, making it wither. Implicit is the acceptance that evil and harm are part of this cosmos at a level that does not entail choice or intention on the part of the cause, a first pass in his response to those who charge the more divine parts of the cosmos, the heavenly circuit and planets, with complicity in moral evil as it occurs among human beings. II.3.18, 1–5 also deals with the presence of evil in the cosmos, with the bold statement that it would be imperfect without it.

32, 32–44 *This All is . . . of bigger ones*: If one had doubts about the possibility of malevolent action by parts of the cosmos against other parts, Plotinus tries his best to remove it here. He begins with the principle that the whole cosmos as one living thing preserves each part, but since the parts are many and diverse, they can prey on one another and harm one another in a multitude of ways. One principle is that each part has its own end, including the need to preserve itself. Thus, one part will use other parts as food, which means they are similar enough without being the same. Another principle is that each part in its own self-interest uses what is similar and destroys what is different. Each part also gives benefit to other parts, insofar as they are capable of taking advantage of its operations, but when the other parts are unable to absorb the impact of its activity, they are destroyed or maimed. His examples of plants withering at an approaching fire or small animals crushed in the stampede of larger ones indicate once more that these negative effects have no choice or intention behind them. The survival of the fittest seems the rule in its most brutal form, although there are other passages where the largess of nature dominates his imagination, as in the prolific nature of the vegetative soul coming from the sun at Chapter 35, 40–43.

32, 44–52 *The generation and corruption . . . it the same*: The final section of this chapter reintegrates the parts into the whole and gives the salient differences between them. Plotinus begins with the changes characteristic of life as it appears on earth, the generation and corruption of sensible beings and the alterations they can undergo during their limited spans of life. In contrast, the cosmos as a single living thing has by nature a life that he describes as unimpeded. He means that it does not have the limitations of earthbound sensible objects, so its life is by nature complete and this is the end toward which all other living things are directed. While sensible beings have their own ends, as he has just argued rather forcefully, these beings do not exist by themselves and thus they and their particular ends are subordinated to the one end of the whole. This subordination to the whole has two interrelated consequences: their lives do not, and cannot, go on forever and they do not have the power to stay the same. The cosmos, by contrast, is different precisely in the sense that its singular motion is eternal and complete, giving it a sameness lacking to its subordinate parts.

II.4.3, 9–10 describe matter as taking one form after another in the sensible flux, and II.4.8, 14–16 describe the qualities of living things, such as size and shape, as coming from their form. While the context of II.4 deals with the spatial characteristics of sensible objects, their temporal attributes have the same limitation, implied here under the rubric of their coming to be and passing away and the changes they undergo (see VI.9 [9] and III.7 [45]).

32, 47–52 *Since it was . . . it the same*: This section is particularly difficult to translate smoothly. As a strategy, I have translated *onta* nominally as "beings" in two instances (32, 48; 50–51) and verbally in two others (32, 49; 50); two phrases, *to . . . echein* (32, 50–51) and *to . . . echon* (32, 52), following L-S, A. III. c. inf. (q.v.), as having the means or power to do something, I have translated by using "keep," highlighting the contrast between the two different cases.

Chapter 33

This chapter takes up Plotinus' complementary assumption, the interdependence and coordination of the parts of the cosmos. The heavenly circuit acts not by chance but rationally, providing harmony between agent and recipient and order in the heavenly array. The image of a dance captures the intricacy of this order in the changing arrangements and states of the heavenly circuit. The dance includes the movements of the dancer and his limbs, as well as the musical accompaniment, with the dancer looking beyond himself toward performing the whole dance. The planets and other heavenly bodies act in the same way, or give portents and signs. Indeed the whole cosmos acts as one living thing, with its parts configured differently to produce many effects, and these effects are not outside it but within. This configuration in the heavens provides for further affections received by living things on earth which is in harmony with the heavens by its link to the whole, but is also a living thing having its own actions and necessities.

33, 1–7 *Since the heavenly circuit . . . of its movements*: In examining the singular and complete motion of the All, Plotinus argues that it expresses the *logos* immanent in a living thing, excluding anything happening by chance or at random. This presence of reason has two aspects, the harmony with recipients on earth and the order among the stars and planets. The order can be seen as the configuration of the *phora* and its accompanying planets, changing according to various cycles. To each of these configurations corresponds one disposition after another on earth, from changes of seasons to particular affections that one thing receives but not some other. The immanence of this reason implies for Plotinus that it cannot be the result of deliberation and planning, and he chooses the image of a dance to illustrate this. As he moves through the description of the dance, it will thus be necessary to show how Plotinus indicates subtly but carefully that the dance derives from a reason that precedes and is outside it.

33, 4–6 *To every position . . . one disposition after another*: Position (*schesis*) and disposition (*diathesis*) are similar in meaning, but *schesis* derives from *echo*, with a sense of having a certain position, while *diathesis* is from *tithēmi*, with the reciprocal sense of being placed. The two terms tend to be linked together in the next few chapters, indicating the current position of the stars and the resulting conditions on earth.

33, 7–25 *Since even in dances . . . the dance fully*: He begins by turning directly to obvious aspects of dances as we experience them, their external elements, the accompaniment of flute or song and incidental things such as props, lighting, and so on, whose role is so obvious as not to merit detailed analysis. The viewer sees all these as part of one thing, the performance of the dance. Next, Plotinus turns his full attention to the dancer in particular, or rather to his limbs. It is almost as if the limbs are independent or detached, each taking different positions in the sequence of the dance, exerting or relaxing in turn, held tight or free as the figures of the dance change. Plotinus sees the dancer as not focused on these motions of the limbs but on the dance itself, capturing the spontaneity of the motions, which would be interrupted if the dancer turned his attention to what each limb was doing at a particular instant rather than on the dance as a whole. Thus these movements are controlled by the dance itself, even as they bring the dance toward its completion. Further, it is not the dancer who states how the particular movements express the dance, but the critic appreciates how each movement contributes with precision to the performance as a whole. In the dance, moreover, the whole body of the dancer works in coordination to bring it to completion. Plotinus is separating the planning, calculation, and practice that precede the dance, or are noted by the critical viewer, from the performance itself in which the *logos* of the dance takes on a life of its own with each limb having its necessary position for each part. Gurtler, 1987, 139–186, notes that not directing one's attention to an activity one is engaged in can be seen in Plotinus' discussion of the difference between *parakolouthēsis* and *sunaisthēsis*. The time for attention to the details is in practicing; the performance has a different dynamic. Armstrong, 1984, IV, 240–241, notes that Plotinus is describing a solo pantomime dancer and indicates the aptness for capturing the active, dynamic nature of the cosmos.

33, 25–41 *One must indeed . . . own internal necessities*: In applying this analogy to the *phora*, Plotinus includes both actions, like the warmth of the sun or the moon's pull on the tides, and signs and portents, where there is no direct action, but the kind of evocation that occurs in a dance as well. The configuration of the whole heavenly circuit, the sphere of the fixed stars or highest parts, is always changing; this can be observed in the night sky as different groups of constellations dominate in one season after another. These changes in the sky have effects on earth associated with them, especially in terms of climate. There are also changes of position, the precise place in the sky where constellations occur at different moments, whether at their rising, at zenith or at their setting. One needs to add, of course, the positions of the planets as they wander through in terms of their own motions and cycles. Plotinus affirms that this cannot be the work of the configured stars and planets, but of the All as the configuring agent, producing these configurations within itself. The alternative, that the stars and planets are responsible for the configurations, positions, and figures, would not yield the unity that we see, as in the dance it is not the hands, fingers, arms, or legs that produce the figures and their different positions, but the one dancer, following the *logos* of the dance. Finally, he briefly describes how these affections are received here, which depends on things here on earth being living things that can act and be affected in terms of their own nature and the necessities that go with that. While this gives a precise overview of the image of the dance, details will be added in the course of the discussion in the subsequent chapters.

The translation of chapters 33 and 34 is complicated both by the terms used and the penchant of Greek to refer to them solely by the article. The strategy for the translation follows: figure (*to schēma*, 33, 37;38; 34, 13;14;20;27;29), configuration (*hē schēmatisis*, 34, 18; *ho schēmatismos*, 33, 16;20;33; 34, 7;15;19;24; the endings make them abstract substantives, Smyth, 1980 [1920], #840), configuring or being configured (*schēmatizo*, 33, 16;34;35; 34, 21;27; *metaschēmatizo*, 33, 29). The genders of the nouns are crucial in determining the most likely antecedent for the lone article, pronoun, or participle; sometimes the "antecedent" comes after.

Chapter 34

This chapter takes up the last lines of chapter 33 with a short qualification of the influence received in our own case as living things that are affected but also act from our own necessities. Our bodies are affected as sharing in the body of the cosmos, but we are also not entirely identified with the body, so that we are like skilled workers, receiving instructions that do not eliminate our own initiative. Plotinus then returns to an examination of the configurations of those stars we observe moving at different speeds, that is, planets, including the sun and moon. The point at issue is whether the different effects of the configurations are due to these, with their different speeds, or to the living thing as having configured the sphere of the fixed stars. The same figures do not produce the same effects, either deeds or portents, when the planets are part of the configuration, so the fixed stars cannot be the sole cause, but the planets have their own input, similar to the workers and their master in the opening lines. Finally, he returns to the image of the dance, broken down into three parts, the figures of the dance, which direct the movements of the dancer, the limbs of the dancer, by which these figures are manifest, and the third part as the effects of the limbs executing the dance on their constituent parts, such as the tendons and veins affected along with the fingers. Thus we have the one living thing producing the figures, the particular motion of the stars and planets which execute those figures, the latter adding their own spin, so to speak, and finally the affections received by things on earth, with their particular responses.

34, 1–7 *Since we give . . . totally to another*: Initially this opening section seems an interruption or digression, but it plays a significant role in understanding the discussion to follow. Plotinus is specifying a point made at Chapter 32, 4–14 about how a part participates in the all; bodies participate completely, but living things only insofar as they have bodies. Human beings thus are under the cosmos in terms of their bodies, but not as souls in their own right. In this case they function like free laborers, taking instruction from the employer, but having appropriate latitude to make their own contribution.

34, 7–17 *But it is necessary . . . a different nature*: He turns immediately to the heavenly bodies that run at different speeds, the planets, including the sun and moon. Plotinus is contrasting the sphere of fixed stars, with their configurations (the constellations), and the other bodies that move against that background from one constellation to another along the zodiac. This passage makes clear that he has been talking about the planets, which is confirmed by II.3 [52] where he names them and gives their supposed astrological character and influence. Enclosing the word in brackets alerts the reader that in most cases only articles, pronouns, and participles appear in the text. The motions are not set by the single living thing in configuring the sphere of the fixed stars, mentioned in the previous chapter (33, 25–41), but nonetheless their motions are rational and their different positions belong to the one living thing; as a result things on earth are also affected sympathetically by them. These wandering stars, especially along the ecliptic, change the configurations of the fixed stars and this observed phenomenon leads to a series of questions about the figures and about their sympathetic affections especially in living things here on earth. Do these affections derive from the figures in the sphere of the fixed stars or are they consequences of the distinct motion of the planets against that background? Is it the figures that have influence, or the figures and these planets that enter them at different times and in different positions? The evidence indicates that the same planet configured in different figures yields different effects and portents.

34, 17–26 *About this, one . . . cases only portents*: In answer to the questions raised, whether it is the figures or the planets, Plotinus opts for both. This attribution to both has been anticipated in 34, 1–7, where he spoke of the independence of human souls, using the analogy of skilled workers and their employer to indicate a degree of independent action. The planets, having souls closer to the Intelligible than human souls, would *a fortiori* have greater independence. Implicit in the argument, however, is that the planets are lower than the fixed stars in the outer sphere, which are eternally the same. Planets are like skilled workers, while that sphere is like the employer. Thus, their analogy to human souls is stronger and their influence on them greater than that of the fixed stars. In terms of the cosmology of his day, Plotinus is interpreting the cosmos as the living thing that causes the sphere of the fixed stars, the constellations they compose, and their different positions at different times. While eternal and unchanging, its effects on earth vary according to times and seasons. He places all other heavenly bodies, to which we might add more occasional things as comets and shooting stars, as manifesting an independence from this initial and eternal configuration of the one living thing and with an influence that is perhaps more subtle as subordinate to that larger and more powerful motion. Human souls, in the astrology of the day, are especially apt for picking up the subtle influence of these wanderers in the sky.

Platonic background for this is especially strong in the *Phaedrus*, in Socrates' second speech or palinode, where he associates different types of souls with specific planets, the gods of the Greek pantheon. Elements of this also appear in the *Symposium*, in the discussion of the daemons, intermediaries between the divine and the human; the role of the daemons is mentioned at Chapter 30, 30–32 and treated at 43, 12–16. The astrological background introduces planets as favorable (Jupiter, Venus, and the Moon), unfavorable (Saturn and Mars), and ambivalent (Mercury and the Sun); Ptolemy, *Tetrabiblos* I, 4-5, divides them into pairs of opposites, with favorable planets associated with warmth and moisture, the unfavorable with cool and dry, and the neutral as depending on the configuration of planets with the Sun and their synodic cycle. See http://en.wikipedia.org/wiki/Tetrabiblos (last modified

March 4, 2015) and notes in Igal, 1982, 380, and Brisson, 2005, 267.

34, 17–21 *The particular configuration . . . Even better, to both*: Taking *kai* (34, 18) as adverbial rather than conjunctional; and taking the subsequent phrase (without *kai*) as parallel, with *ten autēn* referring back to *schēmatisin* and *allēn* to *diathesin*. I have also followed Igal, 1985, 433nn193–194, in dropping the question marks at 34, 20 and 21.

34, 26–33 *This account thus . . . affected with them*: The conclusion brings the discussion back to the analogy of the dance. The motion of the heavenly sphere relates to the configuration directing the movement of the dance as a whole, the hands and other limbs of the dancer also have a crucial role in executing the dance, and finally there are the third parts accompanying the fingers affected by the motion of the hand in executing the dance, such as the tendons and veins, representing the consequences of planetary movement on living things on earth.

34, 30–32 *The third parts . . . in the dance*: For this reading, the comma after *sunepomena* has been suppressed and *ta merē kai ex hōn tauta* are taken as predicates. The powers of the planets will be similar to the power of the dance, evoking a response in living things open to receive their influence but with the limitations of the recipient determining whatever might be deficient or evil.

Chapter 35

This chapter begins with the "aspects" used in astrology to specify particular effects of the planets. While Plotinus does not deny these planetary configurations, he argues that their effects cannot be due to either the bodies of the planets or their choices as souls. Summarizing previous chapters, he reminds us that the cosmos is a single living thing and its life is rational and harmonious with a single, ordered structure. As a consequence, the configurations of the planets among themselves and with the sphere of fixed stars must also be rational, analogous to a dance. The activity of the cosmos is thus the figures as well as the planets configured, with powers that have their specific effects. Further, the cosmos as a whole has a single end, a choice within which all other choices occur. If some good follows from the actions, for example, of the sun, it is because the sun is looking toward the same good as the whole cosmos, which is the Intelligible World. The effects, moreover, are received by living things on earth according to their capacity to receive. Some individuals are frightened by a certain figure, while others are not, just as some see the beauty in a certain face and others do not. All beings have a power to act and some to be acted upon. The variety of possible interactions between agents and their corresponding receivers explains the differences that emerge from the same actions and why these effects are so particular. Finally, those things acted upon function as substrates in which the received powers from active beings have the ability to act in their own right. Human crafts serve as examples of this ability, especially as our reason uses the innate powers of natural objects to produce things with wondrous effects.

35, 1–19 *How then do . . . their rational natures*: In asking how the powers work, Plotinus alludes to some of the specifics of astrology, differences in triangles and of one planet from another. The triangle refers to one of the astrological aspects, which indicate the relation of the planets to one another as seen in the night sky, 180° from horizon to horizon, which is half the full 360° of their orbits around the earth. The aspects are measured from the rising of the planet in the east, so that if two planets rise together, they are in conjunction; the other aspects are the sextile at 60°, the square at 90°, the triangle or trine at 120°, the angles indicating how high a planet is above the rising planet, with opposition occurring when one planet is setting as the other is rising, 180° different. The sextile and trine indicate the fraction of the full 360° circle that these figures represent. Ptolemy, *Tetrabiblos*, gives a full account of the mathematics involved and of the astrological assumptions to which Plotinus takes exception. These aspects indicate the major relations of the planets on which the astrological importance of their effects was based. Plotinus does not dispute the mathematics, but gives a different explanation of their influence, eschewing the astrological claim that the effect depends on whether the planets can see one another or on the division of the planets into moist and dry, diurnal or nocturnal, and male or female. In III.1.5 and II.3.1–6 Plotinus critiques these astrological assumptions; II.3 is particularly detailed in its critique. Thus their effects cannot be due to their bodies, as he has indicated earlier in pointing out that all heavenly bodies are basically composed of fire, nor can it be choice, since these divine beings are constantly aware of the intelligible and hence do not need choice (cf. Chapter 31, 30–58). He recalls the assumptions behind his own explanation, the cosmos as a single living thing so that sympathy will be the key for understanding how one part affects another. The cosmos is also necessarily structured and ordered by reason, with nothing random possible. With these two principles, the figures and configurations of the stars can have effects that are multiple, although always coordinated, and without involving the absurdities and determinism that Plotinus finds among the astrologers.

35, 13 *Fixed degrees over time*: *Arithmous*, L-S, xii, [q.v.], astrology, mostly plural, "degrees traversed in a given time."

35, 19–24 *While some figures . . . this particular animal*: Using the analogy of the dance summarized at 34, 26–33 (dancer, limbs, veins and tendons), I have construed the passage with minimal violence to the words and their grammatical forms. *Ta men schēmata* is thus parallel to *ta de . . . alla [schēmata]*, contrasting the sphere of the fixed stars with the planets, likened to the limbs (*melē*) of an animal, taking *alla* as it appears in the mss. rather than as construed with the following clause. For that clause, I construe *allas* with *dunameis*, while *tas* is construed with *hōs zōou merē*; *to . . . sunteloun* explains what is particular to these parts (*autois* referring to *merē* rather than *melē*, as in HS_2) as not having choice, thus the actual bodies of the planets as parallel to the veins and tendons in the fingers of the dancer. II.3.9 also discusses the double nature of the cosmos and everything in it, as composed of body and soul; that context also mentions the double nature of the sun's influence, its physical warmth and its vegetative power. While the possibility of planetary influence rests in the soul of the planet, the actual influence depends on its body as the locus of its dispersion. That this body does not contribute to the nature of the planet follows from the nature of matter and body developed in II.4.8–12, where Plotinus argues that all the qualities of the composite are contained in the form, with body and matter providing the place where the nature of the form can appear.

35, 19–37 *While some figures . . . employer is looking*: This section begins with a sentence that has not been easy to comprehend. Part of the difficulty is that translators have not noticed that Plotinus moves back and forth between the image of the cosmos as a living thing and an individual animal, with its specific shape, including its limbs and their physical components. In Greek, the same word is used, *zōon*, but in English calling the whole cosmos an animal would not sound right (although it works, for example, in Spanish). The parallel between an animal and the cosmos as a living thing returns at Chapter 45, 1–10, where Plotinus makes explicit what is implicit here, that for the cosmos some of its parts are in fact also living things in their own right, while for an animal even its most basic parts have some kind of consciousness of it as a whole.

The figures (*ta schēmata*) both of the sphere of the fixed stars and of the planets are thus seen as analogous to the parts of an animal. The sphere of the fixed stars is like an animal's overall proportions and dimensions, with its motions and positions, so that the recurrent motion (*phora*) of the cosmos in orderly progress across the sky appears like any animal with its size and motion. The next short clause compares the figures of the planets to the limbs of such an animal, set apart from one another and configured in relation to the animal as a whole, with the planets appearing to have their own motions against the background of the fixed stars. The motions of the legs of an animal capture the epicycles of the planets in Ptolemy's model of planetary motions, moving in swift circles against the background of the stars moving in their more stately orbit. See http://csep10.phys.utk.edu/astr161/lect/retrograde/aristotle.html (accessed March 25, 2015) for an explanation and visualization of this planetary motion.

The "limbs" also allude to the analogy of the dance, in which the limbs of the dancer, especially the hands, are the most expressive parts for the audience, although small parts relative to the whole body of the dancer. The planets also take on an expressive importance because of the way they are set at different intervals in constantly changing configurations with the figures of the zodiac and one another. Finally there are those powers of the living thing without choice, like the veins and tendons of the dancer. These powers refer to the actual bodies of the stars and planets, what allows them to be in time and space and to be composed, in the case of the stars and planets, of fire. Both of these factors allow these stellar beings to act, but their nature comes from the Intelligible and not from the bodies with which they are associated in the sensible cosmos.

Plotinus applies this discussion to the cosmos as a whole, whose one choice includes all the choices of its parts within it. These choices, many as they are and in conflict as they may be, are all directed to the same one end as that of the whole cosmos. The basis for this is Plotinus' assumption that the cosmos is like an individual living thing since it has one soul. He then returns to individual animals and gives four examples of their activities: appetite, anger, growth, and generation, where the specific ends of some animals are counter to the ends of others, amplifying the discussion in 32, 23–58. Thus, appetite indicates the need of one animal that is satisfied by taking something from another, anger (32, 29) in one animal is aroused by the provocation of another, growth (32, 35) is nourished by another, and generation (32, 45) produces something other than its sources. These particular examples refer to animals on earth, but Plotinus has already alerted us that they have analogues in the heavens as well (32, 30), and reaffirms that it is the whole living cosmos that works all these things in the parts. The cosmic soul, moreover, does not choose these diverse actions, as he stated at the beginning of the chapter, but they come about because of the order and structure it gives to the cosmos by seeking or looking toward the good. For our part, he states, choice also seeks this good beyond immediate passions and by so doing contributes to the one end of the whole cosmos. He will explain later how even wrong choices are interwoven by the whole into its own perfection (Chapter 45, 29–34). His point here is to emphasize the autonomy of the parts, referring once more to those working for another, following directions and improvising on their own, while coinciding in looking to the same good (Chapter 34, 3–7).

35, 37–61 *If then the sun . . . these figures do*: At this point Plotinus indicates that the sun and the planets do not act from choice. The reason is different from those powers residing in their bodies examined in the previous section that lack choice and do not contribute to the nature of these beings. In the case of these celestial beings they do not have choice because they do not need it. The explanation for this is in terms of their two acts, the act by which they are what they are and the act which flows from them and is present in their bodies and beyond. The first act he describes as the sun looking above, while the second is the warming that comes from it to the earth and within that second act the presence of that part of soul that is essentially generative, the vegetative soul. The other planets, and indeed the sphere of the fixed stars, similarly act without choice as looking toward the Intelligible, producing a second act which is like an illumination. Their configurations in different unities produce different dispositions in the things affected on earth, effects related to other aspects of the soul, especially the sensitive soul.

Plotinus turns to the things here on earth to limn what these different effects can be and what kinds of things can be affected. His first example is of figures that frighten. He mentions some of the curiosities of this reaction: the frightened individuals have no previous experience of this figure that would warrant fright, these same individuals are not frightened by other figures, and other individuals are not frightened at all by this figure. The causality is not physical or corporeal, the premise of the astrologers, but rather has its origin in the soul. It is also not based on the choice of the planet, so that the planets are not causes in a deterministic sense and are thus not culpable for any human deeds supposedly done under their influence. It comes about because of the sympathy operative in the cosmos, but here specified in terms of the specific sympathetic relation between this individual and that figure. They are attuned to one another. The next examples are in the realm of vision, that the beauty of a particular face strikes one individual but not another and that colors, more fundamentally, strike the eye with their activity. All these phenomena have the same source, the sympathetic relation of one part of the cosmos to another. This means that the influence of the configurations of the stars and planets has a similar nature rooted in the soul. Plotinus in this way counters the materialistic determinism of Stoic sympathy and the fatalism of the astrologers in their explanations of planetary influence. He is careful to indicate that the influence of these heavenly bodies corresponds to lower levels of the soul only, the vegetative and sensitive, leaving the intellectual part free of interference. These lower aspects also take into account the psychosomatic character of the operation of sympathy active in the cosmos; for example, the physical warmth of the sun is associated with the vegetative soul and the illumination of the planets with their effect on human beings by means of perception, visual and otherwise. Igal, 1979, 315–345, discusses Plotinus' synthesis of Platonic and Aristotelian divisions and powers of the soul. The sensitive and vegetative powers form part of the true self, and are also powers of heavenly bodies, precisely as powers properly of the soul.

35, 61–69 *So in fact . . . many wondrous results*: From his examples, seeing frightening figures, or the beauty of a face, or even simple colors, Plotinus draws the parallel between planetary influence and ordinary sense experience. They have the same structure of sympathy between objects, one acting as agent and the other as recipient to that action. He has noted that the nature of the recipient allows for some to react to a particular figure or beauty and for others not to be affected by them. Now he argues that the nature of planets, as beings in a fuller sense than faces and colors, clearly gives them the power to act. All beings have this power to act by means of that first act that makes them what they are, and coming from this act is a second act that flows out from them, to a greater or lesser extent. It is this second act that is poised to influence some other object, whether it is the figure of a planet in the heavens, the beauty of a face on earth, or the color reflected from some object. It is, moreover, the nature of some objects not only to act but to be acted upon that allows this circuit to be completed. The completion of the circuit is not, however, the end of the story, since the recipients as substrates have powers because of the figures present to them. To illustrate this, Plotinus uses the example of powers present in us that are not derived from the qualities, such as hot and cold, of the elements from which our bodies are composed. These powers are, on the contrary, generated by different qualities that are derived from our rational faculty and the power of Nature. In other words, these powers are the work of crafts, both those that produce artifacts and those that cooperate with Nature. These crafts utilize, moreover, inanimate objects such as stones or the natural power inherent in plants to produce their amazing results. This is not so much a reference to magic and witchcraft as it is to Plotinus' consistent and insistent argument that magic and such things are simply applications of what is generally true of all crafts, where their effects are due to the natural sympathy among all things in the sensible cosmos. This interpretation runs counter to Brisson 2005, 268n393, who refers to the magical properties of stones and plants, but misses the point that the properties of stones and plants, even magical ones, have their source in reason and Nature; that is, precisely in the soul, reason in the human soul and powers in stones and plants coming from the soul of Nature.

Chapter 36

This chapter continues the reflection on the cosmos as a living thing in terms of human beings as living things who have the ability to comprehend the works of Nature. The All contains a rich diversity of both rational natures and powers. This is illustrated by looking first at how these natures and powers appear in human beings: the eye with its power and the bones of hand and foot with their powers. We are ignorant of the rational nature of these parts of the body and their corresponding powers unless an expert has studied and explained them. The All by comparison is much more complex, but it did not need to be so; it could have come about like a house, soulless and built from a few basic materials. The All is, however, everywhere awake, everything in it is variously alive, and everything that can exist must be part of it. It follows from this that even things we call inanimate are actually alive, since we designate as living only those things that appear to be self-moving. Thus within us there are parts with a hidden life that give us marvelous powers and even spur us on to great accomplishments. The All is infinitely more complex and its life is enriched by the living things within it. These living things are not produced by the choice of the All, since its making is more primordial than choice, but they all serve it with their abundant powers.

36, 1–15 *The All is . . . in this All*: This section fills in some of the details about the nature of the cosmos as one living thing. It employs a two-pronged argument, that knowledge of the complexity of the cosmos is parallel to knowledge about the complexity of the human body which relies on the study of experts, and that the amazing diversity of the cosmos did not need to be so, but is evidence that it is everywhere alive. The parallel with knowledge of human anatomy is a particular application of the analogy of the cosmos as a living thing with an individual living thing with which we should be familiar, but with the added twist that the familiarity derived from ordinary experience is actually innocent of this complexity, which only emerges in the study of experts, such as Galen (AD 129–c. 201/216). Igal 1985, 437n205, refers to Galen's *De Usu Partium Corporis Humani* (On the use of parts of the human body), trans. and ed. by K. G. Kühn (1754–1840). Kühn's edition of Galen's writings (Leipzig, 1821–1833) functions as the standard text for citation purposes.

Plotinus is not focused on the details of this study, but rather on the complexity it reveals about human anatomy and the particular power in each part of the body and by implication, as we shall see, how all these parts work together for the welfare and flourishing of the human being. Human anatomy, however, is a mere trace of the complexity of the cosmos itself, especially in the motions of the various heavenly bodies, the study of which is also the work of experts, especially Ptolemy (AD c. 90–168), as we have already seen in previous chapters. The complexity revealed in the Ptolemaic system functions as evidence that the cosmos is not soulless, like a large and complex house fabricated from only a few materials, but is completely alive, the second branch of the argument. This life extends in various degrees to all its parts and anything alive must, in turn, be part of it. The source for this idea is, of course, Plato's *Timaeus*, where the cosmos is a single living thing (30d3–31a1) which the demiurge produces with a single end (34b–36d). Plotinus' image of the possibility that the cosmos could have been like a soulless house, made with only a few basic materials, is a typically humorous or ironic rejoinder to the Stoic view of the cosmos.

36, 5–8 *There is no part . . . in the All*: Some details here need explanation; *ho mē echei [dunamin] kai ou tēn autēn de echei*: I have read *dunamis* as object of the first *echei* and as modified by *autēn* (36, 5–6); instead of translating the latter phrase as "and not having the same power [as another part]," I render it positively. I kept the *en tō panti* suggested for 36, 7 in HS_2, then followed Igal 1985, 437–438n206, in dropping the dashes (36, 6 and 7) and the punctuation after *ekeinōn* and placing a comma after *panti* (36, 8).

36, 15–27 *From the above account . . . by their powers*: The resolution that inanimate things can be present in the ensouled cosmos indicates that Plotinus understands the previous sentence as establishing that every part of the cosmos is alive in different ways, so that living is an analogous term that refers to an activity that can be shared in varying degrees by anything in the ensouled cosmos. Our usage, he points out, restricts the application of the term "life" to those things that we experience as self-moving. The life in other kinds of things is thus hidden from us, just as in a living human being, for example, there are parts that we do not regard as living and yet they are the source of enrichment for the kind of life we possess. Restricting the account only to the parts already mentioned, the eye and the bones in hand or foot, and taking these as alive rather than as lifeless physical, or perhaps mechanical, components allows Plotinus not only to see their life as coming from the presence of the human soul but as already being ensouled. This is in contrast, for example, to the Aristotelian notion that the rational soul in a human being subsumes the powers of the sensitive and vegetative souls. Plotinus insists, however, that the soul is not an entelechy, so a multitude of souls can be present in the same living thing. He further claims that the advantage of this view is that the multiplicity of souls moves human beings to such things as the study of human anatomy or celestial astronomy. This means that the eyes, hands, and feet have, in some sense, a life of their own. Thus they come to the attention of physicians like Galen when they do not function as we would like, either from disease, accidents, or age. They have an independence that is not merely physical, as in the case of the components of a computer or car, but precisely as alive and not under the total control or choice of the human being of whom they are parts. In a more complete way, the All has living things within it, but they are not like the parts of a human body, since they are in fact produced by the All, although not from its choice since its production of things is prior to choice. These living things, nonetheless, serve the All by their powers and this service refers back to the opening lines of Chapter 34, where laborers work for a master but without losing their independence. Finally, Plotinus assumes that unity and activity both have their roots in the nature of soul and thus something completely soulless would be unable to act and indeed could not exist since it lacks even the most accidental kind of unity. His analysis of matter in II.4 and III.6 presupposes these ideas in accounting for the peculiar nature of matter, as having a kind of existence that prevents it from being a thing and thus not having an activity or unity proper to itself. Even the simplest of bodies, by contrast, have a unity and activity traceable to the soul in the forms and *logoi* present to those bodies, part of the structural diversity of the All that opens this chapter.

Chapter 37

The discussion examines the implications of power in the All and its parts, their role as agents. After the cavalier way the parts have been described as bringing harm and destruction to one another, Plotinus begins with an affirmation that all these parts are essential for the All. The text then turns to fire and the whole range of things that we think we understand until we try to give an account of their nature and especially their active power. Our investigations run into difficulties unless this power is traced back to the All. Generally we do not bother to investigate familiar things but only those whose powers stand out as strange and extraordinary; then we want to know how each of them functions. Everything, however, is actually amazing, as an expert's account and explanation would show us. Everything has three aspects: a certain irrational power, a share in soul alongside the soul of the All, and being surrounded by and being part of the All. Everything has a power for doing, but some have more and some less, with heavenly bodies exercising more power with their clearer nature. These greater beings produce many effects but these effects are not produced by their choice nor are they aware of them. Living things can be generated without choice, without lessening the progenitor, and without awareness of the effect. As choice and awareness go together, so too do the lack of choice and awareness.

37, 1–11 *For the All . . . in full their powers*: The affirmation that nothing in the cosmos is disposable also means that everything belongs to the All as its own. This is the premise that these chapters are attempting to tease out and the topic brought up next applies it to the power and nature of the ordinary things of our experience, like fire, which cannot be explained except in relation to the All. Nothing exists in isolation, but is essentially interconnected as part of the All. The things that make up the sensible cosmos are not, for example, like Cartesian ideas, understandable on their own by a sort of immediate intuition, but can be understood solely in terms of their relation to the All and to one another. The passage then reflects on human knowing. We do not tend to investigate the obvious, but what appears different or puzzling, or as the Stoics said, what is unusual amazes us. This point is already present in the previous chapter about human anatomy, but now it is extended to anything at all. If an expert presented something we have taken as obvious and began explicating all its powers and how they came about and what they can do, we would be duly amazed. Echoes of this attitude permeate Augustine's (AD 354–430) discussion of time in *Confessions*, XI.1. It reflects the ancient and medieval sense that Nature and the cosmos always elude our grasp, and that our knowledge is thus never complete or linear in its development, but can be surprised by imaginative leaps that allow us to see things in a new and different way. So, for example, Einstein's theory of relativity looks at space differently from Newtonian physics, going beyond it while also indicating its continued relevance within a specific context.

37, 11–25 *We need to say . . . of the effect*: Where Chapter 36, 1–2 describes everything in the All in terms of reasons (*logoi*), this section begins by noting that each of the things in the cosmos must have a certain irrational (*alogon*) power. This irrationality is the first of the characteristics that describes things in the sensible cosmos and is perhaps surprising or paradoxical at first glance, but is part of Plotinus' basic understanding of the nature of the cosmos, particularly in its relation to matter as the substrate or receptacle. The very corporeality of the cosmos depends on matter as without form or logos in any sense. The irrationality of matter allows forms to appear in it, but these forms become distinguished in time and space by this contact, becoming the bodies that inhabit this cosmos. Their association with matter, however, gives them a "certain irrational power," illustrated in previous chapters in the vivid description of the harm and evil some things can inflict on others, as can be seen in the accounts of matter in II.4 [12] and III.6 [26], as discussed in Gurtler, 2005 and 2013.

The next characteristic indicates that each thing also shares somehow in soul. If the first characteristic is surprising in the irrationality of having a body, the surprise continues with this rather minimalistic description of how these bodies share in soul. It does not say they each have a soul (although some of them surely do), but only that they share in soul "somehow," adding that they do so "from" or "alongside" (*para*) the whole cosmos as ensouled. The context, of course, is the earlier discussion in 32, 4–13 where Plotinus defines the different ways the parts of the cosmos as bodies share in soul, the soul of the All or other souls as well. The present chapter also follows 36, 15–27 by leaving the whole range of the soul's presence open so that distinctions can be made about the powers that specific corporeal beings have in terms of their own natures, whether as agents or recipients. The third characteristic emphasizes that each part is both surrounded by the All and is part of it. This principle is fundamental for Plotinus' explanation of how one part can affect another, since it presupposes that all the parts are not only within the same cosmos, but are actively related to one another since that cosmos is alive with soul. The alternative to soul's presence throughout the cosmos is the total indefiniteness of matter, where there is no possibility of change and interaction. These are the premises, as it were; what follows are the consequences.

The first consequence is the fact that some parts are more powerful than others "for doing" (*pros to dran*). This difference occurs both among things on earth as well as things in the heavens. Differences on earth are dependent both on the nature of the particular body and of the soul present to it. We have seen so far that size and position can give power, but also reason in the human soul; more will be added as the discussion continues. The planets and stars, moreover, have a nature that for Plotinus and his contemporaries gives them a power to do things that surpasses anything on earth. In some sense, this continues to be true in terms of the energy that the sun or a star can produce and the effects this can have on earth, which we realize includes more than the light and warmth noted by the ancients. In another sense, it indicates Plotinus' assumption that the composition of the heavenly bodies in terms of fire gives them a clearer nature since that element is closer to the Intelligible than the other elements. The following section analyzes the way in which these heavenly beings exercise their doing. First, he claims that the effects coming from them do not happen by choice, since these beings are above choice, summarizing the claims of the previous chapters. Next, he reminds us that these beings do not turn their attention toward the effects that come from them, even if it is an outflow of their soul.

The context is Chapter 35, 37–50 where the sun is doing some good for things on earth but is nonetheless looking constantly toward the Intelligible. Implicit is the rejection of both hearing and seeing on the part of the stars and planets, since their effects do not depend upon their hearing prayers and then choosing to produce some effect, and since they are not attentive to what comes from them, they do not need to see. This lack of attention to what they are doing is indeed characteristic of our own activities when we are most completely engaged in doing them, as indicated in Gurtler, 1988, 139–183, in the analysis of perception (*antilēpsis*) and conscious awareness (*parakolouthēsis*). It is forms of *parakolouthēsis* that are used in 37, 21–25 and it is restricted by Plotinus to contexts related specifically to a type of human consciousness where one part is aware of or follows the activity of another. At I.4.10, 19–32, Plotinus uses the example of reading to indicate that this kind of awareness (*parakolouthēsis*) would detract from and interfere with the activity and is thus inferior to the consciousness (*synaisthēsis*) that characterizes any being in its self-activity, which can be attributed to Intellect and, with qualification, even to the One. For scholarly clarification of Plotinus' terms for consciousness and their relation to one another, see Cobb 1936, Mossé-Bastide 1959, 1972, Schwyzer 1960, Warren 1961, 1964, Graeser 1972, and Gurtler 1978.

Chapter 38

The account turns from the agents to the recipients and falls into three parts. Plotinus first considers the beneficial effects that come from the All and particular planets either in the natural course of their motions or as prompted by such things as prayer. These effects should not be examined in terms of those heavenly agents but of the nature of what is done. First, benefits for the life or other needs of sensible things indicate the natural flow of influence from greater beings to lesser ones. Second, if the effects are unpleasant, especially at the birth of living things, this should not be traced to the planets but to the substrate of the living thing itself, especially as that substrate limits its immediate and future development. He mentions again that the mixture of planetary influences is beneficial for life, but naturally useful effects may not suit this individual nor is the whole cosmic order directed to what a single being might want. Plotinus mentions briefly that we also add to (and perhaps subtract from) what we have been given. Third, the general effect is the harmony of all things, where even opposites can contribute to one another. The defect or lack in a particular living thing is due once more to its not mastering its matter. In sum, some effects, those that are positive, can be attributed to the planets; others, especially unpleasant ones, to the substrate; and others can be added by the individuals themselves, presumably for good or for ill.

38, 1–7 *The effects, then . . . to the lesser part*: The effects come from the All or from its parts, the stars and planets, and they may come either from the different life of the All or as instigated by such things as prayer to the sun and other planets, mentioned at Chapter 30, 1–5. This different life is the unchanging motion of the all in its eternal stability, discussed earlier at Chapter 32, 50–52. The occasional nature of prayer and other such activities has a role, although so far that has not been spelled out and is mentioned here without any commitment on Plotinus' part as to how or whether prayer affects the planets. The crucial point in the present context is that the examination needs to look at the effects themselves and not their reputed sources, either the All or one of the planets. The movement of the analysis must go from effect to cause, *a posteriori*, and not from cause to effect. Beneficial effects are the first to be analyzed, with the simple explanation that they show the natural influence flowing from the greater to the lesser parts of the cosmos. In this case, therefore, one is free to attribute the cause of these effects to the All and the planets, although this does not in any way counter the previous argument that such causality is not the result of their choice. The different life of the All is Plotinus' shorthand for the exclusion of choice in the production of any effects.

38, 7–16 *When something unpleasant . . . been given us*: The alternative class of effects is called "unpleasant." The choice of this neutral and minimal term is a way of indicating a whole range of effects that may for one reason or another warrant a negative evaluation. Stronger terms, such as evil or harmful, bias the argument toward seeing the heavenly causes as engaged in the doing of evil or toward a melodramatic account of experience. Plotinus has clearly set himself the task of excluding divine beings from any concert with evil, and we have also experienced his detached realism in describing the harm and brutality present in nature. The argument is also directed precisely at the core of astrology that planetary motions and positions at the moment of birth determine one's fate. His counter-argument is simply that the substrate is incapable of receiving the benefit that always comes from the heavens. The substrate in this instance has both the sense of the corporeal component of the living thing but also the living thing as the recipient of affections. Thus some of the unpleasant effects can be due to bodily defects in the living thing, while others relate more to the living thing's comportment with the world. Physical blindness is different from an insensitive character, but the cause of both lies within this particular living thing as composed of body and soul. Proximate causes are thus more crucial than the more remote causality of the heavenly circuit. The mix of influences from the planets, each giving something beneficial, does not benefit everything, since it does not necessarily suit certain individuals nor give them what they want. Two separate issues are included in this phrase, that individuals are not receptive to a particular effect, echoing Chapter 35, 49–61, and that they may not want the benefit, emphasizing the role of choice especially in human beings. The next sentence, that we add things to what is given us, also implicitly introduces the factor of choice, which Plotinus seeks to preserve against astrological fatalism and which thus grounds how it is possible not to want some benefit.

38, 17–23 *Nevertheless, all things . . . on their own*: The final section of the chapter reiterates a constant thread in the analysis, that everything that occurs is unified and harmonious, even to the point of reconciling opposites. Thus, if one thing lacks something or is defective, its form has failed to master its matter and it is thus far ugly. Plotinus' lack of sentimentality on this issue may not appeal to one's emotions, but his argument is not without merit. He clearly does not see the need for a perfect universe to be perfect in its details, and has much of the philosophical tradition behind him. Gurtler, 2002 and 2006, indicates that Plotinus' theodicy is rather consistent across the *Enneads* and has its own logical rigor in tracing evil, whether metaphysical or moral, to the presence of soul in the body. The latter article contrasts this sense of moral evil with the very different model rooted in the Biblical tradition, where moral evil has its origin in the soul as personal. Plotinus, for ontological reasons, cannot see evil as possible for the soul as incorporeal, and even less for Intellect. In summary, effects can be traced to various sources. If they are good, they are in line with the natural order of the cosmos; if not so good, look to the limitations of matter or the choice of individuals.

Chapter 39

The way in which all things are woven together is examined further. The affirmation that everything is set in array together and they all contribute to a single end is the basis for portents, one thing signaling another. The reference to virtue presiding over the choices and destinies of individuals find its roots in the ontological dependence of earthly things on those of heaven and, in turn, of the whole sensible cosmos on the intelligible as more divine. This precludes spermatic reasons as causes determining the destiny of individuals, since they are purely corporeal and are incapable of producing anything beyond themselves. The comprehensive and productive reasons are prior, in the heavens and in the Intelligible, and from them can come whatever is in the whole cosmos, what is brought to perfection from matter, and the interaction of the things generated. The reason operative in the All is like the order and law in a city, stemming from the knowledge of how the citizens will act and making laws that promote the interweaving of these actions, with appropriate incentives and penalties. Similarly portents are not so much about predicting, but indicate that effects in a cosmos ruled by reason can give signs of other things. Thus, one thing can be known from another, cause from effect, consequence from premise, composite from its parts, since the same reason makes them all together. This role of reason solves the difficulties of earlier chapters on the complicity of the planets in evil by introducing the role of individual things on earth to explain the presence of evil in terms of their corporeal substrate or the additions these things bring to what they receive from above.

39, 1–17 *Since all things . . . a common harmony*: Plotinus turns from the analysis of the effects of the higher on the lower to their power of giving portents or signs of things here on earth. The context once more is the astrological theory that these signs indicate that the stars or planets determine the character and actions of individuals. The opening sentence, however, states his own assumptions in opposition to that theory, that everything in the sensible cosmos is set in array together and serves a single end, and for that reason they can all be indicated by signs. Next, he quotes the phrase, "virtue has no master," from the Myth of Er in the *Republic*. The context is the return of souls to earth, which combines the soul's choice of a particular life, human or animal in the myth itself, and the destiny that the fates oversee, with virtue having the role of guaranteeing justice. This passage deftly combines choice and destiny to counter both the fatalism of the astrologers and the determinism of the Stoics. Plotinus first interprets the myth to conform to his own Platonic ontology. The cosmic order consists of the dependence of the lower on the higher, moving from things on earth to the heavenly circuit and then from the whole sensible cosmos to the more divine beings of the intelligible cosmos in which they participate. This ontology allows Plotinus to explain the origin of sensible beings in the higher, intelligible causes without eliminating their own causal contributions as beings.

It is this latter factor that introduces his second move to attack the Stoic theory of spermatic reasons, whereby each thing comes about by the reasons immanent within Nature universally and absolutely, in an unalterable chain of causes that determine all things materialistically. In III.1.7, "On Destiny," Plotinus argues that the Stoics, despite their efforts to give individual humans some kind of choice, cannot escape the determinism of an all-determining nature that controls all causes. In the present context Plotinus mentions only that spermatic reasons cannot generate anything beyond themselves, which are specified as the sensible things that come to be, their perfection in the whole from matter, and their interaction with one another. Behind these three statements is his assumption that bodies, however intricately arranged, can never add up to something unified and thus alive. Unity comes from the form and the form always traces back to soul and Intellect, from which it gets its power to unify. The form, even the forms of the elements, is already a unity beyond the multiplicity of corporeal components, whether these things are the simplest of bodies or the most complex of living things. These forms, moreover, function within the unity of the whole sensible cosmos as depending on soul and as appearing in the indefinite nature of matter, so that the perfection they bring to generated beings is always part of the perfection of the whole, a common theme in the preceding chapters. Finally, the capacity of sensible things to interact with one another is a further indication that the whole sensible cosmos and all its parts are alive and essentially active. Plotinus discusses these issues throughout the *Enneads*, with attention to the indefiniteness of matter in II.4 and III.6, and to the relation of forms to bodies in VI.4–5. The three points listed here have also been discussed previously in IV.4: (1) things generated in 32, 4–13; 44–52; 36, 15–27; (2) their perfection in the whole in 35, 25–37; and (3) their mutual activity in 31, 25–48; 32, 13–22; 44–52. Gurtler, 1988, 91–133, presents Plotinus' discussion of Stoic materialism and his transformation of Stoic sympathy.

In contrast to the spermatic reasons of the Stoics is the reason in the all. This reason does not function deterministically, but establishes the order or law in which the choices of individuals can take place. Following Plato's account in *Statesman* 305e and *Laws* 904a–905a, the reason of the All anticipates, as it were, how individuals will act and makes laws that will interweave these actions toward a common harmony. While the reason of the All functions intelligently and is thus analogous to the way a human lawgiver formulates laws through careful deliberation, one must always keep in mind that in the All there is no deliberation or reasoning in the discursive sense, but the All by fixing its gaze on the Intelligible establishes a cosmos that mirrors this intelligibility in a multitude of ways. In III.2.17–18, Plotinus speaks of the harmony of the cosmos in terms of the unity of a drama. The image, while different, emphasizes the unity of a story, and it thus complements the lawgiver used here. Plotinus, in that later work, carefully distinguishes the reason in the soul of the All from the Intelligible, accounting in this way for the imperfections that have played a part in the present treatise as well. Thus the reason in the soul does not have the complete perfection of the Intelligible, but is nonetheless more perfect than human reason.

39, 17–23 *Giving a sign . . . the other together*: After this *discursus* on the role of reason in interweaving the cosmos, Plotinus finally turns his attention to the signs and portents that prompted the discussion. He concludes that when one thing gives a sign of another, this is not primarily about predicting the future, but manifesting the sympathetic unity of the cosmos. It is thus like many other activities, none of which make the predictive claims of the astrologers or the deterministic ones of the Stoics. They center instead on how one thing can be known by another: by reasoning from effect to cause and from parts to the composite whole, or in reverse, from premise to consequence. All of these are possible because reason in the cosmos is the common cause of them all.

39, 23–32 *If these arguments . . . what is provided*: The final section of the chapter indicates how the arguments presented solve the problem set out at the beginning of this part of the treatise, that the gods are causes of evil. This is not the case: (1) since their choices are not in fact the causes (31, 48–58; 37, 17–25), but the effects come from natural necessities, of some parts in relation to others (38, 5–7) and as a consequence of being in one living thing (32–33); (2)

generated beings, particularly human beings, add things by their own choice (38, 16–23); (3) the influence of the planets is beneficial, but in being mixed here something else comes about (38, 12–13); (4) life is not for the sake of the individual thing but the whole (32, 25–52; 38, 15–16); (5) the substrate may receive a benefit but may not be able to master it and thus experiences it negatively (38, 11–12; 22–23). This summary paves the way for specific discussion of particular issues, such as magic, prayer, portents, and the presence of evils, all areas where Plotinus will apply the points he has established in these first chapters.

IV.4.40–45 Seventh Problem: The Susceptibility of Souls to Benefit and Harm

Chapter 40

The first issue discussed is how magic works. Plotinus lists three factors: sympathy, the natural tendency in similar and dissimilar things, and the diversity of powers in the cosmos. The true magic is rooted in the natural tendency in things, expressed by Empedocles' Love and Strife. This magic does not need anything but Nature itself to work, with Love as first magician and alchemist, imitated by human beings through drugs and spells. The natural tendency to fall in love can be assisted by an erotic art that uses natural substances to effect the growth of love in individuals intertwining them like plants. A second method is to use figures, the position of the planets, to bring about a certain end by inducing a similar configuration by the magician in those who are to be led to one another. The practitioner in this case uses spells and incantations to bring to bear powers within the cosmos as a single living thing. A third method examines these incantations in terms of the natural tendency of music to attract the powers in the cosmos, as the moans of the sick can induce concern and care in another. Music works on the irrational part of the soul in its power to charm and so does not depend on choice. Similarly, choice is not involved in prayers directed to the planets. As with those cast under a spell or mesmerized by such things as snakes, the irrational parts of their soul are affected, but not the ruling part. So also with the planets, whatever power comes toward the magician or another from them does not involve their choice.

40, 1–4 *But how do . . . one living thing*: In this list of the ways magic works, sympathy has the first place since it indicates the fundamental principle operating in all of Plotinus' explanations for the possibility not only of our experience but also for the operation of any of our crafts (Chapter 31). The natural tendency for harmony among similar things and opposition among dissimilar things functioned earlier to indicate how beneficial influence comes from one part of the cosmos to another and also how different things harm and destroy one another (Chapter 32). Finally, the diversity of powers in the All that contribute to its perfection emphasizes the complexity of the whole cosmos, the interdependence of its parts, and the degree of autonomy that allows them to add their own contribution (Chapters 34–35).

40, 4–9 *Many things are . . . on one another*: Following these premises, Plotinus observes that magic is actually the manifestation of the nature of the cosmos, understood here in terms of the Love and Strife of Empedocles. This preamble to the discussion of magic thus rests on the second premise about natural tendencies that can be either beneficial or harmful. In this context, the thrust of the argument focuses on the positive side rather than the negative, as was the case in Chapter 32. In addition, the way in which human beings imitate this facet of nature relates directly to the different kinds of crafts, producing artifacts, cooperating with natural processes, and influencing the soul, mentioned in Chapter 31. The argument also indicates Plotinus' strategy of seeing magical arts not as esoteric, but as in continuity with ordinary human activities and experience. Finally, when he describes Love as the first magician and alchemist, he is not denying the continuity between the erotic art and other crafts, but he is conveying a tinge of disapproval.

40, 6–7 *Magician and alchemist*: The Greek *goēs* and *pharmakeus* present a problem for translation. Armstrong, 1984, 261, uses "wizard and enchanter," which seems to me too strong for the context of the ordinary and pervasive workings of Nature. "Magician" easily translates *goēs*, but *pharmakeus* is more difficult. Translating it as "druggist" strikes a pedestrian note, while "poisoner" remains too negative; by opting for "alchemist" I have attempted a balance between an ordinary sense of craft and a slight note of disapproval. The disapproval applies especially in its human manifestation, but also to Love, as we can see from Plotinus' analysis that the influence involves appeals to the lower parts of the soul and not to its higher, rational nature.

40, 9–27 *Because there is . . . of accomplished musicians*: The natural propensity to fall in love is the work of Love, imitated in different ways through the drugs and spells of a magical erotic art. Several different methods are then examined in turn. The first is the use of natural substances, like the love potions of literature. Different individuals are brought together and these potions bring about falling in love, affecting the souls of the two, at least the lower parts, so that they cling to one another inseparably, intertwined like plants in a hedge. Second these masters of the art of love can use elements of astrology, configuring their clients so the powers of the planets can be quietly induced in them. In an aside, Plotinus notes that the magician in this case is functioning in terms of the sympathy in the cosmos, since standing outside the cosmos would render the spell useless, a point that is also central in the account of sensation in IV.5.8. The magician thus can exploit knowledge of the parts of the cosmos and their similarities and differences to lead one individual to another. A third method is the tune of the spell itself, which is traced to the natural influence of music on the human soul, specifically its lower parts. This influence is likened to the moans and gestures of the sick in rendering others benevolent to their needs. The charm of music does not proceed from choice, since it relates to the irrational soul.

The analysis of music in Chapter 40 is clearly about the effects of music on the lower soul. In three earlier treatises, however, the role of music in the soul's intellectual ascent is paramount; in I.6.3, music appeals to the rational part of the soul, especially in its mathematical nature (I.6.3, 33), later in I.3.1–3, the musician, lover, and philosopher can all make the ascent, with the Platonic premise that beauty is the route most immediately and widely available, and in III.6.4, 43–52, music is used as an analogy for the soul's presence to the body. The discussion in I.3.1, 30 emphasizes the mathematical character of music, with the soul guided beyond rhythm and figure, with their intervals and harmonics, to the beauty separate from their sonic matter. There is no contradiction, but an indication of the double character of activities that receives articulation in IV.4.30–5.8, where one activity, like light, is directed to the higher soul, while another activity, like heat, has a more directly corporeal influence, both coming from the same sensible source

40, 27–32 *One must not . . . from that planet*: Following this examination of music is a brief comment about prayer to the planets, which are also characterized as without choice and without being affected. Plotinus indicates that those under the power of a spell and those mesmerized by snakes and other such things have no sense or awareness of it when it is happening, but they only come to know of it afterward. The planets similarly may have a power flow out from them to an individual but are themselves unaware and more importantly remain even more completely unaffected by any of this. The examination of prayer continues in the next chapter.

Chapter 41

This chapter makes explicit that the planets do not hear prayers. The effect takes place because of the sympathy in the cosmos. Three analogies are used to illustrate this. First, when a single string is plucked at one end, the other end vibrates as well, so when two parts of the universe are put in line by something like prayer, there is a sympathetic transfer between them. Second, when one string is plucked, another tuned to the same scale vibrates as well. As on another lyre, this vibration occurs despite the distance between them that is overcome by the sympathy of the same attunement. The All is more pervasively a single attunement, even overcoming opposites, because opposites are ultimately similar as parts of the one whole. Third, harm may come unintentionally in this sympathetic relation, as anger accompanies bile and enters the nature of the liver, unintentionally bringing harm, as in a relay, where the first runner in lighting a torch from a fire does not intend harm to the third runner when passing the torch to the second, but the second runner passes it to the third in a way that injures the third as unable to receive it.

41, 1–9 *But the sun . . . of their opposites*: The question of hearing by the planets has been mentioned several times (Chapters 30, 1–4; 31, 29; 37, 21–25; 38, 1–7), but this is the first text to exclude it explicitly and offer an alternative explanation. Sympathy, one of the three premises of Chapter 40, 1–4, is analyzed as the way in which prayers are answered. The first analogy, of a single string that is plucked, represents an immediate and direct link between the planet involved and the effect produced. In this instance, one suspects that the prayer has received, as it were, an immediate answer. In the second analogy, where the vibration of one string on a lyre is picked up by another string that is in tune with it, especially as on a different lyre, adverts to a more complex situation that does not have the same immediacy. One might say that if the first string vibrating refers to the power in the heavenly body, which is always active, then the harmonic vibration of the second string refers to the recipient on earth, who may need a number of things to be properly receptive. Besides being tuned to the same scale, this attunement must occur when the two are in the right position to produce the effect or when intermediate links are also properly in tune. The mention of the single attunement of the All, including similar and dissimilar things (the second premise in 40, 1–4), alerts us also to the complexity of the relation of attunement between different bodies in the cosmos.

41, 9–15 *Many things harm . . . to receive it*: This final section of the text brings up a further problem, that the effect may in fact have unintended harmful consequences, illustrated both in the analogy Plotinus mentions and the poor state of the text as transmitted. First, there is the example of anger, which, when associated with bile, changes the nature of the liver. The liver is by nature sanguine, so the harm here is to enflame the liver and to change its nature from tranquil to choleric; for a resume of this theory see: http://en.wikipedia.org/wiki/Humorism (last modified March 18, 2015). According to this understanding of the humors, anger is stirring up yellow bile, thought to come from the spleen and associated with fire, and this bile is in turn adversely affecting the liver, which for Plotinus is the locus of the appetitive part of the soul. The medical theory has sources in Praxagoras (born c. 340 BC) who distinguished arteries and veins, Herophilus (c. 335–280 BC) who distinguished sensory and motor nerves, and Galen (AD 129–216) who associated the account of the parts of the soul in the *Timaeus* with medical theory to locate the rational soul with the brain, the irascible with the heart, and the appetitive with the liver. See Igal, 1982, 90–91, for a discussion of Plotinus' familiarity with these sources and his care to correct Galen's account for philosophical accuracy, and Igal, 1979, 315–345, for placing the irascible and appetitive parts of the soul in the "other man" rather than the "true man."

Second, an analogy is introduced that one expects is meant to illustrate and clarify what is happening, but this is not quite the case with the present state of the text.

The image seems to be a type of relay, in which the lead racer lights a torch from a fire and hands it on to the next member of the team who then hands it on to the third but in such a way that this third racer is harmed, as being unable, or perhaps we might say unready, to receive it. If this is a reasonable account of the image, the question remains, how does it illustrate what is happening to the liver? It may be that anger, as a state of the soul heating up the blood in the heart, does not seek to change the nature of the liver, but by stirring up the bile, a fiery substance from the spleen, it has the unintended effect of altering the liver.

We need to move now from the damaged liver to the damaged text. Since the text is not crucial for understanding Plotinus' thought, one can presume that the copyist did not intend the damage to mislead later scholars, but accidentally introduced changes that have that effect. Igal, 1985, 310nn54–55; 445, suggests that the background is a torch race (*lampadēdromia*), with Plotinus imagining three contestants, the first who starts the race, the second who receives the lighted torch, and the third who in receiving the torch is injured. The argument is that the first does not intend the harm and is thus only accidentally its cause; this much is clear, but accounting for the details in the text remains a challenge. The first part, "and also, for example, when someone, taking a flame from a fire, injures a third party," only specifies the *allon* of the text as the "third party." The second part, "the first had planned that the flame not go where the second who received it made it go, at least as it was passed from that individual to the other," depends on Igal's conjecture that *ē elthein ē* should read *mē elthein hē* (41, 12–13), with the relative adverb translated as "where." This also takes *mēchanēsamenos* (41, 12) as "had planned" and reads *metatethen* instead of *metatithen* (41, 14), an aorist rather than present participle. One of the *ti*'s in 41, 13–14 seems superfluous and without explanation. Finally, "but when it reached the third, the flame harmed him, if he was unable to receive it," I have rearranged so that the last phrase, *eis hon metēnechthē*, construed temporally, is placed at the beginning of the clause.

Chapter 42

The discussion continues to reply in the negative to earlier difficulties about memory and sensing in the planets. Those difficulties came from the assumption that choice is involved in their influence. They do not, however, need to assent to prayers, since their influence is always active, with or without the prompting of prayer. This chapter makes explicit that their influence is not something occasional and due to human effort, but is instead constant and due to the nature of the All as a single living thing. Prayer and magic are thus like other crafts, such as medicine, that tap into the power of Nature in various ways, for this power is naturally active and available for those who seek to utilize it. Plotinus next traces this power to the nature of the All, which permeates all things and gives to all its parts since none of them are alien to it. Even if the part is evil, the All does not hold back, reinforced with the example of evildoers drawing water from streams and the argument that the nature of a giver neither discriminates nor is aware of who is receiving the gift: it just gives. Those who misuse the All for evil, however, are pursued by a justice both persistent and thorough. In the last section, Plotinus shows how the All and its celestial parts are impassible to the affections arising within the cosmos. The ruling principle of the All is by its nature impassible to any affect, but the body of the All is also impassible, since nothing in it is outside its nature. The planets are similarly unaffected, since their choices remain free and their bodies remain unharmed. The influence from them is the kind of activity that diminishes neither their souls nor their bodies, which remain the same, and anything subtracted from them or added to them is so inconsequential as to escape notice.

42, 1–10 *There will also . . . or of spells*: The chapter begins by noting that the previous argument also entails that there is no need for memory in the planets, the initial issue at 30, 13–23 (based on the exclusion of memory earlier at

IV.4.6–8), nor for sensations transmitted from here, a secondary issue raised at 31, 29–30. The discussion addresses those who hold that the planets hear and remember, because their assent to prayers seems to involve deliberate choice. The argument thus shifts from the relation of sympathy between the individual on earth and a particular planet, to whether this influence is due to prayer and the planet's assent to the prayer. In answer, Plotinus articulates what has been implicit all along, that the activity of the planet is constant and derives from its own nature as a particular kind of being with its own life. The influence, moreover, is the secondary activity coming from a being as the overflow of its first activity. Such an activity is always flowing out from a being, especially one of divine nature, and depends neither on its choice nor on an external stimulus to be operative. Plotinus moves, finally, to incorporate this activity with similar powers within the one living thing that all function without choice and have their influence with or without the extraneous assistance of some skill or craft, referring back to the discussion of craft at 31, 15–24, especially as cooperating with the processes of nature. It also recalls the premises at the beginning of 40, 1–4, of the many powers and natural disposition of things to benefit or harm other things. Plotinus once more points out that prayer and magic are not different from other crafts, such as medicine, which share in the powers already present in nature. He leaves the reader to infer that prayer is not affecting the planets, but is instead bringing the individual in tune with the influence of the planet already available.

42, 10–19 *And the All . . . with a relentless law*: These next sections move beyond the issue of prayer to the discussion of the nature of the All and the planets within it as giving and as unaffected. The nature of the giving of the All returns the argument to the principle of two acts in order to understand the constant activity of the All in the context of the influence flowing from it to all its parts, a topic broached at 31, 3–8 about actions and affections and their relation to Nature and craft. Plotinus subsequently argued that the effects of the sun and planets are beneficial unless the substrate of the recipient is unable to receive them or introduces something of its own to them (Chapter 38). The present passage turns from these effects and their recipients to the nature of the All as the benefactor, which, by its first act of being what it is, constantly causes a second act to flow out that is available directly to its parts or indirectly when one part draws on the resources of the All for its own purposes. As in previous discussions, Plotinus indicates that there is no limitation on which parts are able to draw on the services spread out by the All, even when those parts are evil and intend further evil. He supports this with an example from our common experience and an argument about the nature of giving. The example is that evil people draw water from streams for themselves, which surprises no one and which could be multiplied by other examples of the availability of nature's resources to all indiscriminately. The task of the argument, however, is to explain why this is so in terms of the nature of the givers. Giving depends on that first act, by which something is itself, and from this first act there is a necessary and constant outflow of the second act, which is beneficial in its essence as containing life, form, and intelligence. To exclude certain parts of the cosmos from the benefits of this second act could only happen by not acting at all, which is both contrary to the nature of these beings as good and to the nature of giving as unconditional and without calculation. Plotinus has been careful to show the essential goodness of this second activity, so that any evil is traced to the substrate, the additions that come from the recipients, and the complexity of the interrelation of the parts of the cosmos. He adds again here that any evil committed will be brought into harmony by the inexorable justice in the All, reinforcing earlier discussions of the effects at Chapter 38 and the work of justice at Chapters 35, 27–37 and 38, 17–23. The goodness of divine beings, such as the sun and planets and more so the All itself, is assumed in terms of their nature and perfection. This goodness flowing from them becomes articulated in the medieval principle that the good is self-diffusive (*bonum diffusivum sui*), and in Plotinus includes these cosmic souls as in constant contact with the goodness of the Intelligible, which in turn is even more closely in contact with the One. An early exposition of the two acts occurs in VI.4.7, 8–23, and is explained in Rutten, 1956, 100–106, Clarke, 1952, 167–194, and Gurtler, 2008, 113–127.

42, 19–23 *We cannot assume . . . the All itself*: This section examines the second issue, the impassibility of the All and its celestial parts, particularly as souls. The impassibility of souls has been examined in III.6.1–5, where Plotinus shows how affections, virtues, and other states associated with the body can be reconciled with the impassibility of the soul. While the major focus in that treatise is on the human soul, its application to stellar souls and the All-Soul follows easily. Plotinus begins with the assumption that the All cannot be affected. The difficulty to be resolved turns on the nature of the All as composed of body and soul, both of which Plotinus argues are impassible. This is different from the account for human beings, whose soul is impassible but whose body is not. He begins with the complete impassibility of the ruling part of the All-Soul and moves directly to the more complex situation of its parts, which are the corporeal elements that conjointly constitute its body. The ruling part is impassible because it is always looking toward the Intelligible, freeing it from any affection arising within the cosmos, aspects of which have been discussed in IV.4.10–13 in terms of Zeus as demiurge. Affections do, however, occur in the parts of the All, which includes its lower souls, vegetative and sensitive, as well as the bodies within it. We have seen already that activities go out from the sun and planets in terms of their vegetative and sensitive souls (35, 37–50), but here he is dealing with the different situation of affections occurring in these lower souls as well as in the bodies of one planet or another. I restrict the argument to these beings as the harder case; affections in sensible things on earth obviously occur, but the All-Soul is remote from any possibility of being affected by them. Thus, when an affection occurs in one of the planets or its lower souls, such affections reach them (*hēkein*), but do not trigger a separate affection in the All, since these parts are, as he says, not beyond the nature of the All. These parts are the ways, as it were, the All deals with the affections that arise, and when they reach these parts that is sufficient for reaching it.

42, 22–23 *What happens . . . to the All itself*: There is a slight problem with this passage, where *to genomenon* has seemed to some superfluous; I follow Igal, 1985, 310n58 in construing it as the subject of *einai*, with *apathes* meaning "to cause a sensation."

42, 23–30 *Next, for the planets. . . added escapes notice*: The case of the planets is slightly more complicated. As parts, he says, affections reach them. They are parts in both senses, as having within them the lower souls, vegetative and sensitive, and as having particular bodies. They themselves, however, are unaffected, since their being is of such perfection that these affections do not produce the kind of need or difficulty that is true of human beings or other animals, so there is nothing that affects their choice, with the rational part of their souls fixed on the Intelligible. Their bodies are also unharmed, since their proper nature is composed of fire and they rest securely in their proper motions, so that they are completely immune to alteration from these affections. Finally he examines the influence or effects that flow out from these planets, once more in terms of body and soul. This influence is, as we have seen, in terms of their vegetative and sensitive souls as well as of activities such as light and heat. In terms of the principle of two acts, these second activities are non-reciprocally related to the first. They are constantly flowing out, but do not diminish the first in any way, specified here by saying that their souls are not diminished and their bodies remain the same. In addition, there is no perceptual change in these beings, since whatever flows from within them is imperceptible and whatever is added to them from outside escapes notice.

42, 29–30 *It goes imperceptibly. . . added escapes notice*: Plotinus is very precise, using *anaisthētōs* for internal awareness and *lanthanontos* for attention to externals. See Gurtler, 1988, 139–183, for the conditions under which Plotinus holds perception to take place; the All and the planets may have the necessary conditions, but they do not have the sufficient condition, which is the need to pay attention to these affections. These affections are thus present but they pass unnoticed, as do vast numbers of our own affections and sensations.

Chapter 43

The discussion of how different souls, human and daemonic, are affected continues the argument at the end of the previous chapter. Plotinus states that the human soul, like its sister souls above, is not affected in its rational part nor changed in its opinion by magic and drugs. When the irrational part of the All that is in the human soul is affected, the individual is affected insofar as his attention is turned toward that irrational part. Love potions, for example, do not make the soul fall in love, if love means giving assent to the love of another. The soul can also use counter chants and incantations to release itself from the effects of an incantation on its irrational part, but this release may not ward off damage to the body, including death, even if the soul remains unscathed. Daemons also are not impassible in their irrational part, so one can reasonably attribute memory and sense to them. Their susceptibility to magic and being summoned by spells derives from the fact that they allow themselves to come close to sensible things by turning toward them. This serves as a general principle: anything that turns toward another is under its spell and can be led by it, while anything that is only turned toward itself is free. As a consequence, the whole practical life and all the practical activities we engage in are under a spell since these things enchant us. Their enchantment is not due to magic, but to Nature deceiving and linking us to one another by its own magic potions.

43, 1–12 *How is the sage . . . departure from Nature*: Plotinus singles out the sage as the one who can be impassible to the effects of magic and drugs. As engaged in the philosophical life, the sage has learned to identify with the All and thus the rational part of his soul is directed toward the Intelligible, so that the principles of his reason are stable and not swayed by changing affections that result in shifting opinions. In V.1.2 Plotinus provides a description of the soul's identification with All-Soul and discovery of its own nature, especially as capable of knowing both itself and the higher realities (V.1.1). The notion of the two selves is used to explain the lack of awareness of our identity and of exercising our intelligible nature, with the higher self as directed toward the Intelligible and the lower self toward the sensible (V.1.12 and I.2). In I.2 Plotinus distinguishes the different kinds of virtues, civic and purificatory, which serves as background for this chapter.

Igal, 1979, 315–345, analyses the irascible and appetitive parts of the soul, derived from Plato's tripartite soul, as the image of soul that is separate from the true self and identified with the "other man" as the shadow of the true self. These irrational parts of the soul thus remain exposed to the effects of magic as also does the human body, making the position even of the sage different from the planets, which are impassible in these parts as well. First, however, he indicates how the sage is immune to certain effects of magic, those from love potions and incantations. Since he defines love as a deliberate choice, the sage is immune to the effects of potions at the rational level. Incantations, moreover, may be overcome by counter incantations. This section concludes that, relative to the body, the sage is as susceptible to death, disease, and bodily harm as anyone else, whether these are caused by a drug, Nature itself, or the All in its complex workings. The human body can thus be harmed in its proper nature, since unlike the bodies of the planets it is composed from corporeal elements that are not pure but are corruptible by their very nature.

43, 7–8 *By counter chants . . . from those powers*: Armstrong, 1984, 268–269n1, points out that this may refer to the sage engaging in casting spells of his own, but there is also a strong sense that the philosophical life is itself a countermeasure to such incantations, which has support from Platonic background in *Charmides* 156–157 as well as Plotinus' own usage later in V.3 [49] 17, 18–20. Porphyry, *Vita Plotini*, 10, also reports Plotinus' experience of Olympius' attack against him which was turned back not by a counter incantation of Plotinus but by his own strength of soul.

43, 12–24 *Daemons, further, are . . . potions it offers*: The second section begins with a reference to the daemons, answering a query raised at 30, 30–32. Like the planets, the daemons are impassible in their rational natures, but unlike them they can get involved with persons and places by turning toward them, acquiring memory and sensation in some form. In this way, these beings are like human beings, susceptible to magic and the summons of incantations. III.4 presents an early discussion of daemons, particularly those associated with human souls at various levels in terms of the center of consciousness operative in each individual. Plotinus seems to be using the term here with a wider meaning than the particular Platonic context of III.4, including their relation to other animals and places.

After this very brief mention of the daemons, the text reverts to the discussion of human beings. In context, then, the mention of the daemons serves only to articulate the general principle that one is under the spell of whatever serves as the moving cause of one's action, bringing one under the enchantment of that object, which can lead one wherever it wants. Only the sage as moved by himself alone escapes this kind of enchantment, and Plotinus now contrasts the sage not with those who are victims of magic and drugs, but with those who are dedicated to the practical life and its activities, becoming enchanted by these activities. This enchantment, moreover, is the work of Nature, as expressed in feelings and the sympathetic links we have with one another. For Plotinus, this magic is far more pervasive and deceitful than the limited work of magicians.

Chapter 44

The sage is further contrasted with those engaged with the practical affairs of life, especially as attention to them puts one under a spell. The sage has characteristics that set him apart: his unity, contemplation, and reason are directed to the Intelligible, and thus his life and task are centered there, where they ought to be. Those not directed there do not act from reason but their starting point is the irrational and their premises are passions. Human life consists of certain passions and activities responding to them. First, there is the desire for marriage and the care of children, or indulging the pleasures of the passions. Then there are actions triggered by anger, or political action and desire for office prompted by ambition. Fear drives some to avoid pain, but various desires drive others to acquire in excess. Finally, the force of Nature urging us to preserve life grounds the response to these bodily needs and the social concerns emerging from them. These describe the arena for the beautiful actions of the human life, depending on their relation to the contemplation of the Beautiful. Some say either that these actions cannot come under a spell or that contemplation is also subject to spells. Plotinus argues that if they are done as far as is necessary with the soul directed to the beautiful in itself, they are immune to spells. Recognizing the necessity of these actions means not focusing on their effects nor on things other than oneself, but that such actions rest on the force of human nature and the natural urge to preserve the life of oneself and others. Suicide in fact indicates that one is under a spell. The opposite attitude that leads inevitably to coming under a spell is described as focused on the beauty within the actions, which are only traces of real beauty. This spell is the deception that what seems true is taken for the truth or what seems good is taken for the good, which is the magic of Nature that turns one to the form in things and by irrational impulses leads one where one does not want to go. To be immune from spells means that the rational part of the soul controls the other parts and does not take as good any of the goods they present, but what it already grasps as good, neither being deceived by the irrational nor driven by the passions.

44, 1–6 *This leaves contemplation . . . premises are passions*: The contrast between the life of the sage and the life of action continues with the sage alone free from spells, precisely as self-directed. The argument is essentially that the sage is actually functioning as the true self, grounded in the Intelligible. This self is unified and is the object of the sage's contemplation, while the life of action is divided into multiple selves that have their gaze directed to the external objects of the sensible cosmos. The result is that reason in the sage is not deceived, and so his task to construct his own life is done as it ought to be. The life of action, by contrast, is not concerned with the task of making a unified self or with being at one with the real self. Instead, Plotinus argues, the principle of such a life is irrational, since it is centered in the inferior soul and its parts, the irascible and appetitive, and so its premises are the passions present to those parts and the opinions based on them, with the result that reason is not the guide of its action. The background for this section is Plato's *Republic* VIII–IX, where the philosopher and the tyrant are contrasted in terms that parallel Plotinus' more terse description. For Plato, the philosopher is unified precisely as ruled by the rational part of the soul, which keeps the irascible and appetitive parts within their proper limits. The tyrant, by contrast, is a many-headed monster who is at war as much with himself as with others and is ultimately unable to satisfy even the desires of the irascible and appetitive parts that dominate his soul. Plotinus shifts the irascible and appetitive parts outside the real soul to the inferior soul added on with the body. This inferior soul is the locus for misfortune precisely as susceptible to the enchantments of Nature's magic luring it through its irrational parts.

44, 4–5 *He makes his . . . is not there*: I have taken *to ergon poiei* in light of L-S IV.4 (q.v.), where it has the sense of "attending to a matter." The next sentence, however, has fared less well, with *ekei* translated "here" and *ou to hautou* as "no self-possession" (Armstrong, 1984, 271), presumably reading *ou to [echon] hautou*. I have construed it as parallel to the preceding clause, so *ou to [ergon poiei] hautou*. The contrast seems, then, that the life of action is not centered "there" in the real soul, and so the task has slipped to the inferior soul as irrational and the place of passions.

44, 6–16 *Nature's magic can . . . us to live*: Plotinus next lists a series of passions and responses to them that make up human life. They occur in pairs, with one side positive and the other negative. The last in the series, however, is without a contrasting side and analyzing it first may give a key for interpreting the others. The text states that the inherent urge to preserve life directs us toward those activities that fill up some lack in Nature with regard to certain basic physical needs. Given its use again some lines later (44, 21–24), this does not seem to be something that Plotinus regards negatively, but as a necessary component of the human soul's activity on earth. As in the previous chapters, these activities should come from the first activity of the being and should be beneficial in their nature, although particular effects may be accidentally harmful. The complication for the human soul, however, is that it may not always function in terms of its first act; that is, it may not be in contact with its real self and thus the activities that come from it may lose even this inherent beneficial nature.

With this distinction in mind, the list of activities can be taken not as things that the sage avoids by his contact with the real self, but that the sage and the practical man regard and do these activities differently. Further, the pairs of activities can be seen as evaluating activities that seek to provide assistance for basic needs that Nature overlooks, especially concerned with the survival of oneself and others. The first pair concerns marriage and children on the one side and pleasures on the other, with the contrast between the necessity of marriage and children for human survival as opposed to indulging in pleasures that have no value outside themselves. The next set contrasts actions provoked by anger, or other such passions, with the ambition prompting political action and the desire for office. Here again the contrast rests on actions that concern the individual in isolation with those actions where the individual is exercising responsibility for the common good. In the last set, where fear drives one to avoid pain and passions lead one to acquire excessively, the contrast is that bravery in relation to such fear has a value in preserving life, both for oneself and for society, while a life of luxury does not. This list, therefore, is about those areas of action that constitute human life, fleshing out the task of making a life either as one ought or as based on the irrational. Their value is thus determined by whether they derive from the rational principles of the sage or the irrational principles of the inferior soul. It also shows that Plotinus is not here distancing himself from the ethical reflections of the Greek tradition, especially as found in Plato and Aristotle, both of whom see contemplation as key in constructing a complete human life. Plato's description of the nature of the philosopher in the central books of the *Republic* indicates how even the virtues only have value in terms of looking toward the good; Aristotle also argues in

Nicomachean Ethics 10.6–8 that contemplation is the highest activity, integrating the self and supplying principles for the practical life. In I.2–3, Plotinus presents his own integration of different aspects of Platonic and Aristotelian views of the virtues. See Gurtler, 2003, 801–834.

44, 14–16; 21–24 *Finally, those actions . . . under a spell*: The key term is *oikeioō* and *oikeiōsis*, a Stoic technical term that means being "endeared by nature" for something or an attraction or propensity for something (L-S, II.1.b for the verb and L-S, A.2 for the noun; q.v.). At 44, 16, *oikeiōsasan* is an aorist participle modifying *bian*, translated "inherently urging"; at 44, 23–24, the nouns are translated as "the inherent urge," in order to emphasize the parallel between the two passages. Two other terms, *chreiōdēs* and *endeia*, also present problems, since their meaning seems fairly close. For the former, L-S, A.II (q.v.), gives the translation "needy" in relation to parts of the body and for the latter, "want" or "lack," yielding here that certain activities fill the gaps nature leaves relative to needs of the body. The result is to highlight, in a way that other translations have not, that the human body, as opposed to the bodies of the planets, has certain needs that human activities are by their very nature set to address, especially with Nature giving us the urge to preserve life, individual and social. Plotinus used the term, *oikeios*, earlier at 32, 38, where he describes how the many living things naturally seek to preserve their own lives even when they harm or destroy others, taking from the other what is akin (*oikeion*) and destroying what is alien (32, 32–40). The present context presents the more positive side of this kinship. Brisson, 2005, 273n486, takes note of this Stoic term and cites Brunschwig, 1997, 553, as emphasizing that Nature is exercising a particular action on a living thing rendering it familiar or near to itself, and also to others. It should be noted also that Nature provides these activities, rearing children, forming groups, and certain emotional reactions, to other animals as well, although operating in them at the more basic level of instinct rather than choice. Inwood, 1985, 184–194, brings out the Stoic background of the term in relation to human and animal action as resting on the instinct for self-preservation, but also as grounding justice and social bonds, the two dimensions that Plotinus clearly has in mind. He translates *oikeios* as "orientation," but I think "inherent urge" captures its more primordial grounding in Nature.

44, 16–24 *But if, on . . . under a spell*: This section starts with the objection that either beautiful or noble actions are in themselves immune from spells or that the contemplation of beautiful things is itself susceptible to spells. If the previous analysis is correct, the topic of beautiful actions does not emerge from thin air, but captures the positive series of actions listed in the immediately preceding lines, including political life and the desire for office, which scholars have taken as an instance of Plotinus' disdain for political involvement. For example, Brisson, 2005, 273n485, refers to Porphyry's *Vita*, 7, 29–51, where he mentions particular individuals involved in Roman politics whom Plotinus encouraged to take up a life dedicated to philosophy. This passage does not entail, however, that Plotinus discourages every individual from any involvement in politics, even a sage. It is important to note, moreover, that the Greek *kalos* has both aesthetic and ethical connotations, with the Platonic tradition preserving the aesthetic side even in the ethical arena of practical or moral action. In the present context, the actions under consideration are those present in any human life at the urging of Nature. They thus express the role of the soul in bringing order and beauty into the sensible realm, connected to the contemplation of beautiful things, rather than actions that stand out as noble. The analysis, then, attempts to show that the beauty in these actions is only apparent and depends on the unchanging nature of beauty itself as the object of contemplation. These actions do not have intrinsic value, but manifest the integral unity of the life of the sage, emphasizing the sage's contemplation of beauty, in which the sage is not merely refraining from evil but goes beyond the practical life to a contemplation that reveals kinship with Intellect and the divine (cf. I.2.6).

Since the objection sees no difference between the life of practical action and contemplation, these next two sections are designed to show exactly what the difference is. The argument begins by saying that if such actions are done only so far as is necessary, while keeping beauty itself as distinct, one is not under a spell. The explanation that follows is intriguing. First, the role of necessity in these practical actions is central. They are done because they need to be done, not because of the effects that may occur, and this necessity comes from within the self, and not from things in the sensible cosmos. The necessity is then defined in terms of the last item in the list of actions in the previous section, as the force of human nature and the natural urge to preserve the life of others and oneself. Plotinus is holding that both this force and urge come from the contemplation of the Intelligible, but he is leaving us to figure out how and why this is the case. As mentioned in the previous section, the principle of two acts is once more crucial for understanding what he means. The first act is that which makes us be what we are, designated here as the force of nature, while the second act is set to preserve the life of ourselves or others, something necessarily flowing out of the first act. This pattern makes us most like the more divine beings in the cosmos that Plotinus wants us to imitate. Finally, the section ends with a brief comment that this naturally urged propensity excludes suicide, since suicide would actually indicate that one is under the spell of some external object. Stern-Gillet, 2013, cites texts that indicate Plotinus' ambiguous attitude toward suicide and political involvement under conditions of duress. The present passage is not about an extreme situation but the sage's ordinary involvement with this life

44, 25–37 *But if, on the other . . . drawn anywhere else*: The second section spells out, so to speak, the contrasting attitude of someone only engaged with the practical life, with no contact with the real self in the intelligible. Such an individual sees actions as inherently beautiful, and so is already under their spell by choosing these traces of beauty. The argument, not surprisingly, is very Platonic, taking the instance as if it were the real thing on multiple levels: traces of beauty for the beautiful itself, apparent truth for truth itself, what is not good for the good itself. This is the deception of sensible things that by their nature appeal to irrational impulses, drawing the individual to the form within them rather than to the intelligible form, and leading the individual unwittingly into slavery, whether by vice, addiction, or ignorance. It is exactly the situation of the dwellers in the cave in *Republic* VII. The sage, by contrast, is neither deceived in his reason nor driven by his appetites, but already grasps the truth. Plotinus is not claiming omniscience for the sage but rather that his operative rational principle comes from contact with the Intelligible. This means that his deliberations remain stable without being deceived by appearances or swayed by the appetites of the inferior soul. Contact with the Intelligible is not expressed in terms of propositions, but as seeing those intelligible beings which are indeed beautiful, true, and good. It is to make the journey out of the cave, however briefly, which reveals to the sage the nature and relative value of things in the sensible cosmos and so gives him the principle by which his actions to preserve life can be accomplished without falling under the spell of Nature's magic.

Chapter 45

This last chapter explicitly concludes this phase of the discussion, reviewing and summarizing preceding themes. It begins with a look at each animal as contributing to the All according to its nature and disposition, as agent and recipient. Each animal with its parts is parallel to the All with its parts. The parts of an animal bring it to perfection by their particular functions, accepting their places and roles and interacting with other parts according to their nature. Each part has a kind of consciousness of the whole animal and if it were also an animal would have a function of its own different from what it has in the whole. This point has direct application to human beings, who not only interact with things through their bodies but introduce their other nature as souls, with powers relating directly to intelligible beings outside the sensible cosmos. Since we relate in different ways to the Intelligible and sensible worlds, what we give and receive is different and ambiguous. We cannot, for example, give the good if we do not have it, nor could we receive that good without a capacity for it. Evildoers are recognized for what they are and their contact with the Intelligible is blocked by the weight of their own nature. The actions of the good, by contrast, are in accord with the Intelligible so intimately that they appear like puppets in the hands of nature. Both reflect the power and order of the cosmos, under the inescapable control of justice. Evildoers are oblivious of justice and go unawares to their fated place, while the good are conscious of justice and know ahead of time where necessity will take them, firmly hoping for the company of the gods. Returning to the contrast between small animals and the cosmos as itself living, Plotinus notes their difference in scale both in size and duration so that the parts of an animal have little consciousness of one another and are not alive on their own, except perhaps briefly, while the cosmos is so vast that its parts are alive and have motions and interactions equally vast. We can see this in the motions of the sun, moon, and planets and can surmise that the changes in our souls have similar effects on how our souls will be ranked, with the head or the feet, as better or worse, in harmony with the workings of the All. The soul that does not choose for itself better or worse things here, receives that pure, intelligible place that was in fact the object of its choice. The punishment of evils, on the contrary, operates like medicine, treating them with drugs or surgical amputation to restore the health of the whole.

45, 1–10 *From everything we . . . as a part*: When the analogy between the whole cosmos as a living thing and the animals of our experience was introduced in Chapters 31–32, the thrust was to understand the nature of the All as a whole with parts present in it, each part contributing to its perfection. In this last chapter, the thrust is in reverse, an attempt to clarify the nature of animals with the more limited function of their parts and particularly the human animal and its unique place in this cosmic scheme. The parts of animals are thus understood as contributing to the perfection of the whole animal as far as their nature and condition allows and they do this almost as animals in their own right, using the analogy of how the parts of the cosmos function. Hence these parts render service to the whole animal, consent to their position and purpose in it, act as agents and recipients in relation to one another, and have a kind of consciousness of one another and the whole. This description repeats the point made at 36, 15–27 that everything in the cosmos is alive, even things we do not usually speak of as living, and then Plotinus adds that if these parts were also animals, they would have a function of their own independent from their function in the whole. One purpose of this description is to reaffirm his opposition to the materialism of the Stoics as well as the determinism and fatalism he maintains they share with the astrologers. Another purpose, however, is the application of this insight to human beings as living things within the whole. Plotinus keeps moving back and forth in his use of the analogy, from the parts within an animal to animals themselves as parts within the whole cosmos. It is interesting to note that modern biology allows us to see the validity of his insight, that within an organism are a multitude of organisms, bacteria and microbes of one kind or another, that in part are essential parts of the whole organism and in part have an independence which can make itself felt dramatically, for example, when we are sick.

45, 10–26 *This latter point . . . Nature on strings*: The application of the analogy to human beings has its first pass in this section of the chapter. Two points are made immediately. First, that our actions in the All are not merely physical—bodies colliding and interacting with the benefits and harms graphically depicted at 32, 25–52—where different things as parts can harm and even destroy one another without any conscious intention or choice determining their actions but merely by positioning their bodies in such a way that another body ends up in harm's way. Second, Plotinus states that we introduce our other nature, our souls, which join us to higher beings outside the sensible cosmos and its merely corporeal interactions. He adds that our souls and dispositions connect us to the daemonic realm immediately above us and then to the real beings beyond it. His wording is very careful: our souls and dispositions. Mentioning souls indicates our nature, but mentioning dispositions brings in the contrast in the previous chapters between the sage and the practical man (43–44), with this ambiguous situation now receiving further definition. He continues that we cannot overlook what sort of people we are. This comment may be no more than his usual exhortation to discover and acknowledge our identity as souls, the theme of several early treatises that deal with the exhortation to ascend and move away from involvement with the sensible world, especially in the moral sphere: I.6, VI.9, V.1, I.2, as discussed in Gurtler, 2005, "Self and Consciousness," 113–129. In the present context, however, it also raises the more radical difference between the morally good and the morally evil. This difference is then defined precisely in terms of giving and receiving different things. Again, the use of "giving" is not accidental, as it refers back to the discussion of the benefits coming from the All and the planets, who always give what is beneficial but their nature as givers also implies that in giving they do so indiscriminately, so that their gifts can be used for good as well as for evil (Chapters 41–42).

While those higher beings are carefully preserved from any responsibility for harmful effects in general and from any complicity in human moral evil in particular, Plotinus now has the task of explaining the strange presence of moral evil among human beings. The next two clauses address the ambiguity in the human situation. First, we cannot share or give what we do not have, the good; second, we could not receive the good without having some capacity for it. As souls in human bodies, we are not automatically active in relation to the good, whether of the All-Soul or of the intelligible world, so in that sense we do not have the good. As souls, however, we are the kind of beings capable of the good. Plotinus introduces the image of puppets to illustrate this, which may interfere with the point he is trying to make since it seems to reduce humans to mere instruments in the hands of Nature. His contrast, however, uses the image in a decidedly different way. He first describes the evildoer as "recognized for what he is," a passive phrase with the subject not specified. At Chapters 39, 2 and 42, 19, and just below at 45, 28, virtue and justice are mentioned as charged with interweaving everything in the All so that evil is brought into harmony and order. Plotinus seems to emphasize, moreover, that what happens to evildoers is accomplished in an appropriately impersonal way, pushing themselves into what holds them in the sensible cosmos and removing their contact with the divine by the pulls of their own nature. The good, on the contrary, by their acts of giving are like the divine beings above, and are instead pulled by Nature like puppets on strings. The point of the image is not that the good are passive with Nature pulling the strings, but rather that the strings show their continuity with the divine powers flowing into them. The evil, for their part, have severed these strings and fall like puppets in a dead heap. Both cases together indicate Plotinus' location of choice in the ambiguous nature of the human soul, able to align itself with its real self in the Intelligible or to be captivated by objects and activities centered in the inferior soul.

45, 18 *There is no way we can overlook*: "*Lanthanomen*" must be a first person plural, but both Armstrong, 1984, 277 and Igal, 1985, 450, translate it impersonally; Brisson, 2005, 191, renders it correctly.

45, 27–52 *How wonderfully is . . . not be diseased*: Justice works its silent ordering thoroughly and wonderfully. Part of the wonder in Plotinus' description is the contrast between the impersonal mode operative for evildoers and the fully human engagement of the good. The evildoer pays no mind to justice and is led unknowingly to his fate. This makes explicit what was implicit in 43, 16–24 and 44, where the practical man is left deliberately indefinite, an assortment of multiple selves, as opposed to the sage, who is unified and contemplates his real self. The sage has constructed his life in tune with justice and thus his departure from this life comes at an appropriate time and the dwelling necessarily awaiting him is filled with the hope of being with the gods, about as personal as Plotinus gets about this transition, described in greater detail in IV.3.24–IV.4.5.

His task in this section, moreover, is to explain how this justice can actually work and he turns once more to the analogy of small animals to the whole cosmos as a living thing to understand further the different fates of human souls. The emphasis here is on their small size, so that their parts have only slight consciousness and since they are not animals themselves they cannot live on, except briefly in a few cases. The context for this text can be found in IV.4.29, 3–7, which examines whether or not there is a trace of life in the body when the soul departs. Igal, 1985, 420–421nn158–159 and Brisson, 2005, 160 and 262nn305–310, discuss Plotinus' own theory of the soul's presence to body, whether as being warmed or illuminated, with reference to Aristotle's *De Anima* in the background; IV.4.29 is also important in the immediately following discussion of sensation and light in IV.5.7. In IV.4.29 and IV.5.7, 56–62, the trace of life concerns the vegetative soul, but in the present passage the issue turns to the distinct fates of the good and the evil, one identified with the higher soul and the other with the inferior soul, with its irascible and appetitive parts and its association with body. In addition, the analogy with the whole cosmos takes on a very different role in these lines as opposed to the beginning of this chapter; there Plotinus emphasized how life so permeates these animals that their parts are almost animals themselves with a kind of consciousness, but here this consciousness is minimized and their parts have no life of their own. Plotinus is not being inconsistent or contradictory, but this emphasizes the suppleness of his images, which with subtle shifts can reveal the marvelous nuances implicit within them. They have this adaptability precisely because they attempt to mirror the complexity he sees in Nature, which reveals itself in often contradictory ways that nonetheless bear witness to the wonderful order that finds expression at the beginning of this section (45, 27).

In contrast to the small animals and their nearly lifeless parts, the cosmos itself appears so vast that its parts are free living things whose motions and interactions are similarly vast, illustrated by the changing positions and orderly motions of the sun, moon, and other planets. While Plotinus has earlier argued strenuously against any causal role of these planets on human behavior, he now claims it is not unreasonable that human souls are like them in changing position and character and not unreasonable that human souls are similarly ordered by what they experience and do. They are, however, not ordered like the planets against the sphere of the fixed stars, but in relation to the human body, some ranked with the head and others with the feet. This ranking, further, manifests the harmony in the All, which encompasses better and worse. The harmony is, of course, the working of justice which none can flee, but so far it is not quite clear how it is actually accomplished. The final lines apply this ordering to the two different cases of the good and the evil. The soul of the sage does not choose for itself anything in the sensible world, regardless of whether it is better or worse. The soul, thus, does not identify itself with the things of its sensible life, but has instead chosen a different place, the intelligible as pure and itself as present there. It is ranked with the head, which Plotinus holds is the part of the body upon which the real soul is present and operative. Evil souls, on the contrary, are not even mentioned, since Plotinus only speaks of punishments and how they are applied analogously to the medical treatment of diseased parts of the body. Some diseased parts can be treated with drugs; others with the more drastic means of surgery. It is perhaps helpful to think of these drugs in terms of homeopathic medicine, where the drug is similar to the disease it is treating, and of amputation as removing a diseased part and allowing it to decompose, while the patient continues to live. The patient, however, is not the soul of the evildoer, but the All as having these infections within it. Like the parts of the animal that have no consciousness and life, the inferior souls of the evil linger in a shadowy existence for however long it takes for the evil they have introduced into the all to be removed and cleansed. Thus, if we see them as ranked with the feet, what remains of them are like footprints in the sand, waiting for the waves of the sea to wash them away. Despite his clear and repeated statements about justice pursuing the wicked relentlessly, Plotinus is not at all interested in describing the details of this pursuit. For an imaginative rendering of punishments as drugs or amputations, Dante's (AD c. 1265–1321) *Inferno* and the paintings of Hieronymus Bosch (AD c. 1450–1516) and other Flemish artists can provide appropriately excruciating details of punishments fitting the crime and surgically precise tortures.

Plotinus has presented a sustained argument occasioned by issues that seem to have minor importance, both for him and for us, the memory of planets and their complicity in human evil. Behind these surface problems lies the fundamental issue of a materialistically determined universe, where all action is fated. Plotinus' argument, therefore, presents a marvelous account of the complexity and unity of the cosmos that is directed against the determinism of the Stoics and the fatalism of the astrologers. The cosmos as a living thing, with its source in Plato's

Timaeus, includes everything in its embrace, using Stoic sympathy to fill out the implications of Platonic imagery. The way in which the parts of the cosmos interact by means of sympathy allows Plotinus to take the issues of the discussion, like planetary influence and magical human arts, and show how they produce the results they do, but at the price of blending them into the most natural and ordinary sorts of activities. The real, and more dangerous, magic is the work of Nature itself, seeking to deceive and enchant human beings in their most ordinary activities. This work of Nature, however, is precisely the means Plotinus uses to argue for human choice and the responsibility of the individual for the actions and character that constitute a human life. Unlike other beings in the cosmos, the human soul has a peculiar ambiguity, since it can function in terms of its nature as soul or in terms of its presence in the body. While this element of choice is explicitly addressed only a few times and then only briefly, all the arguments in these chapters are designed to establish and safeguard it. The influence from the planets, for example, is always beneficent, but in the case of human beings, we not only have the limitations of the body in receiving it but can introduce changes on our own that turn that benefit to harm. Our nature as souls allows us to understand Nature and its workings, a gift of knowledge which is available to all, with the clear possibility that it can be used for good or for ill. While Plotinus exhorts us to identify with the true self, he reminds us that even if we do not, the order and harmony of the cosmos work relentlessly to bring what evil we do to justice.

Nevertheless, the choice he articulates has its limitations, the limitations of Greek philosophy. I have used choice deliberately, since it does not import notions of the will and freedom of the will. The will is usually taken as having its roots in the nature of the soul, but Plotinus has argued clearly and insistently that the soul by its nature has no choice. It is in that sense something like Kant's pure rational being, which without the interference of experience would always choose the moral law. The more perfect souls in the sensible cosmos are all free in the precise sense of not needing this kind of choice. The root of freedom in the human soul, thus, does not lie in the soul but in its peculiar situation in relation to the body. Human beings are influenced by the body, but they are able to bring in their other nature, the soul. It is this situation that allows for choice, a choice that Plotinus defends against the fatalism of the astrologers, who see human character as determined by the direct, physical influence of the planets, and the theory of the Stoics, whom Plotinus argues cannot ground the choice they allow in a cosmos in which all causality operates completely deterministically.

IV.5.1–8 Eighth Problem: The Nature of Vision and Light

Chapter 1

This final section of the treatise returns to another issue mentioned earlier, whether seeing needs a transparent body between the eye and the object. The argument begins with a statement about the nature of sensation as dependent on the body, since the soul functioning without the body would be in the intelligible world. The soul consequently needs to come in contact with sensible objects by means of something similar to them, precisely the organs of the body. These organs are similar by their nature as corporeal and thus allow a kind of unity with corporeal things and a common affection with them. The contact between organ and object can be either immediate by touch or at a distance by sight or hearing, raising the problem about the role of the body between them for sight or hearing. Plotinus poses a series of questions with brief responses that set the parameters of the discussion for this section of the treatise. (1) Is Aristotle's transparent body between eye and object necessary? No, such a body impinges accidentally and contributes nothing to sight. (2) Given that dense earthy bodies hinder and subtle ones do not, do these finer bodies cooperate or at least not hinder? No, all such bodies hinder. (3) If the body is struck first is it not necessary for it to be affected for the affection to reach the eye? No, since the eye is naturally capable of being affected, the body between does not need to be affected, or at least not in the same way. This last point is illustrated with the shock of the torpedo fish and the role of the fishing rod between it and the hand; the rod does not receive the shock, but in its absence the shock would not be felt by the hand. Finally, sympathy is introduced as the solution to be investigated. The eye and the object are related sympathetically and their similarity allows the one to be affected by the other. The body between is not similar and at best is affected differently; if it were possible to have nothing between, the eye would be affected even more easily.

1, 1–13 *Since we deferred . . . occurs with them*: Plotinus returns to the discussion of the soul and sensation, posed at IV.4.23, which is summarized succinctly in these first lines. In that earlier context, sense organs were presented as between the non-corporeal soul and the corporeal qualities of bodies. These organs are able to mediate between the soul and the qualities since the qualities coming in from the bodies are united in form; for example, the color or shape of the object, which is the affection that the soul can use to assimilate it with the forms it has within. Thus two issues from that early discussion are featured, the transparent body between the eye and the object perceived at a distance (IV.4.23, 43–48) and the assimilation of the organ to that object in terms of the affection produced in it (IV.4.23, 20–29). In the background stand Plato and Aristotle. *Timaeus* 45b–c speaks of the connatural continuity between the organ and the object that makes a kind of unity between soul and object possible, and *De Anima* 2.7.418b4 proposes that the transparent body necessarily mediates between organ and sense object.

There are details of the Aristotelian theory to which Plotinus objects, particularly the role of the transparent body as being affected and thus necessary as the medium transmitting the form from object to organ. On the one hand, Plotinus thinks that Aristotle's theory does not account for some of the details of the functioning of sight, particularly seeing at night, as we will see in Chapters 3–4, but on the other hand, there is the more fundamental disagreement about the nature of light as an activity that makes sight possible. For Aristotle, light and its relation to the transparent body between is understood in terms of the principle of act and potency. Light and various bodies—air, water, glass, ether—are all transparent and this transparency is not due to any of these bodies, but rather the transparent is something common and separate from them and is related to light as potency to act. Thus a transparent body is potentially active and the illumination of light moves it from that potentiality to active exercise, the condition for seeing. Brisson, 2005, 274n10, presents an excellent summary of the role of the transparent in Aristotle, relying on Merker, 2003, 136–166.

For Plotinus, by contrast, light is a second activity flowing out of a luminous source and this activity is capable of moving through the intervening body without affecting it. This makes light different from warmth, for example, which does move through the intervening body by changing it directly (Chapters 2, 50–53; 4, 25–28). Light, thus, is closely related to the nature of sympathy developed in the previous section of this treatise (IV.4.30–45), where the affection can go from one part to another directly, with the intervening part unaffected as dissimilar. With this different understanding of the nature of light, Plotinus does not need the transparent body since it is the sympathetic nature of the cosmos that allows for the activity of light to be present simultaneously at its source and at the object illuminated.

In discussion with Carlos Steel when I presented a paper on this topic at Leuven (2 May 2013), he objected that Plotinus was not giving a scientific explanation in the style of Aristotle. His claim was that Aristotle is indicating the path of causality from the object to the eye, while Plotinus asserts that the action just jumps over the intervening body. This does not do justice to Plotinus' account. He differentiates different kinds of activities, some of which may function within Aristotle's model of act and potency, while others do not. His theory of the two acts provides a model designed to deal with causality functioning in a vertical and direct fashion, as it were, rather than a horizontal framework of change or alteration. The distinction is, therefore, not about scientific explanation, but about the premises or assumptions of particular explanatory schemes. Plotinus' principle of two acts is no less explanatory than Aristotle's principle of act and potency.

1, 13–17 *If then there . . . and the color*: Plotinus first develops the notion of the contact essential for sensation. Contact seems clearly related to touch, but even in that case it still needs to be investigated in the present context of sensation and the soul. The question alerts us that Plotinus does not regard touch as unproblematic, although it is addressed explicitly in this treatise briefly at 2, 53–56 and more fully at 4, 14–49. Contact in relation to seeing or hearing, by contrast, is the first question that Plotinus formulates, since they both involve a distance between the organ and the object that makes the contact a problem. This first question, then, is whether a transparent body, as the Aristotelian account insists, is actually necessary and, if so, what specific function it has.

1, 17–19 *I answer that . . . those who see*: The first answer is brief and blunt: this body might impinge accidentally but contributes nothing. The word for impinge, *nussō*, was used by the Stoics with regard to sensation where it introduces some kind of interference; Galen, 10.221, 390; 13.565 (Kühn edition), also uses it in relation to a lesion in the nerves. In short, Plotinus sees the transparent body not as something that is instrumental in making sight possible, since it does not contribute positively to it and may interfere in some circumstances. An example of a body impinging on sight can be seen in a stick partially submerged in water, since the two different transparent bodies, air and water, cause the stick to appear bent. Although the body discussed explicitly in the text is not specified as transparent, the preceding context and the following question on earthy bodies indicate that Plotinus is concerned with the transparent bodies deemed necessary for sight in the Aristotelian account.

1, 19–22 *But, if when . . . do not hinder*: Since earthy bodies block sight when dense, but as they become subtler vision improves, moving, for example, from opaque or translucent bodies to motes in the air, the question arises whether these finer bodies are cooperating with sight or at least not hindering its operation.

1, 23 *I answer that . . . these bodies hinder*: The response states that these bodies, however fine, block seeing at least minimally. Earthy bodies, unlike transparent bodies, cannot be merely neutral but have a degree of dissimilarity with the source of light and the illuminated object such that they necessarily block light as an activity from reaching an object that can be illuminated. The consideration of these bodies indicates that Plotinus is not eliminating any role for transparent bodies, but is insistent that the role be different from the active role given them by Aristotle. It is also possible that Plotinus is taking one of his frequent, ironic jabs at Stoics and other materialists for their rather dense accounts of sensation.

1, 23–27 *But, if the . . . not reach us*: The next question shifts from a consideration of the nature of the body between, whether transparent or opaque, to its role in the transmission of the affection. Aristotle is again the source, since he holds not only that the eye, for example, is affected by the color of the visible object, but that the color first affects the transparent body, which in turn affects the eye (*De Anima* 2.7.419a17–21). The affection is further understood as being struck on the air, like the impression of a ring, which is then propagated out. The example of someone standing between us and the object, but who sees the same object and presumably sees it first, is taken as evidence that the impression is in the air and affects that individual and only then us. This type of transmission of the affection is linear, with each section of air being impressed by the affection as it moves through it.

1, 27–34 *I answer that . . . feel the shock*: Plotinus counters with his own theory that the body between in the case of sight does not need to be affected, since the eye is naturally capable of being affected by the object directly, with the proviso that the body between may be affected differently. The burden of this treatise is to show why this is the case and Plotinus will contrast sight, where the air between does not need to be affected, with being warmed, where the air between does indeed need to be affected. Thus, one can see a fire directly without the air in between being illuminated, but to feel the warmth of the fire that air needs to be warmed first. The illustration in the present passage is the shock received from a torpedo fish, which the hand feels but not the rod in between. The rod serves as a conductor but is itself not changed: it does not burst into flame or quiver in reaction, but allows the electricity to jump from the fish to the hand. The following sentence seems to backtrack a bit, stating that one cannot feel the shock without the direct contact of the rod, implying that it is affected, which Plotinus disputes by pointing out that the shock can sometimes go directly from the fish in the net to the hand. While this instance does not involve the rod, the fisherman's contact with the fish through the net seems still to hang by the thread of the line between them or perhaps by their presence together on the boat's deck. In describing the situation with this intricacy, Plotinus acknowledges that the body in between plays a role, but that role does not include the actual transmission of the affection by being similarly affected.

1, 17;22;27 I have inserted question marks in all three instances to make the questions more explicit, while suppressing the question mark in 1, 19, as the response to the first question.

1, 34–40 *In any case . . . some way itself*: The previous discussion of transmission introduces the sympathies Plotinus has discussed previously in IV.4.30–45, especially at 32, 13–25. Its plural form alludes not only to the sympathy between objects in the cosmos, but the sympathy of the cosmos itself as a living thing. Sympathy establishes the context in which the natural similarity between the object and the eye allow for their assimilation to one another, with its role emphasized by the extreme statement that, if there were no body between, the eye would be affected even more easily, the opposite of Aristotle's contention that a void between makes sight impossible (*De Anima* 2.7.419a20–21; see *Physics* 4.6–10 for Aristotle's discussion of the existence of a void and its purported role in the motion of various objects). This statement, however, is not a denial of the medium, as has been the common interpretation, but a way of emphasizing that whatever is in between need not be affected in the same way as the eye in direct relation to its object. I highlighted the twofold character of sympathy in the present passage and also argued that it does not exclude a medium earlier in Gurtler, 1988, 117–119, citing Bréhier, 1928, Clark, 1942, Armstrong, 1984, and Igal, 1985, who tend to exclude the medium in any sense.

Sympathy, therefore, joins with the structure of the two activities to clarify the subtlety of the arguments and their context. The series of questions with their terse responses thus has the goal of indicating why the body between does not need to be affected: it does not contribute to sight, it always hinders, and it does not transmit the affection. The transparent body, however, may be affected in another way, which may or may not be related to the source of light, and occasionally this affection may even interfere with sight. Sensation, in this preliminary discussion, is primarily about contact, and contact at a distance remains precarious and problematical.

Chapter 2

The chapter begins with a brief review of the account of seeing in the *Timaeus*, turning from the Aristotelian transparent body to the Platonic light between eye and body. For Plato, the eye has its own visual ray of light that flows out and joins the daylight to go straight to the object. This combined ray of light is then modified by the light from the body, and returns to the eye. At this point, Plotinus argues that this theory does not need a body between. He then mentions two theories, one Stoic, where sight is caused by impact, and the other Epicurean, where images pass through the void, which give stark alternatives for understanding the transmission of the affection. Before examining these theories in detail, the discussion returns to an analysis of sympathy. Reminding us that a dissimilar body hinders sight at least minimally, he argues that a similar body, as being affected, interferes completely with sight by establishing a continuous body between the organ and the object. The situation is like setting a log on fire: the surface is burned, but not the interior of the log. This lack of continuity for sight raises a dilemma for understanding the nature of sympathy, since sympathy is posited on the continuity of all bodies in the cosmos, but in the case of sensation, that continuity is denied in terms of the dissimilarity of the intervening body that falls between the eye and the object. Plotinus then distinguishes the essential continuity of the cosmos from the accidental continuity of sensory affection. In the case of the visual ray, if the air in between were continuous, there would be an interaction of the air and the ray, a reciprocal replacement by the air to help propel the beam in its trajectory. Plotinus points out that this is not how air functions in relation to certain bodies. A stone, where the element earth dominates, is not propelled by a reciprocal replacement in the air when it moves downward to its natural place, but passes through the air merely by dividing it. Fire with its upward motion is similarly not enhanced by the less quick motion of the air and thus also passes through it without a reciprocal replacement on the part of the air. The next two examples turn to living things, the upward growth of trees, which depends on the tree and not external things pushing it, and our lateral movement through air, which is not advanced by the air moving around us. If these bodies can pass through air without its assistance, the forms in the visual ray can even more easily pass through air without affecting it. Finally, if the air needed to be affected first, we would not see the distant object but the affection in the air nearby, just as in the case of warmth coming from the fire. But vision is not like touch, so when the object is placed on the eye it cannot be seen. The explanation is not that the air is potentially transparent and light actualizes it, but rather that air is essentially dark, so that vision depends on light as an activity that needs only to travel through the air without essentially changing it.

2, 1–11 *If then seeing . . . light flows straight*: The Platonic theory of vision receives attention next and is summarized extensively in these initial lines. The background consists both of the general account of sensation in the *Theaetetus* and the specific account of vision in the *Timaeus*. At *Theaetetus* 156d–e and 182a–e, Plato describes sensation as two quick motions taking place between two slow motions. The slow motions are the animal and the object, each producing one of the quick motions, the one through a specific sense organ and the other by one of the particular qualities of the object. These two quick motions together constitute the sensation, which is infallible at the precise moment it takes place. At *Timaeus* 45b–d and 67c–68d, the quick motions of seeing are analyzed. The motion from the eye is the visual ray (*opsis*; see L-S II.e, for this meaning, with reference to *Timaeus* 45b, 46c) that is an attenuated fire that does not burn. When daylight surrounds the eye, this internal light flows out, joining the daylight and moving straight to the object. There is a third kind of light in the object that allows it to be seen, modifying the beam of light from the eye, which delivers the result to the soul (see Archer-Hind, 1888, 156–157). Plotinus' brief summary follows this account very closely. He begins with the visual ray (*opsis*) flowing out from the eye and joining with the light surrounding it. This joint light goes directly to the object and is the quick motion between the eye and the object, as the Platonic theory requires. The colored object underlying the act of sight emits its quick motion that modifies the light beam from the eye. Since it is this modified beam that constitutes sight, Plotinus asks whether there is any need in this theory for a transparent body between them in addition to these motions that together and simultaneously constitute the act of seeing. His answer is that those who hold that visual rays (*opseis*) flow out do not in fact need such a body between to guide the visual ray, but they may have posited it for extrinsic reasons, like keeping the beam of light from falling, an unnecessary concern given that light from the eye flows straight to the object.

2, 11–12 *Those who allege . . . a body between*: This brief mention of the Stoic view, that the cause of sight is the impact (*enstasis*) on the object by the light, implies the need for some kind of body, which the Stoics describe as a sort of cone of illuminated air between the eye and the object, functioning like a cane between the two. While this merits no further attention here, it returns in the following chapters where the Platonic account of sight is examined in terms of reciprocal replacement (*antiperistasis*) at 2, 33–45, and of the soul using light like a cane at 4, 39–61. In these instances, Plotinus resists assimilating sight to touch, using the Stoic account to criticize possible misinterpretations or weaknesses of the Platonic theory in the *Timaeus*.

2, 12–15 *The champions of images . . . dispute the hypothesis*: This strangely favorable comment about the Epicurean thesis that images (*eidōla*) move through a void emphasizes Plotinus' position, mentioned at the end of 1, 38–39, that having nothing in between captures his denial of any positive role to a transparent body between the object and the eye. It also looks forward to his use of the void in 6, 3 and 15, where he discusses the relation of light and air, and of *eidōla* at 7, 44–49, under the formality of reflections in a mirror that indicate how the activity of the reflected object is present in the mirror without affecting the air or space in between. This Epicurean account thus functions to sustain his disagreement with Aristotle on the role of the transparent body and to clarify the nature of the Platonic visual ray and its content.

2, 15–21 *Those who say . . . than the surface*: The Platonic theory is now interpreted in terms of sympathy, with Plotinus first reminding us that the body between, presumably transparent, continues to hinder, impede, and weaken the sympathy. He then adds that if the body between were actually similar to the organ and the sense object, that kindred nature would weaken the sympathy completely since it establishes a continuity in which the affection necessarily has to modify everything in its path. He illustrates this with a body continuous in depth, like a log. When this log is set afire, the surface burns immediately but the fire may not reach to the interior of the log at all. The continuous nature of bodies and their interference with sympathy presents a problem that Plotinus needs to address so that the operation of sympathy can be understood correctly. The dilemma is that sympathy assumes the continuity of all the bodies in the cosmos, but that a sympathetic affection between two bodies includes both their similarity to one another and their dissimilarity from the body between them. The dissimilar body thus needs to be discontinuous, and his task is to explain how this is possible.

2, 21–33 *But if the parts . . . in between anywhere*: The explanation of sympathy depends on the analogy of a living thing, as we have seen in IV.4.32. Parts of an animal are in sympathy, but dissimilar parts in between lessen the sympathetic affection. The degree to which these dissimilar parts lessen the sympathy is determined by the nature of the animal. Thus some parts can prevent excess, like the eyelids blocking a bright light or the hands a loud noise. Their role in preventing excess is evidence that they are not similarly affected. Moving from an animal to the cosmos as a living thing brings out Plotinus' dilemma. He is arguing that sensation is possible at a distance, because both we and those objects are in one cosmos and belong to it, a position developed in multiple ways in IV.4.30–45.

This possibility rests squarely on the continuity among the parts of the cosmos as a single living thing.

Plotinus distinguishes at this point the essential continuity of the parts of the cosmos from the accidental continuity of sympathetic affections between parts. The parts of the cosmos, all the bodies within it, have their existence as belonging to that one living thing and must necessarily be continuous with one another, including the transparent bodies between some parts and others. The sympathetic affection between two similar parts, however, is accidental. The affection does not always exist and its existence depends on the similarity of the two parts and their difference from the part in between, since the affection is an activity that flows from the one part to the other, from agent to recipient, as he argued in IV.4.32, 23–25; 35, 53–55; 41, 1–9. This affection cannot take place unless the recipient is in tune with the agent. All these factors indicate the accidental character of the affection. Taking the affection as if it were essential is to assert that everything is affected by everything and a transparent body between becomes impossible, or superfluous. This superfluous condition actually describes the situation of the intelligible cosmos, where everything is transparent to everything else. In the sensible cosmos, by contrast, bodies in space and time are typically not transparent but dense in varying degrees, so the possibility of sensing things at a distance depends on the similarity of some parts and their difference from others, depending especially on the transparency, or lack of density, of the bodies in between.

2, 33–48 *If someone says . . . it without division*: The discussion of continuity is now applied to the case of the visual ray and the air through which it travels. Plotinus indicates that certain bodies can move through air without affecting it, since they only divide it. In the background is Plato's theory of reciprocal replacement by air to explain the motion of projectiles, objects that have more than one mover to keep them going as if in continuous motion (*Timaeus* 79b–e), a theory criticized by Aristotle because it demands that all the members of a series (the projectile and the segments of air) move and are moved simultaneously, but for a projectile only its motion needs to be explained, with the source of its motion being sufficient (*Physics* 8.10.267a12–20; see Boeri, 2003, 276). Plotinus' examples are not projectiles, but the motion of natural bodies, the downward motion of earth and the upward motion of fire, and of living things, the principle of growth in a plant and the choice of a human being. He does not comment on Aristotle's critique of Plato, but uses it for his own purposes to discount the need for the forms in visual rays to be moved by the air.

Aristotle's discussion of the void in *Physics* 4.8.214b12–215a22 provides another facet of Plotinus's argument, as it too discusses the natural motions of earth and fire in relation to a void, concluding that a void renders such motions impossible. Plotinus agrees that these motions are indeed not caused by a void, but maintains that air in fact functions like a void so that if the interval between contained nothing, or were a void, sight and other such sensations would occur more easily. A stone falling through the air, in Plotinus' scheme, is simply not supported by the air, and otherwise leaves it unaffected. The stone's downward motion is natural and does not need to be explained by the theory of reciprocal replacement, where the air displaced by a projectile moves behind it and acts to propel it. The falling stone does not need this series of additional movers. Similarly, fire naturally moves upward without needing the reciprocal replacement of the air to propel it, especially since its motion is much quicker than that of the air it would be displacing. Trees also grow upward in terms of the nutritive power within them and are not being pushed upward by anything external. When we move through air, moreover, there is no reciprocal replacement, but merely the air moving around us as we go forward. These examples give evidence that bodies of different kinds move through air without any need for the reciprocal replacement of the air to move them along. If bodies can move through air without affecting it in any way other than dividing it, then affections such as forms in the visual ray are even more capable of passing through it without modifying it, since they are not even dividing it in the way bodies do.

2, 48–61 *But if the forms . . . and of itself*: This section draws out a consequence from the previous argument: if the affection can pass through the air without affecting it, then the air does not need to be affected first and, more crucially, the affection can reach us without the air being affected at all. At this point, Plotinus introduces the difference between light and warmth. Feeling the warmth of a distant fire clearly depends on the air in between being warmed first and we actually feel the warm air nearby and not the distant fire. Seeing the distant fire, however, is not dependent on the air nearby, but comes directly and without delay, so that we are seeing the distant fire where it is. The two activities are different, one essentially dependent on changing the air from cold to warm, the other allowing the form of the object to pass through the air without effecting any change in it at all. Plotinus distinguishes these two sensory experiences in terms of touch. Seeing necessarily operates at a distance, but its knowledge is direct since it receives the form all at once as a whole. Touch, however, demands immediate contact with what is nearby, but needs memory and reasoning to yield knowledge since it receives the different qualities of the object part by part, recalling or inferring the nature of the whole (see Appendix: IV.1.1, 29–41, qualities as secondarily divisible, and 2, 11–19, sensing as able to unify them). In the case of seeing, placing an object on the eye, the immediate contact of touch, in fact prevents seeing. Air is then needed not as something to be affected but only to establish the distance between the eye and the object that allows for sight. Plotinus speculates on how this is the case. It is not, as in *De Anima* 2.7.419a10–13, that the air is potentially light as transparent, but rather that it is actually dark in its very essence. Light, further, as an activity overcomes this inherent darkness not by moving air from a potential to an actual state, but merely by its nature as an activity. Air, as establishing the distance between organ and quality, is thus a necessary condition for sight, but light, by overcoming the darkness of air and revealing the form, is the sufficient condition. When that distance collapses by placing an object on the eye, the combined darkness of the air and the object prevent sight. The advantage of this thesis, for Plotinus, is that it accords with the experience of light, which can be seen when it is dark without illuminating the air nearby, the topic that begins the next chapter.

Chapter 3

This section reviews many of the same issues, but draws out different aspects that build up the case Plotinus is attempting to make about the nature of sensing at a distance, especially of sight. He begins with the case of seeing objects at night—fires and stars and their particular shapes. Since these objects are seen where they are, some at great distances, and since the intervening air is dark, seeing them cannot be due to an affection of the air. That would be claiming to see the bright by means of the dim. It also cannot be due to daylight, since starlight and even fires on earth are visible at night. The body between, relative to sight, may just as well be nothing at all. To clarify, it is not so much that there is nothing in the interval, but that an actual void would destroy the sympathetic connection of a living thing toward itself and of its parts toward one another. Sensing is therefore the ability of one part to participate in the power of another, even at a distance, within the sympathy of the whole. The test of this thesis is postulated in imagining a cosmos outside this one and unrelated to it, could it be seen? The final section returns to examining evidence, the evidence of sensing itself. The thesis that a transparent body brings the affection to the eye necessarily gives the affection a corporeal character, like warmth in the air. This means that the visual ray brings only a small portion of the object to the pupil, what fits the portion of air directly connecting the two. Plotinus claims instead that the whole object is seen and all those in the surrounding air see it from every angle. This holistic kind of affection cannot be due to the body, but to the necessities of the soul of the cosmos as a single living thing.

3, 1–15 *The clearest evidence . . . nothing in between*: Seeing lights in the darkness of night seems obvious, but giving it an adequate account escapes Plato and Aristotle. In *Timaeus* 45d, Plato holds that the absence of the surrounding daylight causes the cessation of seeing and encourages sleep. The overt target, at least for now, continues to be the Aristotelian thesis that the transparent air is activated by light, and sight occurs as the affection moves through this activated body of air, whether during the day or at night (*De Anima* 2.7.419a23–25). At night, however, the transparent body is not activated, so seeing fires and stars and their shapes tells against the theory, since the transparent air should not be able to transmit them to the eye in its darkened state, even for someone holding that theory. Instead, Plotinus argues, fire in illuminating its form takes away the darkness from this form, but not from the air. The argument then makes explicit that this is not just about heavenly bodies that are by their nature composed of fire, but that even fires here on earth obviously can be seen in their own form, the particular shape and color of the flame, and further they can be seen even when the stars are not visible and thus cannot illuminate the sky, as is evident in the light from beacons and lighthouses on the darkest of nights. This point also counts against the

Platonic claim that sight is the joining of the light of the eye with daylight. Plotinus is for the moment not disputing that the light of the eye joins with the light outside it, but expands that outside light to include starlight as well as the light of more modest fires here on earth. At the same time, he is arguing against the possibility that the transparent air is actualized by starlight or the light of fires. If someone insisted that the illuminated form in the visual ray reaches the eye because of the air, this is claiming that perception is caused by the dimness of the air and not by the brightness of the fire. Plotinus observes, building on his previous thesis that air is essentially dark, that the air in between remains dark and that the fire is seen from afar without illuminating the intervening air, as if nothing were in between, the very thing Aristotle sought to avoid.

3, 15–26 *But one might . . . will discuss later*: This section repeats the earlier contention at 2, 15–21, that the absence of a body between eye and object is actually a denial of the sympathy of the cosmos rather than that this intermediate body is instrumental in producing the affection in the eye. That the activity of one body in the cosmos has the power to influence another at a distance depends on the fact that both are in the one living thing, which was mentioned earlier in the case of magic in IV.4.40, 14–20, where the magician can lead one individual to another because all three are parts of the one living thing. Plotinus proposes the test case here of seeing another living cosmos outside this one, but puts off examining it until later in Chapter 8. These two sections, therefore, give evidence that seeing is not dependent solely on daylight and is not based on the illumination of the body in between, but that the role of the body between is tied instead to the sympathy of the cosmos as a living thing. The last section gives further evidence for this sympathy.

3, 26–38 *Now, however, we . . . self-sympathetic living thing*: Plotinus begins by noting that if the air between were actually affected, the affection must be corporeal. The argument alludes to the example of corporeal affection already mentioned at 2, 50–55, warmth in the air. While that earlier context emphasized that this perception is by contact with the air nearby, the present context brings out other consequences of this direct contact. It is like an impression, with each part of the air receiving only part of the original object. The warmth I receive is directly related to the air between me and the fire and is necessarily different from what someone on the other side of the fire receives. The application is that the visual ray connecting the pupil and visible object has only so much of the object as bodily fits that portion of air between the pupil and the part of the object directly in line with it. It is like looking through a narrow tube, or that cone of illuminated light posited by the Stoics (cf. 2, 11–12).

In contrast, Plotinus states that the whole object is seen and all those whose vision is not blocked see it from any angle, and most importantly see the whole visible object, such as the face. Several things are packed into these few words. First, the focus has shifted from the relation of one part of the object to the pupil of one eye, to all those who can see the object from any vantage point. The visual ray is not like warmth in the air, which is a quality of the air, but, as has been stated already, it contains the form of the object. This form necessarily captures the whole object, so that it cannot be limited to any one perspective, but includes all perspectives at once. This wholeness implicitly gives sensation a social dimension, which becomes explicit when Plotinus mentions those in the surrounding air see it. Unlike feeling the warmth of a fire, where I may be warm but you are still chilly because of your location, seeing an object is something we do intrinsically together and where our positions are interchangeable. It is this shared experience that is part of the necessities of the soul: the possibility of sensation depends on the nature of the cosmos as a single living thing and the possibility of my sensation depends both on that cosmic factor and on my relation to others experiencing the same object. Our sense experience is fundamentally a social endeavor, with each of us complementing the experience of the other.

Chapter 4

This chapter turns to an analysis of how the Platonic theory works, with each of its elements receiving attention, the visual ray, the daylight in between, and the light of the object. He distinguishes first the difference between daylight and air as occurring between the eye and the object. The role of air is excluded at least for the moment, and daylight is examined as not being affected and as not a body. He then examines the visual ray, which Plato describes as ensouled in moving out to the object. Plotinus has argued that this visual ray does not need the daylight between, but an unintended consequence is that this makes seeing akin to touch, the ensouled visual ray brought into immediate contact with the object. The following sections analyze the implications of this from various points of view. First, he considers the role of the interval, having previously shown that a body in the interval hinders and interferes with sight. With the bare interval, the contact of the visual ray and the object looks like a case of touch, making the object inactive, but this is impossible. Touch and sight are then contrasted. In seeing a fire, for example, the fire is present immediately in the air and to the eye, while its warmth comes more slowly through the affected air and is perceived by touch. A solid body, blocking sight, is moreover warmer than the air and thus from contact with it we can infer the presence of a fire even though we cannot see it. Next, the roles of object and organ are reversed: the object has the power to act and the organ to be acted upon. Anything in between becomes an obstacle. Sunlight, moreover, can be seen at a distance, present to us and the air at the same time, so the air nearby does not need to be affected by it, against the theories of Plato and Aristotle alike. On the hypothesis of those theories, there is no explanation for seeing stars and fires at night. The Stoic theory that in seeing the soul remains inside and light is used like a cane allows Plotinus to examine more fully the nature of touch, with the touches of the cane involving a prior state that is immediate before this touching can be used by memory and reasoning to provide knowledge. Thus touch is indirect and not immediate, while sight is immediate and direct, so light does not function like a cane, even in the ensouled version of Plato, but seeing is direct and immediate.

4, 1–10 *But how is . . . will consider later*: The opening words of this chapter duplicate the opening of Chapter 2, with one small addition: how? Plotinus is moving gradually to indicate the limitations of the Platonic account and replace it with his own. The first problem analyzed is the nature of what is between the eye and the object, air and light. He summarizes the results of previous arguments, that the transparent body between, in this case air, is at most accidentally affected (2, 8–9; 15–21; 46–53; and 3, 1–4). The task now is to examine the role of light in this Platonic theory, which involves three separate elements, the visual ray going out from the eye, the daylight occuring between the eye and the object, and the light of the object that modifies this visual ray. Air has been eliminated from the role of carrying the visual ray at 2, 8–10, on the grounds that visual rays do not need to be supported by such a body but flow straight to the object. Plotinus then adds that he will examine another argument for the necessity of air for the presence of light later, in Chapter 6. The argument resumes with the statement that the ensouled visual ray does not need the daylight between to see. This refers to the sun's light, which is not affected in the Platonic theory but acts as the light between the eye and the object that allows the visual ray to move out and be modified by the light from the object. This light is not between as a body since light is not a body, but merely as allowing the visual ray to see at a distance. At this point, Plotinus does not mention that he has already qualified the role of daylight by analyzing seeing at night, where the light from stars or fires allows for the activity of the visual ray or, perhaps better phrased, allows for sight.

4, 10–17 *Now, however, we . . . there [at the object]*: These lines capture the sense of *Timaeus* 64d that the visual ray is an extension of the body out to the object, and is thus ensouled as if a part of the body (see Archer-Hind, 1888, 156 and 237). This ensouled visual ray does not need the light between, daylight, to perceive, and leads Plotinus to draw the inference that this turns seeing into a form of touch, with the visual ray in direct contact with the body and with daylight not being affected at all. Given his resistance to understanding sight as a form of touch, the next sections subject this Platonic theory to a more thorough examination, especially where it seems to confound seeing with touch.

4, 17–22 *We need to ask . . . this is impossible*: Since seeing is by definition at a distance, there has to be something in between, with the alternatives here denoted as an interval or as a body in the interval. If the body in the interval is carrying the visual ray, it would be easier if that body were removed, so the visual ray can fulfil its function directly, repeating the argument already made at 2, 8–10 and subsequent places where the role of the body in between has been shown to be more a hindrance than a help. The empty interval remains the only alternative and the visual ray, according to this theory, moves through it to the object. Plotinus interjects the claim that this takes the object as idle or doing nothing. It is the ray that goes to it, and sight is accomplished when the ray reaches the object. This is not what the theory of *Timaeus* or *Theaetetus* actually state, even in his own summary earlier at 2, 1–10, so Plotinus is shifting here to a critique of that theory based on his own understanding of the role of daylight and analyzing the role of the visual ray in terms of that change, which implies that its contact with the visible object is beginning to look a lot like touch. His critique, ironically, seems based on the Peripatetic theory of sensation that the action of the agent occurs in the patient, where the agent is the object sensed producing the sensation in the animal and its organ (*De Anima* 3.2.426a). This background explains why he says that it is impossible for the object to be idle and do nothing and why the subsequent analysis ends up reversing the initial, Platonic movement of this chapter that goes from the eye to the object.

4, 22–38 *Touch, in fact . . . on this hypothesis*: Even touch, however, is more complicated, giving more information than merely the proximity of the object; Plotinus in fact turns the tables and takes touch as more like and even dependent on sight, so that, if it could function with nothing in the interval separating it from the object, touch would also sense it at a distance. The argument begins, however, with a couple of comparisons that seek to indicate the contrast between sight and touch. First, sight is contrasted with feeling warmth, already noted at 2, 53–56. Plotinus' statement is strangely phrased: we and the air in between sense the fire together. This implies that the visual ray is not going out to the fire, but the fire is somehow already present in the air and in the eye before its warmth can be felt by touch in that nearby air. Second, the solid body of 2, 19–20 (and 5, 19–22) returns. In that earlier context, it was used to indicate that the interval cannot be a solid body, since its continuity would interfere with seeing, paralleling the way its continuous mass blocks the transmission of a fire from the surface to the interior. In the present context, however, a solid body in the interval, is used to make a different point, since it can become much warmer than the air, so that we can infer the fire that warms it even though we do not see the fire because that body is effectively blocking our vision. Disparate points are being made. In the first comparison, sight takes place directly and immediately, whereas touch is indirect and takes time as the warmth travels through the intervening air and changes it. In the second, the solid body blocks the visual form of the fire, but its warmth serves to indicate the presence of the fire more definitively than the warmth in the surrounding air. In both cases, Plotinus is showing that the activity of the object is crucial for sensing in general and seeing in particular. Seeing thus cannot be understood solely in terms of the visual ray going out from the eye to the object, but it and the senses generally are acted on by the object. Looking at sensation from the direction of the object, he thus concludes that, if the object is already active and the organ ready to be acted on, there is no need for something else in the middle to act on the organ, if the object is within the range of the visual ray.

Finally, sunlight comes to us and the air around us together, and this includes the case where we can see sunlight at a distant point on the horizon, even though it is not near the visual ray and thus cannot activate it according to the Platonic theory. That is, sunlight is not in this case joined to the visual ray, but we actually see it and the object it is illuminating at a distance. The point is repeated, perhaps with a nod toward the Aristotelian theory as well, that the air is not affected; the transparent air in between has not been illuminated or moved from potentiality to fully active exercise. Thus, the role of the sunlight in either theory has not taken place and nonetheless we see. Plotinus now adds the conclusion from 3, 1–15, that the hypothesis that sight depends on sunlight, however differently it operates according to each theory, cannot explain seeing stars and fires at night. Finally, while this has analyzed the nature of sight in contrast to touch, the complication of touch itself has not yet been delineated.

4, 27–28 *A solid body . . . not through it*: This sentence has been consistently translated in such a way that the solid body is immediately dropped, with air replacing it in the second half of the sentence. The result is that the solid body is left dangling, with no role in the argument, or is identified with our body (Armstrong, 1984, 297n1), losing the thrust of the argument. Maintaining the solid body as governing the whole sentence allows for the contrast to emerge between air and the solid body in relation to sight and touch. First, we see the object immediately through the air, even before it has been warmed. Second, if a solid body is between us and the fire, that body is warmed more than the air would be, so we can infer the presence of fire on account of it, but we cannot see the fire through it. This contrast between the immediate character of sight and the inferential nature of touch continues in the following section.

4, 38–49 *If the soul . . . in other places*: The last section deals with the alternative hypothesis, not that the soul moves out through the visual ray, but that the soul remains in itself and uses light like a cane to reach the object, the Stoic view alluded to at 2, 11–12. This theory changes seeing into a violent act, where the light strikes the object and the color of the object pushes back, the way a cane acts through the medium of air, for example, detecting aspects of the surface by its thrusts and the different kinds of resistance it encounters. The next lines, with their enigmatic "at first" and "later," seem explainable on the analogy of how a cane is used by the blind. To be able to use a cane later to navigate a particular route with its different surfaces, there needs to be an earlier experience more direct and not dependent on the cane, perhaps especially with a guide having sight assisting the blind individual. The cane can then by used, with its touches or tappings, to remind one of the route, where the walkway ends and the street or grass begin, and to deduce which way to turn when one has reached a particular surface or to calculate how much farther one has to travel. Seeing does not function in this indirect way, relying on memory or reasoning, but on the direct apprehension of the object's form. The final lines draw the application of this analysis for the ensouled visual ray as the light going out to the object: if it needs to be affected when directed toward the object, that affection will then need to be brought back to the eye, but that involves severing the affection from the sense object, so one is not sensing the object but only the affection in the visual ray. This takes the ensouled visual ray as functioning like touch, with the need for memory and reasoning to infer the relation of this affection to the object, the very hypothesis already disproved that the air transmits the affection at 3, 26–38. In conclusion, the arguments and analogies of this chapter show the direct and immediate character of sight and the indirect character of touch, with the involvement of memory and reasoning to function. Plotinus has further indicated, consequently, that the Aristotelian and Platonic accounts, and even less the Stoic account, are not equipped to explain adequately how vision takes place, since they all seem to involve some mediating element which from Plotinus' point of view inevitably reduces sight to a form of touch.

Chapter 5

This chapter takes up the problem of hearing with three questions. Does the object making the sound affect the air near it and then affect the air all the way to the ear? Is the air in between affected only accidentally, with the sound going directly from the striking of the two bodies to the ear? Is the air struck first and the struck air then affects the ear? It is this last view that Plotinus criticizes, since it makes the sound dependent on the air itself rather than on the two bodies that strike each other. Since the air is one body and the strike one action, this theory does not explain differences in voices and sounds, which do not depend on the air (or the strike) but on the kind of objects struck. While air and the striking of objects can explain differences in volume, other differences are not reducible to them, but to the different qualities of the objects striking against one another. Air can be responsible for sound, however, when it takes the condition of a solid body, against which something is struck. Generally, the striking together of two bodies is sufficient to explain the production of sound and the internal sounds of animals, such as the grinding of teeth and of bones, are clearly produced in the absence of air. These brief comments show the similarity of sight and hearing, where the affection is related to the kind of consciousness within a living thing.

5, 1–4 *About hearing, do . . . arrives at sensation*: When Plotinus finally turns his attention to hearing, brought up at 1, 15–16, he presents three views in succession, beginning with Aristotle's view that air is the body between that is affected by the object making the sound, and this motion affects the adjacent air until it reaches the ear, causing sensation. The two alternatives that follow are in fact different ways of understanding how the air is affected, whether accidentally, as Plotinus wants to argue, or as that which is actually responsible for hearing, as the Stoics held.

5, 5–8 *Or: is the [air] . . . reaches us immediately*: Plotinus' account takes the air as affected only accidentally, since it is in the middle, and if the air were not there, the sound of the two bodies striking against one another would immediately produce sensation in us, the same explanation he gave for sight. The sticking point for Plotinus is that each hearer hears the whole sound, not part of it, so the sound cannot be parceled out like warmth from a fire any more than sight could be parceled out in that fashion. This empasis on wholeness is key to understanding his position and his use of Aristotle in the attack on the Stoic account of sound.

5, 8–10 *Or: is the first . . . already [struck] differently*: This Stoic view presents two moments for sound, as described by Igal, 1984, 463n31. First, there is the moment when the sounding object strikes the air and, second, when the struck air is moved in waves and concentric circles to bring the sound within it to the ear. Plotinus spends most of the rest of the chapter attacking this Stoic theory, since it radically separates the sound we hear from its source.

5, 10–18 *In this view . . . also sound differently*: Aristotle, *De Anima* 2.8.419b19, postulates that air and water are not responsible for sound, which is due instead to the two bodies striking together. The Stoic view, however, as Plotinus reports, traces the sound not just to the two bodies clashing together but the effect of that clash on the air, striking it and forcing it out rapidly. In the Stoic theory it is this strike on the air that then strikes the subsequent portion of air until the sound reaches the ear. This is parallel to their theory about sight, with its cone of illuminated air between the eye and the object, while here the sound moves within waves and concentric circles from the objects clashing together to the ear. It is noteworthy that these Stoic theories take sight as moving from the eye out to the object, but sound as moving from the objects to the ear. The first bit of evidence Plotinus raises against this Stoic thesis is that if the striking is simply air moving, this account will have difficulty explaining the differences in voices and sounds, such as bronze having a different sound when it strikes against bronze as opposed to some other object. Brisson, 2005, 277n49, notes that the distinction between voice and sound can be found in Plato's *Timaeus* 67b–c and Aristotle's *De Anima* 2.8.420a20–b16, 2.11.422b29–31.

5, 18–27 *The air, however . . . no air between*: While voices and sounds are different, the air and the striking are one. Plotinus follows Aristotle, *De Anima* 2.8.419b21–22, in holding that a strike on the air makes a sound only when the air is in a solid condition, against which the strike hits both quickly and forcefully, so that the air stands fast before flowing, as in the cracking of a whip. Ordinarily however the striking of the bodies against one another is sufficient to produce the sound that is heard by the ear. The second bit of evidence against the Stoic theory is the internal sounds of animals, like the grinding of teeth or bones. These sounds are produced where there is no air, but where one body is striking or moving against another.

5, 28–31 *Let us conclude . . . within a living thing*: He concludes that this examination of hearing has established its similarity to sight, as summarized at the end of 3, 26–38, where sight is not due to the air being affected corporeally, but to the higher necessities of soul in the sympathy of a single living thing, described here as a certain consciousness in a living thing. As I argued in Gurtler, 1988, 49–84, *synaisthēsis* is a companion term to sympathy, but emphasizes the internal unity of the subject, particularly the unity-in-itself of an unparticipated source and two unities dependent on it, a united whole and the individual unities within that whole. In the present context, the living thing as the cosmic soul is the united whole that provides for the individual unities within it. In the present treatise, sympathy exhibits the external unity of the sensible cosmos available to sight, while *synaisthēsis* expresses the more personal context of hearing, particularly of the words of others through which consciousness is possible at the human level. Hearing in this chapter alludes in fact to different kinds of sounds, voices and sounds in general, and thus divides into hearing noises and listening to a voice, where the attention is directed not only to the sounds but to the speaker and the meaning or communication intended. At the end of Chapter 3, a similar pattern of common experience was pointed out, but centered more on a common perception of the object, open as well to other animals. Here, however, Plotinus alludes very briefly to a higher kind of common experience particular to human beings as bringing in the other kind of soul they possess (cf. IV.4.45, 10–26).

This higher kind of experience receives more complete articulation in other treatises where the parallel between sight and hearing is more fully developed, especially VI.4.12, 1–20 and III.8.9, 26–29. In VI.4.12, for example, Plotinus presents analogies for the soul in certain activities that are everywhere as a whole, such as hearing and seeing. Thus a word spoken in the air is received entirely by the ear, and if there is another ear in between, that will hear the whole word as well, like seeing the whole face in Chapter 3, 35–37. Hearing and sight are used in VI.4.12 as analogies for the soul's presence as a whole throughout the body, illustrating not only its unity of form but its presence as a unified activity. Sound, especially in words or music, is an activity that derives directly from the activity of the soul in the body, the ground of the analogy. In III.8.9, 26–29, he uses a voice present everywhere and as a whole in any empty space to illustrate the nature of the One as present to the intelligible world and also to each sensible thing as a whole, where it is present to each individual at the same time both as a whole and yet not as a whole in the sense that no part contains it completely and exclusively. Although sound has a preeminence in those two treatises, sight is more central in the present treatise, where the whole object is contained in sight in 3, 32–38 and where light is defined as an activity of a luminous body in 6, 13–23.

Plotinus' discussion of music is also relevant for understanding the nature of sound. In IV.4.40, 20–26, discussed above, music affects the lower soul, emphasizing its corporeal nature as sound, the context of the present chapter as well. In I.6.3, I.3.1–3, and III.6.4, 43–52, by contrast, the rational form present in music highlights its mathematical nature and its role in provoking the ascent of the soul. Music thus has two activities associated with it, a lower one related to the body and a higher one related to the soul, much like the two activities in IV.5 associated with fire, warmth as corporeal and light as incorporeal. Finally, understanding the affection not corporeally but as presenting the whole sound to each hearer is the basis for Plotinus' agreement with the Aristotelian account of sound that hinges on the accidental character of the affection in the air, which keeps the sound related directly to the bodies that are striking one another as their activity.

Chapter 6

This chapter returns to the problem of light and air. Plotinus proposes the thesis that light can occur without air, if for instance there were a void between the sun and bodily surfaces. The objection compares the effect of light to that of other affections, which do depend on the air being affected. Plotinus answers that light belongs to fiery, shiny bodies, and not to air. The objection then claims that even the color of these bodies needs to pass through air. Plotinus answers with an analysis of activity and contrasts this with qualities belonging to bodies. The activity can go from its source to the object without the need for a body in between, whether air or something else. Light as an activity thus does not need to be carried by a body to its object nor does it need to be drawn out or forced to come, but moves down by its own nature. The alternative would mean that the illumination would belong to the body illuminated, and not to the source of light. The evidence, however, supports the notion that the illumination depends on the position of the source which determines the comings and goings of the light. The sun as a source of light is then analyzed as the cause of light as a second and external activity, so that the sun remains the substrate of light in the sense that light is completely dependent on it, with the consequence that the illuminated body cannot be the substrate of light in any sense. This relationship is like that of soul and body, the activity of life coming out of the soul and enlivening the body, but not changing the soul at all, where life remains even when a body is not enlivened. There are two final points about the illumination of air before turning to an examination of the nature of light in Chapter 7. First, air can only darken the light, given its earthy nature. As essentially dark, the best thing for air is to get out of the way. Second, whatever affection light produces comes from it, and so color is due to light, with air an inactive bystander.

6, 1–4 *Could light occur . . . it is there*: Plotinus returns here to the question posed at 4, 9–10 about the possibility of light occuring in the absence of air. The problem is not that the air remains unaffected, which has already been demonstrated at 3, 26–38, but that if a void were between the light and the object, illustrated by the case of the sun shining on the surface of bodies, a void as such cannot support or carry the light. Plotinus is invoking here the Epicurean account of vision mentioned at 2, 12–15, where their use of the void indicates that vision as the transmission of images (*eidōla*) is not dependent on affecting the intervening space or body at all, but moves directly from the source of light to the object. The presence of a void rather than air thus emphasizes that the distance or interval between the light and the object may be affected or illuminated accidentally, solely as the space between them, since a void makes clear that the requisite distance or interval has no active role in the transmission of the light, despite any accidental affection it may suffer. He also argued earlier that illuminated objects can be seen at a distance even though the air between is not illuminated. There is thus a two-pronged attack, that the air between cannot be affected, for example, at night when the air is dark and that a void between could not transmit the affection even if it were affected in some other way, combining to eliminate any active role for air, or other transparent bodies, in the transmission of light.

6, 4–7 *On the contrary . . . affected also exists*: The contrary theory states that if the affection of other things is due to air, and light is essentially due to air, then no such affection is possible if there is no air in which light can be an affection. One other affection that is due to air has been mentioned in previous discussion, warmth in the air. Perhaps one could add other qualities as well, a smell or a chill, the wet or the dry, for example; all these seem dependent on the air for their transmission. The objection then comes to this: why is light different?

The translation follows Igal, 1985, 465, in part, but taking *di' auton* as referring to air (masculine rather than the neuter *phōs*) and *ta alla* as subject of *pathonta* (aorist accusative neuter plural); Armstrong, 1984, 301 and Brisson, 2005, 204, take light as subject of *pathonta* (as if aorist accusative singular masculine, but again *phōs* is neuter), and they insert "light" with the "other things," understood as other transparent bodies, but it is easier to take them as bodies affected in diverse ways.

6, 7–10 *I say, first . . . a luminous color*: Plotinus' response is that light is not primarily an affection of air nor is it essentially related to air, but it is due to fiery and shiny bodies, including stones that have a luminous nature. These stones stand in contrast to other objects that are merely colored over by the presence of light, as described later at 7, 38–41, because they are themselves sources of color and are not merely colored by light in the air. More than likely he is referring to birthstones or gemstones, crystals with distinct colors that seem to emit light as well as receive it. They have associations with the zodiac, and thus also fall under the sympathetic magic that Plotinus analyzed in IV.4.38–42. In brief, Plotinus is arguing here that instances of color dependent on light are not like other qualities.

6, 10–11 *On the contrary . . . without that [air]*: The objection continues by pointing out that the light associated with these luminous objects and their specific colors cannot pass from them to another, to the seer, without the presence of air as the body between them, arguing once more that the presence of air is not merely accidental but essential for sight.

6, 11–22 *I say, if . . . back at another*: Plotinus now moves to explicate his own theory of the nature of light. He begins by examining the nature of a quality, which is always in some substrate or body. The relation of a quality to the body in which it inheres has been investigated in VI.4.1–2, where he sees qualities as possessed by certain bodies, the form of the quality distributed piecemeal in the body and not having any independent existence. If light were a quality in this sense, the task would be to determine what body it is in, with the limitations that implies. He proposes instead to take light as an activity of one body that is present in or to another, with no body in between the two but rather a kind of void, if a void were possible. The activity of the first body jumps over the void and is present in the body beyond the void. This is the thesis that he wants to investigate.

First, he considers whether this light needs anything to carry it from the one to the other. He argues that light by its nature moves straight, which seems the assumption of Plato's *Timaeus*, where light from the eye moves straight to the object. The light from the sun, however, not only moves straight but down, falling to the earth. As related to fire, one might expect light only to go upward, but it is an activity of a fiery body with its own distinct motion. If it moves downward, then, it must do so by moving itself down, as neither air nor an illuminated object is drawing or forcing it down. Thus it is not a quality, an accident possessed by the object, nor an affection, equally dependent on the affected object. A sign of this is that light does not effect anything permanent in the body illuminated, but can come at one instant and go at the next. All of this is designed to show that light, in illuminating an object, retains its complete independence from that object as well as its total dependence on its source.

6, 23 *Where then is it*: The question could be a further objection, or posed by Plotinus to indicate the shift in his argument from the object illuminated to its source.

6, 23–31 *I say, it . . . a kind of activity*: The light of the sun needs only a place to be, as coming from the sun. If it were detached from the sun in some way, the element fire composing the body of the sun would lose its own activity, which is just this light. This detached light would then belong to nothing; neither to the sun, to the void between, nor to the body that is illuminated. From this point until the end of Chapter 7, the nature of light as an activity is examined in detail. To begin, activity is from some substrate, but not into another substrate. The use of the Aristotelian *hupokeimenon* is deliberate. This term is used to explain change, the move from potentiality to actuality, where it serves as the substrate in which change takes place, allowing for the replacement of one form by another. This is not the kind of change envisioned here, where the activity remains attached to its "substrate," the sun, and does not enter the other "substrate," the illuminated object. This activity always has its source as its substrate and cannot exist otherwise. It can, however, affect the other substrate somehow, if it is present to it. An example of this kind of relation is life as the activity of soul, whose presence affects a body by making it alive. This is not an example of Aristotelian change, where one thing comes to be as another ceases, but of a vertical causality, where a higher activity can affect a lower object, but remains independent, unchanged, and undiminished, like the sun in *Republic* 6.508a–509c. This section ends with the question whether light is this kind of activity.

6, 31–40 *For the illumination . . . conclude this question*: Before answering the question whether light is some kind of activity, the illumination of air is given further analysis. First, the illumination of air does not generate light. Whatever light there is comes from the source of light, for air is mixed with earth and thus can only darken the light, reiterating what has been said several times already (1, 23; 2, 15–20). Air for Plotinus is essentially dark (2, 52–61), and thus any modification it gives to the light can only darken it; the best air can do is not get in the way by remaining unaffected. Second, the affection needs to belong to what causes the affection, so color must belong to light itself, and not to air as illuminated, an insight that corresponds to modern theories of light, but without the benefit of the advances in scientific knowledge about the nature of light as refracted into the colors of the spectrum in terms of different wavelengths.

Chapter 7

The discussion continues about the relation of light to its source, with further implications about the relation of body and soul. When light leaves an object, does it perish or run back into its source? If light belonged to the recipient, one could claim that it perishes, like any other quality, but light is an activity that cannot flow away or be detached from its source. To be detached and become part of the recipient implies a transfer much more total than is contained in its mere illumination of the object. Instead, when the source shifts, the light moves with it and illumines whatever object is now in its direct path, so long as no obstacle prevents it. This would be true even if the sun were at a much vaster distance from us than it is.

Next, internal light is compared to the life of the luminous body, the source of its second, outward activity, reflecting it and not separated from it. These two acts belong to any being, and the second act as a likeness exists as long as the first act as its source continues to exist. The strength of the second act, further, depends on the nature of the being in question, some projecting quite fully, others so dimly as to be hardly noticeable. If the second act goes far out, it is simultaneously at the source and at the object illuminated. A digression follows on some of the weaker lights, the night vision of some animals and the phosphorescent character of others. These cases also conform to the theory of two acts. Next, a luminous body is of such a nature that its fiery substance allows it to produce a second act that functions like a form in relation to matter, so that light flowing from it makes a potentially illuminated object actually colored. It does this not by causing a change in the quality of the object, but colors its surface while retaining its independence of the recipient. This is due to the incorporeal nature of light, which comes from its nature as an activity, like a reflection in a mirror. When the light is directly before an object, it is illuminated, but when the source of light moves, the light moves with it, leaving the object in the dark. Finally, the soul giving life to a body has a similar structure, the higher soul as the first act, the lower soul as giving life to a body, and the image of soul as like the color on an illuminated body. Thus when the body perishes, this does not imply that the life that was in it is perishing, but that the soul is no longer present in the body.

7, 1–2 *Does light, then . . . the previous problem*: The questions pursue issues brought up in the previous chapter, whether light perishes, as a quality might when another quality takes its place, or runs back, as an activity returning to its source. Plotinus explores here more fully the nature of activity, the first activity of a being that constitutes its essence, the second activity that flows from it and is dependent on it, and now adds a third activity, which is its presence to the recipient, the color appearing on the object illuminated.

7, 2–13 *So, on the one hand . . . obstacle stood between*: This section begins with the condition under which light could perish, if it were possessed by the recipient as a quality, the assumption of the theories that Plotinus is arguing against, which hold that light is an affection of the air or of the object colored. The evidence against this assumption is the obvious fact that the illuminated color of an object does not depend on the object but on the presence of light itself from a source of light, most especially from the sun. The argument continues with the relation of light to this source. Plotinus claims that light is an activity that does not flow away from its source the way water flows out of a jug. The roots of this principle trace back to the case of the One. Nothing coming from the One can flow away from it, since if it separated itself from the One as its source it would cease to exist. At the same time such activity does not diminish the One, which always retains its own fulness, so the activity is always coming from the One, since the One always remains what it is. From Plotinus' point of view this guarantees the perpetual existence of all things. Parenthetically, he describes what would happen if the activity did flow away, pouring into the recipient much more than is needed merely to illuminate its surface. The recipient would be functioning something like a black hole, drawing within it whatever light came near it. Light, however, remains dependent on the source, so that when the source changes place, the light goes with it to whatever object is now in its path. This dependence indicates that the light, besides not perishing, does not run back to the source, but merely follows the source as its activity. The key to the presence of light depends on whether anything is hindering or blocking the path between the source and an object. When the path is clear, light goes straight to the object.

7, 13–23 *First, the activity . . . to which it extends*: These lines describe the two activities, the first activity of the luminous body within itself and the second activity that comes from it. The first activity is the essence of the source, what makes it be what it is. In the case of a luminous body, it is its fiery nature, described as its life. The second activity, by contrast, extends beyond the limits of the luminous body and is the inseparable reflection of its internal light. Plotinus indicates that this pattern is true of all beings, so that each being has a second activity that is its likeness and perdures as long as that being continues to be, with its first activity remaining within itself and the second activity projecting out, as far as its strength of being allows. This gradation of beings and of the activities that come from them is important for establishing both the difference and similarity between the sun and other luminous bodies—whether stars, fires on earth, or gemstones (cf. 6, 8–10). Some luminous bodies have a strong fiery substance and can be seen at vast distances, others are so dim as to be hardly noticeable. When a luminous body projects far out, its activity is present at the source and at the object to which it projects. The activity, moreover, does not affect what is in between. The sun, for example, illuminates the face of the moon, but it does not illumine the space on the sides of the moon, which remain dark.

7, 23–33 *In the case . . . not directed outside*: These lines are a digression on animals with night vision, projecting light from their eyes, and others that are phosphorescent, producing light from within themselves. Igal, 1985, and Brisson, 2005, list some of the animals that the ancients considered to have these qualities. Aristotle, *De Anima* 2.7.419a5, mentions the eyes of fish, and Pliny (AD 23–79),

Naturalis Historia 11.151, the eyes of cats, goats, wolves, seals, and hyenas; Pliny, *Naturalis Historia* 11.98; 18.250 also mentions fireflies or glowworms as phosphorescent. Night vision does not present a problem, since theories of light coming out from the eyes were rather common, including Plato's account of human vision in the *Timaeus*. The poor firefly, however, merits minute dissection, despite the dimness of its light and the smallness of its size. Plotinus speculates that it has fire compressed inside it, so that when the firefly expands its light shines outside and when it contracts its light is no longer outside, carefully phrasing this to conform to his theory that light as an activity cannot perish, but can only be blocked or hindered from being seen outside. The other option, that the light has run back inside, has also been eliminated as an explanation for other lights not being seen. Plotinus prefers to say that they continue to go out as the second activity, but that some other body is blocking their path to the object. To make this explanation work for the tiny firefly means that its fire sinks to its inside and the rest of its tiny body blocks the light from emerging to the outside.

7, 33–41 *Light from bodies . . . from its activity*: Plotinus returns to the two activities and adds the third activity, the color that appears on the object illuminated. He begins with the second activity as the activity of the luminous body toward the outside. The light within such bodies is defined as the substance corresponding to the form of a primarily luminous body, which means that such a body is composed of the element fire. When a body, luminous in form, is mixed with matter, something potentially illuminated, it produces color. At first glance, this seems to involve direct contact between the luminous and illuminated bodies, but the text continues with the explanation that the activity from the luminous body establishes the contact. The light, as the activity of a body different from the body that receives the color, does not produce the color simply but merely colors over its surface. The color thus retains a certain independence from the receiving body as its matter, since it comes from the activity of another body and the recipient thus remains separate from both the luminous body and its activity. These comments are designed to keep the color from becoming a quality of the recipient, in which case it would no longer depend on the light and its source, but on that recipient.

7, 41–49 *It is necessary . . . actively in it*: Plotinus describes light as totally incorporeal, even though it belongs to a body, its luminous source. As an activity, it is unlike bodies, and so presence or absence are not categories that belong to it, as was stated already at 6, 22, "at one instant it goes away, and comes back at another." The analysis of light is consistent throughout IV.5 and maintains that a body is not needed between the eye and the object, but rather light is the activity that goes from the one to the other and, even more fundamentally, light functions as an activity that is necessarily incorporeal, allowing the object to share in the luminous character of the source of light by the illumination that gives it color. This color is what allows the object to be seen and is not, as such, the particular color that may qualify the object as some kind of pigment qualitatively present in its corporeal parts. In fact, how this pigment appears depends not only on its inherent quality, but on the precise way that light illuminates the object in relation to the eye within sight of it. Plotinus illustrates this difference with the example of the reflection in a mirror, where what appears on the surface of the mirror does not change the nature of the mirror but reveals the activity of the object, especially its pattern of colors, while it is present before the mirror. When the object departs, nothing of it remains on the surface of the mirror. Light similarly washes an object with color that leaves as soon as the source of light is in another place or some object stands in the path between that source and the object. Incorporeality is then not an indication that light is some peculiar intrusion from the intelligible realm, but a precise kind of activity coming from one body and present to another, establishing a sympathetic link between them.

7, 49–63 *But also in . . . there [in that body]*: This final section compares light, and its relation both to the source and the color produced, to the soul and its various levels of activity. This analysis returns to the discussion of light and the soul in IV.4.29, which exhibits the same structure. For soul, this structure is the higher soul, the activity coming from it or the lower soul, and the image of the soul in the body; for light, there is the essentially luminous source, light as its activity, and its illumination of a body as color. Since the soul present in a body is the activity of a prior soul, this second activity remains or continues as long as that higher soul is present. The objection attempts to take the life of the body not as the second activity of the higher soul, but as the product of that second activity, like the color produced by the activity of light on the surface of an illuminated body. The surface of the body, however, is like matter, potentially colored, and actually colored when light, as the second activity, mixes with it. Similarly, the body that is made alive by the second activity of soul, the lower soul, is like matter, receiving that trace of soul as the lower soul mixes with it to make the body alive. As Igal, 1979, 315–345, and 1985, 421n160; 469n44–45, points out, this trace of soul relates to the qualified body of Aristotle, that body which is capable of receiving the lower soul to form the living thing. The discussion then shifts to the perishing of the body, where its loss of life is like the illuminated object losing its color. The higher soul, as it were, is moving away from the body, taking its second activity with it, and with no other adjacent soul able to prevent its perishing, the body is no longer alive, since its life is merely a reflection of the life appearing with the higher soul, which is no longer present to that body.

At IV.4.29, Plotinus indicated that soul gives life to body not on the analogy of warmth but of illumination. If we reflect on these three cases that have been present throughout this discussion, perhaps we can clarify what he means in the present passage more carefully. The relation of soul to body is that of an incorporeal source as well as an incorporeal second activity to a particular kind of body. Soul, thus, remains at the intelligible level, so that its second activity goes out from the intelligible and is present to a certain kind of body, making it alive. This is different from the sun, a corporeal being, that has an incorporeal second activity, the light that comes from it. The presence of soul to body is thus markedly different from the presence of light to body. In the present chapter, we have seen that light affects only the surface of the body, giving it color. In VI.4.3–8, by contrast, Plotinus argues that soul is present to the body as a whole and as permeating it completely from within. Thus the initial objection, that the life of the body is not an activity but the effect of an activity, can be traced to a confusion about this difference, since it takes life as if it were inherent in the body, like its qualities. Although life appears to be much more part of the body than the colors illuminated on its surface, Plotinus maintains that life in fact is completely independent of any body but belongs essentially to the soul.

Light, on the contrary, is incorporeal as an activity, but, as defined by its corporeal source as well as its corporeal recipient, it remains merely the link between them, a link also very clearly dependent on its corporeal source. Light thus functions fully within the sympathy of the cosmos as a single living thing and belongs to this cosmos completely, conforming to the explanation in IV.4.32, 4–13. The life of the soul, by contrast, is the lower soul as the second activity that functions in the body with a degree of autonomy that light simply does not have in coloring over the surface; the lower soul, for example, is able to act as a source of other activities, such as sensing and reasoning. Finally, warmth comes from a source that is corporeal and is also present to bodies, like light, but, unlike light, warmth is a corporeal activity. Some second activities, thus, operate corporeally, limiting them in ways that light is not, since they take time in moving from their source through the intervening body to the object. This feature of time also means that such activities can linger in the bodies they affect, in contrast to the instantaneous character of light. The perishing of life from the body seems to share this temporal characteristic, since traces of life linger in the body after the lower soul as the activity of the higher soul leaves the body—the problem addressed in the final lines of the chapter.

Chapter 8

The account of sight ends with the question of seeing a body outside this cosmos and thus outside the sympathy of this cosmos as a single living thing. Plotinus answers that sensing subjects, sensed objects, and sensations all depend on belonging to a single living thing, so if a body were external to this cosmos it could not be seen, but if it were a part of this cosmos, it would be seen immediately. The objection is then refined: it is not a part, but has all the qualities that are proper objects of the sense organs. Plotinus answers that this cannot be the case if his hypothesis is correct, and seeks to determine where the counter claim is illogical or self-contradictory. He first notes that the situation described of sense organs and their proper objects does adequately correspond to our experience here, and thus will be the basis for examining the counter-hypothesis. The premise for our experience, however, is that as an animal is self-sympathetic because it is one, so the whole cosmos and its parts are related sympathetically because they are one. The objection is further refined to attack this premise: sensation is instead due to similarities. In this case, as the sense organ shares in the likeness of the thing and thus allows the soul to perceive the object because of this likeness, so the All would perceive things like itself even if they were in some external body. Plotinus answers, however, that the likeness and similarity are due to the soul and its sympathy primordially, so that the premise of the contrary hypothesis is actually contradictory, claiming that the external body is different from and unrelated to the soul of this cosmos, and then claiming it can be perceived because they are actually alike.

8, 1–4 *But what if . . . single living thing*: The problem raised at 3, 21–25 is finally examined in this last chapter. That earlier chapter alludes to *Phaedrus* 247b7–c1, where Plato describes the ascent of the soul at its highest point where it is on the outer edge of the fixed sphere of stars and sees being itself. The modification in the objection posits instead a body (a cosmos at 3, 22), that is completely separate and thus breaks the sympathetic connection that Plotinus has argued makes sight and any other sensation possible. The question is then whether an eye looking out from this cosmos would be able to see that other body.

8, 5–7 *I answer, if . . . see [it] immediately*: Plotinus answers with a restatement of his hypothesis that the sensing subject, the sensed object, and the resulting sensation all depend on the sympathy of a single living thing. If this is the case, then if the body is outside this cosmos and thus not part of this living thing, it could not be seen. If, on the contrary, it were part of this cosmos, it is seen immediately. I follow Igal, 1985, 470n48, and Brisson, 2005,

280n89, in punctuating the text differently, moving the comma from after *aisthēta* to after *aisthēseis* in line 5 and understanding *theasaito* from line 2 as going with *ouk an*. In addition I take *tacha* in the final clause not as indicating that it is merely probable that it would be seen if it were a part of this cosmos, but that it is necessarily seen, given that nothing is hindering—the premise of 8, 2.

8, 7–9 *Even if, on . . . to its organ*: The objection continues by specifying the qualities of that body as precisely those that correspond to the sense organs of animals in this cosmos. This reformulation implies the contradiction that a sensing subject and a sensed object do not in this strange case produce the expected sensation. The assumption behind this objection will be made explicit at 8, 19–26, which bases sensation on similarities between the sense organ and the sensed quality that is its proper object.

8, 9–19 *I answer, quite . . . one living thing*: Plotinus replies again that the hypothesis of sympathy precludes sensation in this case and that the contradiction implied by sense organs not being activated by their proper objects is in fact illogical or absurd (line 13, *atopon*). His task, however, is to determine the precise source of the absurdity and thus eliminate the apparent contradiction with his own thesis. He begins by agreeing that in this cosmos, we do act and are affected in the way described, so that our sense organs are activated in the presence of their proper objects. The premise of the objection needs to be examined by referring to the arguments already presented in terms of the nature of sympathy of a single living thing, both for individual animals and for the cosmos as a whole. If that is not sufficient, further arguments may be needed.

8, 19–26 *On the contrary . . . things in itself*: This section examines the contrary position as resting on the premise that sensation is actually based on the similarities between organs and their proper objects rather than on the sympathies involved among living things within the cosmos as itself a living thing. I have made explicit that the similarities (*homoiotēta*, line 19) function as a premise directly opposed to the sympathies that Plotinus has used throughout IV.5 as the foundation of his argument, and also at IV.4.40, 14–19, where a magician can attract and bring down powers only as within this cosmos as one living thing. The subsequent analysis of perception and sensation basically repeats Plotinus' description of sensing in Chapter 1, 6–13 and 34–38, with the animal sharing in the likeness of the object through its organs that are like the qualities perceived in the object.

In the present case, so this argument goes, this cosmos as a living thing should also be able to sense things outside it if they are like the things within it. Taking this whole section as supporting the contrary theory indicates that Plotinus is acutely aware that the source of this illogical hypothesis rests on elements within his own theory of sensation. His task is to specifiy precisely where it is misusing his theory. I have in general followed the emendations of Igal, 1985, 311 and 471, thus reading *on* in line 21, "given that its organ is like it," but take lines 24–26 as drawing the conclusion of the contrary theory that the cosmos, in sensing qualities not in itself (*aisthanētai men mē tōn en hautō*, lines 23–24) and precisely as a living thing (*hē men zōon*, lines 24–25), will perceive these qualities as like the qualities in itself, with Plotinus' rejoinder only beginning with *ē* kai at line 26.

8, 26–34 *I answer, the . . . in the process*: The response begins with the counterclaim that likeness between things is due to the soul as making things alike. Thus likeness cannot be used independently of sympathy because it is rooted in sympathy by necessity. Applying this to the case at hand, Plotinus shows that this other body, as having no relation to the soul of this cosmos, cannot have qualities that are similar to or like those of this cosmos without some explanation. The counter-hypothesis, however, wants to have it both ways. The body does not come from nor is it related in any way to this cosmic soul, but nonetheless it has qualities that are similar and thus open to being sensed. The absurdity is thus spelled out in terms of the inconsistencies of the hypothesis. Plotinus, relying on the earlier formulation of the problem at 3, 21–25, makes explicit that this body must have another soul producing it, since a solitary body with all its qualities cannot exist in isolation from some cosmos and a soul capable of being its cause. By making this other soul explicit, the hypothesis makes the contradictory claims that this other soul is at the same time soul and not soul, akin and not akin, alike and not alike, relative to the soul of this cosmos, and that other soul is source of that body which the hypothesis claims also has a relation to the soul of this cosmos. The attributes of soul reveal additional contradictions, since the hypothesis claims that either soul is all and not all, since there is another soul that is not related to it, other and not other, since these souls are in one way distinct from one another and in another way similar to one another, nothing and not nothing, as not existing within the same world and yet still capable of being in the same world, and complete and not complete, since each soul is source of a whole cosmos and yet not source of that other cosmos outside it. Plotinus concludes that the hypothesis needs to be dismissed and cannot be consistently defended.

Armstrong, 1984, 315n1, claims that Plotinus' rejection of another cosmos caused by another soul fails to take into account his own position in IV.3.1–5 that the hypostasis soul is not identical with the cosmic soul, and so another soul could theoretically be the cosmic soul for another cosmos and that there could be some sympathetic relation between the two (or more) worlds. While such possible worlds are currently popular in some circles, Plotinus' logic is in this instance a little more consistent and coherent. Plotinus does entertain here the possibility of another soul with its own world, but claims that if it is really different then it cannot be perceived by this world and its soul. The sympathetic relation cannot be based on the hypostasis soul, since it is in the intelligible and thus does not provide the sympathetic link necessary for worlds that are corporeal. Sympathy, in IV.3–5, is derived from Stoic usage and maintains its Stoic roots in applying to the particular way the corporeal parts of this cosmos relate to the whole and to one another. Although sympathy for Plotinus is caused by soul, it is necessarily the cosmic soul whose presence unifies the disparate bodily parts of this cosmos and it is as ensouled that these parts can be in sympathetic relation to one another. Thus admitting the possibility of another soul causing another cosmos still faces the contradictions that sympathy only relates the members of a single cosmos to one another.

Another possible understanding of Armstrong's point is that, from the point of view of our understanding of the nature of this universe, the possibility of other worlds with living beings and even rational beings does not seem at all absurd. This admission, however, can still be accommodated by Plotinus' hypothesis, since these worlds are in fact part of one universe and therefore are open to perceiving and being perceived equally. The possibility of other worlds proceeding from the hypostasis soul, however, is harder to maintain on the basis of Plotinus' understanding of reality in its totality. The multiplication of worlds, following the logic of Armstrong, would not apply merely to cosmic souls in relation to the hypostasis soul, but of intellect itself in relation to the One, as I observed already in Gurtler, 1987, 137n17. My study of Plotinus since then has only reconfirmed the correctness of that claim, as such multiplicity would sacrifice the unity of all things coming from the One and lead to an infinity of realities atomistically isolated. This result, however, resembles all too closely Plotinus' description of the matter of the sensible world as infinite and formless. As he argues constantly in the present treatise, the world produced must be one because it derives from a single source and all its parts can exist only by being parts of this one world.

Appendix: Ennead *IV.1.1–2 and IV.2*

Introduction

These two short works both find their point of reference in a key passage from Plato's *Timaeus* about the origin and nature of soul in relation to body. The specific text is *Timaeus* 35a1–3, which reads thus: "From the undivided substance that always has the same state and in turn from that which became divided in bodies, he himself mixed together a third kind of substance from those two." Plotinus sees this as an example of Plato's enigmatic way of speaking (IV.1.2, 50–52), and these two works attempt to interpret it in terms of the nature of the soul as Plotinus understands it. Although they are brief, they interpret this Platonic text in some detail and draw out some consequences that are central to Plotinus' understanding of the nature of the sensible and intelligible worlds and how the soul is situated in relation between them and is able to know them.

Plotinus begins then in IV.1 [4] with a discussion of the primary divisibility of bodies and of the primary indivisibility of Intellect, clarifying their opposite nature in relation to unity and multiplicity. Sameness in the Intellect is identified with the absence of extension and the scattered nature of bodies, and otherness in the divisible is precisely the scattered and localized nature of bodies and their parts. In this treatise, Plotinus seems to go beyond the Platonic paradigm by introducing two secondary natures, the secondary divisibility of forms in bodies and the secondary indivisibility of soul, thus giving four rather than three kinds of substances. In fact, looked at Platonically, there are only the three kinds of substance of the *Timaeus*, the fourth kind folding in the Aristotelian distinction between substance and accidents, with these accidents having no substantial existence of their own. Seamlessly and quietly, Plotinus indicates his synthesis of Platonic and Aristotelian themes which is designed to incorporate the role of Aristotle's distinctions in his more Platonic program, but also to clarify elements in Plato left undefined, like the precise range of the forms present in the intelligible. This combination of Platonic and Aristotelian themes has the further purpose of grounding his attack on Stoic materialism, the central topic in IV.1.2, where their theory of sensation is shown to be inadequate in its two key aspects, the role of the ruling principle and of the transmission to it by other parts of the soul, such as the individual senses. His argument rests on the distinction made between the continuity of body and the unity of soul, derived from his reflection on the divisibility and indivisibility of the *Timaeus* with the one and many of the *Parmenides.* These two distinctions are crucial here, and remain central throughout his writings.

For its part, IV.1.2 draws out some of the consequences Plotinus derives from the nature of soul as combining characteristics of both indivisibility and divisibility. The central issue is the contrast between the continuity of bodies and the unity that only soul can provide in relation to them. The continuous nature of the body is the crucial distinction that negates the possibility of the Stoic theory of sensation, since the Stoics cannot establish the unity requisite for sensation. One aspect of this is the unity of the sentient animal, with the ruling principle (*to hēgemonikon*) as no more than a part of an animal's body. The other aspect is the unity of the whole cosmos by the cosmic soul bringing all the things in the sensible world together and guiding them wisely. While the distinction between the continuity of the body and the indivisible unity of soul remains fundamental in the development of Plotinus' thought, there is little hint in this short treatise of the distinction between the hypostasis Soul and this cosmic soul. To specify exactly the extent of this hint, we need to examine the accounts at IV.1 [4].1, 41–45 and at IV.2 [21], especially lines 9–11. In IV.1.1, 44, Plotinus writes that the nature coming from the primary indivisible "hastens eagerly in progress from itself to the other nature" (*proodō de tē ap' autēs epi tēn heteran speudousa phusin*) and in IV.2 he writes that soul is indivisible in the Intelligible, but "its division is departing from itself and coming to be in bodies" (*kai gar ho merismos autēs to apostēnai kai en sōmati genesthai*, 9–10). The action in both cases is a movement from soul itself toward corporeal nature, a movement that other translations have obscured.[40] From this point, IV.2 continues that "because the whole [soul] did not depart, something of soul did not come [here], a part which is not naturally divisible." The initial action suddenly takes on a meaning that points directly to the distinction between the hypostasis Soul and the cosmic soul, although in IV.2 the text speaks more generally of souls coming to bodies without losing their indivisibility. IV.1.1–2 also speaks both of souls and of that soul spread out over the largest body, but does not explicitly distinguish the cosmic soul from

40 Armstrong, 1984, 13, for example, has this other nature "pressing eagerly on in its progress from the one to the other nature" and later, 21, "its division is departing from Intellect and coming to be in a body." Igal, 1985, 287, has "a partir de aquella hacia la otra naturaleza," and, at 279, "la división del alma consiste en apartarse y encarnarse en un cuerpo." Brisson, 2005, 177, has "comme dans sa procession elle se hâte vers cette autre nature" and at 2003, 494, "La division de l'âme consiste en effet à s'éloigner et à venir dans les corps."

a higher, wholly indivisible Soul. The resistance of the translators, however, to take the movement of this nature "from itself" to the other nature is strangely problematic. It seems that they fear making this secondarily indivisible nature the source of what moves out to bodies, since, if it is distinct from the primary indivisible and these other things come from it, this implies that it does not move itself completely, but part of it remains as their source, parallel to the situation of the primary divisible itself (IV.1.1, 17–29, which these translations also tend to misrepresent). In that passage, the primary indivisible substance is described as "hovering above" all the beings from it, like the center that remains the same with radii coming out of it, the situation of the soul in IV.2. Perhaps then this text serves as the seed from which the distinction of hypostasis Soul from the cosmic soul originates, and precisely as indicating the part of soul from which other souls come, especially with the cosmic soul in first place.

Besides these substantive matters about the interpretation of the text, there are also a few editorial details that need some clarification. One is the reversal of the order of these two works in Ficino's, and subsequent modern, editions. The confusion remains in Henry and Schwyzer, although they print them in proper order. I refer to them by their present position in *Ennead* IV, but often add the chronological number to reassure the reader. The second issue goes back to Porphyry's vacillation in placing IV.2

in its current position. Igal, 1985, 277, points out that it appears in most of the codices twice, at the end of III.9 and again before IV.3, its position before Ficino's reversal. In Porphyry's lists, moreover, it appears between IV.1 [4] and IV.3 [27], and is numbered chronologically as 21. Beginning with the chronological point, IV.2 presents a brief note on *Timaeus* 35a before the long treatise, VI.4–5 [22–23], that explores in great detail the implications of *Parmenides* 131b1–2. This placement highlights the importance of these two texts and their complementary nature in Plotinus' account of the nature of soul and Intellect as many and one. In its placement before IV.3–5, "Problems concerning the Soul," we can see its role as differentiating the undescended soul from soul as descending into bodies, applying careful ontological distinctions in this psychological context.

Synopsis

Ennead IV.1

Chapter 1

1–10 References to IV.7:

1. Alternative theories of the soul: Stoic, Pythagorean, Aristotelian
2. Platonic dualism: soul as intelligible rather than sensible
3. *Timaeus* 35a, soul as the third kind of substance

10–17 Primary divisible: bodies as magnitudes and masses

17–29 Primary indivisible: intelligible substance as indivisible even in thought, analogy of center

29–41 Secondary divisible: forms possessed by bodies as qualities

41–76 Secondary indivisible: soul between primary indivisible and primary divisible not like qualities but indivisible as whole in bodies, divisible as present to bodies

Chapter 2

1–4 Soul is necessarily indivisible and divisible

4–11 (1) If only divisible:

(a) sensation in a part of the body: many souls in the body and cosmos,

11–35 (b) Stoic account of sensation: the ruling part and transmission.

35–39 (2) If only indivisible: soul at center and rest of body soulless.

39–52 (3) QED: soul is necessarily one and many, divided and undivided,

(a) soul as one and the same in many places,

(b) cosmic soul: multiple unity giving life to all and indivisible unity leading all in wisdom.

52–55 In sum, four types of substance: soul as one and many, qualities as many and one, bodies as many and Intellect as one.

Ennead IV.2

1–12 Intelligible World: true substance

Intellect: inseparable and indivisible

Soul: inseparable and indivisible, but also naturally divided in departing from itself and coming to be in bodies.

12–22 Soul as both indivisible and divisible:

part of soul remains indivisible and undescended

soul in body: both divided and indivisible, since it is present as a whole.

Translation

Ennead IV.1 [4] 1–2

1. When we studied the substance of soul, we determined that it is in no way a body,[41] and also that among incorporeal things it is not a harmony;[42] we also ruled out that it is a kind of entelechy,[43] as neither true in formulation nor clear in explaining its essence.[44] When we said, however, that it is of intelligible nature and divine provenance,[45] we were perhaps able to say something accurate about its substance.

It is, nonetheless, fitting to develop [this] further. In that context, we were defining it by distinguishing between the sensible and intelligible nature and placing the soul in the Intelligible. Now, however, assuming that it is in

41 Cf. IV.7.2–8[3].

42 Cf. IV.7.8[4].

43 Aristotle, *De Anima* 413a3–5.

44 Cf. IV.7.8[5].

45 Cf. IV.7.9–12; Plato, *Phaedrus* 230a5–6.

the | Intelligible, let us pursue its particular nature along another path.

Let us say that some things are primarily divisible and predisposed to being scattered by their very nature; these are the kinds of things of which no part is the same as another part or the whole, and a part of them has to be less than all and [less than the] whole. | These things, then, are sensible magnitudes and masses, each of which has its own place, and the same part cannot be in several places at once.

There is, however, a substance opposite to this, admitting no division whatever, both undivided and indivisible, and admitting no extension at all, not even in thought. This [substance] does not need | place nor is it generated in any one of the beings, whether as part or whole, but hovers over all beings at once, as it were, not in order that it may be found in them but because these different [beings] neither can nor want to exist without it. This substance always keeps itself exactly the same, common to all [beings] successively like the center of a circle, | from which are attached all the radii that shoot out toward the circumference and nonetheless [these radii] allow that [center] to remain in itself while they derive their origin and being from it. They thus participate in that point, which is their indivisible principle, but nevertheless, while keeping themselves attached there, they go out [from it].

Thus, there is this primarily indivisible source among Intellects and Beings, and also | that which is completely divisible among sensible things. Then, on the one hand, there is another nature adjoining the sensible, both something near it and in it, not primarily divisible, as are bodies, but nevertheless becoming divisible in bodies, so that as bodies are divided | the form in them is also divided, but it is whole in each of the divided parts, the same [form] becoming many, each of them fully separate from any other, as it becomes fully divisible. [This is the case] with colors, all qualities, and every shape: any of them can be whole in many separate things at the same time | while having no part affected in the same way that another part is affected. Thus we need to suppose that this [form] is also fully divided.

Joined with that fully indivisible nature, on the other hand, there is another substance [derived] from that and having its indivisibility from that, which nonetheless hastens eagerly in progress from itself to the other nature. | [This substance] sets itself down in the middle between the two, [between] the primary indivisible and the divisible in relation to bodies and in bodies. It is not [in bodies] the same way colors and any quality are in many places and in many bodily masses, since the [form] in each [of the masses] is not present fully in another, by however much this mass is | separate from that mass. Even in the case of one magnitude, what is the same in each part has nothing in common to be affected together, because the same form is one thing in this part and something else in that; for it is the same affection but not the same substance.

We say however that what is joined to indivisible substance is above that [bodily] nature; | it is substance but also appears in bodies, in relation to which it happens to be divided, though it was not previously affected in this way until it gave itself to bodies. It comes then to be in these bodies, and even if it comes to be in the largest and upon what is most spread out, in giving itself to the whole it does not cease to be one. It is not | one as a body is one; for a body is one by continuity, with each of its parts different from the others and in different places. Nor is it one as is a quality. But that nature which is at once divisible and indivisible, which we call soul, is not one as something continuous, having parts different from one another, but it is divisible | because it is in all the parts of the [body] in which it is, but indivisible because it is whole in all [of them together] and whole in each one distinctly.

Whoever catches sight of the greatness of soul and catches sight of its power will know how divine and wondrous is its force beyond even the forces of nature. While it has no size, | it is present to every size and is now here and again there, not moreover with something different but exactly with itself, since it is divided and not divided, or better it is not itself divided nor has it become divided, for it remains whole with itself, but is divided in relation to bodies with the proper divisibility of bodies, since they are | incapable of receiving it indivisibly. Thus, division is an affection of bodies, and not of [soul] itself.

2. It will be obvious from the following that the soul needs to have this kind of nature and it is impossible to have a soul different from this, but [soul is] neither only indivisible nor only divisible, but necessarily both in the way [defined] here.

For if it were thus [divisible] | like bodies, having one part different from another, then when one part is affected a different part would not receive sensation of the affected part, but that soul, the soul as it were of the finger, would sense the affection, as being different and on its own. Generally, there would thus be many souls inhabiting | each of us, and further not one soul [inhabiting] this All, but an infinite number of souls separate from one another.

For the [claim of] continuity is useless, if it does not bring about unity.[46] For one cannot admit what the [Stoics] say, deceiving themselves that sensations arrive at the ruling principle[47] by transmission.[48] For first, to speak of a ruling principle as part of the soul is speaking | before probing the issue. How can they possibly divide [the soul] one part from another and call one the ruling

46 Cf. *SVF* Fr. II.441; Alexander of Aphrodisias *De Mixt* 10, Suppl. Aristot II.2, 223.35.

47 *SVF* Fr. II.854 = *Dox Gr* 414.25–27.

48 Cf. Alexander of Aphrodisias *De an*, Suppl. Aristot II.1, 41.5; 63.16; cf. IV.7.7, 7.

principle? By how much or by what qualitative difference will they distinguish each of the parts [of soul], if it is one continuous mass? [Second], will it be the ruling principle alone that senses or the other parts as well?

And if it is only [the ruling principle that senses] and if [the object of sensation] | falls upon the ruling principle itself, in what place will it be located to sense the object of sensation? But if the object [falls upon] another part of the soul, as this part is not naturally adapted to sense, then it will not transmit its affection to the ruling principle, nor will there be any sensation at all. Even if the [object] falls upon the ruling principle, either it will fall upon a part of it | that is sensing, but not the rest, for that would be useless, or there will be many sensations, and they will be infinite [in number] and not all alike, since one says, "I was affected first," and another says, "I sensed another's affection." Where the affection occurred, however, each [of the parts] will be unaware except the first. Or each | part of the soul will even deceive itself into thinking that [the affection] occurred wherever it happened to be.

But if not only the ruling principle, but any part whatsoever senses, why will one [part] be the ruling principle, and another not? Or why does the sensation even need to reach that [ruling principle]? How also will it know the sensations of many senses, such as the eyes and ears, | as some single thing?

If on the contrary the soul were completely one, so that it would be completely indivisible and one in itself, completely escaping multiplicity and division, then anything soul might grasp would not be ensouled as a whole, but soul, putting itself at the center of each thing, as it were, would leave the whole mass of the living thing soulless.

It is then | necessary that soul is one and many, divided and undivided, lest we doubt the possibility that one and the same thing can be in many places. For if we do not admit this, then the nature that connects and directs all things[49] will not exist: the nature that, embracing all things together, holds and leads them | with wisdom. So, on the one hand, it is a multiplicity, seeing that it is many beings, but, on the other hand, it is one [nature], in order that its connecting power may be one: by its multiple unity it provides life to all its parts, but by its indivisible unity it leads [them] wisely. But in those things lacking wisdom, their single ruling principle imitates this [connecting power]. This indeed is the meaning of the divine enigma: | "He mixed a third kind of substance from both, from that which is indivisible and always preserves the same state and from that which becomes divisible in relation to bodies."[50]

49 Cf. Anaxagoras, Fr. B1.
50 Plato, *Timaeus* 35a1–4.

Soul is then precisely one and many; the forms in bodies are many and one; but bodies are only many and the Highest is | only one.

Ennead IV.2[21]

True substance is in the intelligible world. Intellect is the most excellent [part] of it, but souls are also there, for [it is because they are] from There [that they are] also here. That world has souls without bodies, but this one has souls that have come to be in bodies and are divided by bodies. | There, on the contrary, the whole Intellect is together, neither separated nor divided, and all souls are together in that eternal world, without spatial extension. Intellect is then always inseparable and indivisible, but, while soul is inseparable and indivisible There, it is naturally divided. For its division is departing from itself | and coming to be in bodies. It is then reasonably claimed to be "divided in relation to bodies,"[51] because it departs [from itself] and is divided in this way.

How then is it "indivisible"?

Because the whole [soul] did not depart, something of soul did not come [here], a part which is not naturally divisible. So the claim, "from the indivisible and divisible

51 Plato, *Timaeus* 35a2–3.

in relation to bodies,"[52] | is the same as the claim, that the [soul] is from above and attached There but also flows out to things here, like a line from a center. When the soul comes here with this part, it sees how by this same part it keeps the nature of the whole. For even here it is not only divisible, but also indivisible, for its divided | part is indivisibly divided. When the [soul] gives itself to the whole body, it is not divided by [giving itself] as whole to the whole [body], but is divided by being in every part.

52 Plato, *Timaeus* 35a1–3.

Commentary

Ennead IV.1[4]

Chapter 1

This brief treatise begins with a reference back to IV.7 [2], where Plotinus argues against the Stoic view that the soul is a body, the Pythagorean view that it is a harmony, and the Aristotelian view that it is an entelechy inseparable from the body. In IV.7, he placed soul with the intelligible and divine, capturing the ontological dualism of the *Phaedo* and *Phaedrus*. The path taken here depends instead on *Timaeus* 35a, dividing Plato's two kinds of being, sensible and intelligible, in two, yielding four kinds of being. He begins with the primary divisible, sensible magnitudes as bodily masses. The primary indivisible follows, as giving the nature of intelligible substance, compared to the center of a circle. Between these two extremes come secondary forms of each. The secondary divisible are forms, such as qualities and shapes, immanent in bodies. These forms are divisible in relation to bodies and thus become many, the form in one part of a body different from the same form in another part. These forms are only one and whole in themselves precisely as forms. The secondary indivisible is the soul, which is unlike immanent forms in remaining one when present to the many parts of a body, since it is present to it as a whole, or, one might say, it remains within the Intelligible while appearing in bodies. It is, therefore, neither one by continuity, like a body, nor one in form, like a quality that is possessed piecemeal by the body. The soul is divisible only insofar as it is in all the parts of the body, but remains indivisible as whole in all the parts together and in each part individually.

1, 1–7 *When we studied . . . about its substance*: Plotinus gives in these brief lines a résumé of IV.7, covering his refutations of the positions of the various schools and his presentation of the Platonic account. Bréhier, 1928, 179, set the tone in regarding IV.7 as elementary and scholastic, since Plotinus' argues against one position by using resources from another. His attack on the Stoic position, that soul is a kind of body, is the longest section, covering IV.7.2–8[3]; the Stoics remain the main target here as well, with the issue turning on their account of sensation and the unity of the soul needed to explain it. The Pythagorean harmony and the Aristotelian entelechy are both opposed at IV.7.8[4-5], since they make the soul subsequent to or dependent on the body, like the qualities discussed in the present treatise. In articulating the Platonic position, as Igal, 1985, 280, notes, Plotinus depended in IV.7 on the *Phaedo* and the *Phaedrus* to make the ontological distinction between the soul as a real substance (8^5, 46: *ontōs ousia*, *Phaedrus* 247c7), indestructible and immortal (9, 11–12: *anōlethron kai athanaton*, *Phaedo* 88b5–6), and with body coming to be and perishing but never really being (8^5, 48–49: *ginomenon kai apollumenon ontōs de oudepote on*, *Timaeus* 28a3–4). In the subsequent lines of IV.1 [4], these two kinds of being will be divided into two parts, yielding four kinds of being, an account that differs not only from IV.7 but also from IV.2 [21], where soul is intermediate between the indivisible and divisible. As the commentary progresses we can determine whether these two interpretations of *Timaeus* 35a are consistent or not.

I have translated *ousia* as "substance" throughout, after experimenting with "essence" as the alternative. This allows the discussion to feature levels of being rather than differences in definition. With "essence," some contexts clearly required substance, while substance can be used consistently without difficulty.

1, 7–10 *It is, nonetheless . . . along another path*: These lines serve as a transition to the topic of this treatise. Since IV.7 distinguished between the sensible and the intelligible,

Plotinus can now draw out some further details that go beyond that distinction and provide for the way in which soul is able to function in both realms. This development follows a different path that begins with the ontological difference in terms of the nature of the divisible and indivisible, as discussed in *Timaeus* 35a, by introducing secondary modes of each. Igal, 1985, 281, understands this as a new method, different from that of IV.7, but it seems easier to take *hodon* in line 10 as only indicating a different approach that supplements the earlier work.

1, 10–17 *Let us say . . . places at once*: Plotinus begins with the primarily divisible, which has a series of interrelated characteristics. These things are scattered, their parts are different from one another and from the whole, and so a part must be less than all the parts of the thing added together and also less than the thing as a whole. These things are thus many, both different from one another and composed of parts that are also different from one another. Next, they are referred to as magnitudes or masses, emphasizing their essentially quantitative nature, prescinding from their qualities, which will be shortly designated as secondarily divisible. Their relation to one another is thus indicated by the word "place," with each thing having its own place and each part of a thing also having its own place. Later, in the summary comment at 2, 54, they will be called bodies. Plotinus is here emphasizing the divisibility of bodies, each body distinct from others and each part from the other parts within the same body. In the later scholastic phrase, bodies consist of "parts outside of parts," denoting both their quantitative distinction and their spatial separation. See Brisson, 2000, for a discussion of mass (*ogkos*) in relation to matter (*hulē*) and body (*sōma*).

1, 17–29 *There is, however . . . out [from it]*: The primarily indivisible will have characteristics opposite to those of bodies, including qualities. As usual, Plotinus begins with the body and the sensible world as more familiar to us, and then defines the intelligible as different. As bodies were distinguished as parts different from parts and as scattered in different places, this section begins by not admitting division and extension in any way. Each of these two claims is briefly amplified, with this substance as undivided and indivisible and as having no extension even in thought. These comments set the agenda for this section, adding indivisible to being undivided, since even bodies as wholes are to that extent undivided, and excluding extension even in thought, making it different from mathematical entities that are precisely extended in thought. This account implies a different relation of whole and parts, so that the Intelligible is one and many in a way different from the way bodies or mathematical objects are many and one.

The next few lines propose that this indivisible substance does not need place nor does it come to be in beings, in contrast to a body that is situated relative to other bodies as a singular whole, with its parts similarly situated within it by place. First, these beings are not merely parts, but wholes that share in the nature of this primary substance, and, second, this substance is not whole by coming to be in them, but is described as hovering over all of them at once. This substance is then one and many at the same time, and its plurality is neither spatially distinct from its unity nor does it come to unity by becoming a particular being nor all of them together. Plotinus uses spatial imagery, hovering over them all, to argue that it is not a whole like a body composed of its parts, but is whole as independent and not as situated in or possessed by these beings. They, however, neither can nor want to exist without it; they have a dependence or derivation from this indivisible substance that is partial and whole at once and keeps them from being scattered or in any way separate from it or from one another. The last part of this section seeks to illustrate this by the geometric image of the center and circumference of a circle. Indivisible substance is like the center of a circle not as if it were a spatial location, but as keeping itself always the same. Intelligible beings, moreover, as radii shooting out from the center to the circumference, are not spatially distinct from the center, but the image attempts to show that they derive from the center as distinct from it and from one another, while the center remains itself and they remain always attached to it and always projecting from it.

This reading is radically different from Igal, 1985, 286n5–6, and Brisson, 2005, 176, 180n7, who take indivisible substance as hovering over sensible beings, as if Plotinus is here talking about these two levels of reality, the primarily indivisible in relation to the primary divisible. Igal assumes this passage is parallel to VI.5 [23] 5 and V.5 [32] 3, where the relation of Intelligible to sensible is similar to that of the One to the Intelligible, and where the image of the circle and its center and radii has the same function. It is not unusual, however, for Plotinus to use the same image with slightly different applications to suit his purposes. It thus seems more reasonable to take the present section as attempting to spell out the different nature of the primarily indivisible, with the one and many existing within Intelligible Being itself in a manner opposed to the way the many and one are present in the realm of bodies. The brief parallel at IV.2 [21], 16–17 is similarly restricted, but to Soul and the souls coming from it. Armstrong, 1984, 11, leaves the passage ambiguous, not construed to support definitively either reading.

1, 29–41 *Thus, there is . . . also fully divided*: We begin with a summary of the situation so far. The primary indivisible is in fact the source of Intellects and Beings (*tois noētois* *kai tois ousin*), confirming the interpretation of the previous lines, while the primary divisible is in turn related to sensible things. Attention then turns to what is close to and present in the sensible, but is not primarily divisible in the quantitative way of bodies, where each part is separate and distinct. This secondary divisible substance is only divisible when present in bodies, but is otherwise one. It is a form, but the kind of form that is possessed by bodies and possessed by them as many, so that it is whole in each part but not whole in the body as such. Plotinus will examine these forms again in VI.4.1, describing them as possessed by the body in belonging to and divided by its parts and thus as distinct from the way souls are present to bodies as a whole without being possessed by any particular part or by the body as a whole. As described here, these forms consist of all the qualities, like color and shape, which can be present in bodies. They are different from the quantitative and extensional aspects of bodies in their unified nature as forms. Their ontological status as secondarily divisible allows for their epistemological status as perceptible forms, achieving unity in those beings capable of sensing because of the soul present in them. It is also the part of Aristotle's hylomorphism that Plotinus accepts and carefully restricts to sensible qualities and not the relation of the human soul to the body, the point of his argument against soul as entelechy, mentioned at line 3 in reference to IV.7.8[5].

1, 41–53 *Further, joined with . . . the same substance*: Finally, Plotinus comes to the substance of soul, which is indivisible as joined with and derived from the primary indivisible, but which goes out from itself to what is divisible as body. Soul's relation to body, however, is not like that of qualities, which are not only different in different bodies but are also different in a single body, where their separation in the different parts does not give them a common affection. In a wall painted white, for example, the white in each section is separate from any other, such that the wall has no unified affection of the form of white splattered across its surface. The affection or property is the same in each, but the whiteness does not constitute a single substance but merely the juxtaposition of parts that have the same quality. Soul does not relate to the division of bodies in this way.

1, 53–66 *We say however . . . each one distinctly*: Since soul is joined to the indivisible, it retains its independence as a substance, even when it appears in bodies. It is divided in bodies accidentally, as it were, but keeps its substantial unity. In part, this means that the soul is present to body not inertly, like a quality, but actively, like a power, which is the way Plotinus will analyze this situation in VI.4.3–4, on the soul's omnipresence in the body, whether that body is as extensive as the whole cosmos or as tiny as a gnat. Its powers, moreover, may have their locus or starting point of activity in different parts of the body, but they function in union with one another and the whole, examined in IV.3.20–23, where the different senses are the basic manifestations of the soul's activity, with each sense having its proper organ, but with the whole organism receiving the sense impressions in unified fashion. In the present context, the unity of the soul is contrasted to the unity of body, which is merely continuous, or of a quality, which is one in form but divided in a body. The indivisibility of the soul allows it to appear divided in the body but this in no way compromises its indivisible wholeness, present equally to the whole body and to each part. Plotinus' understanding of the different types of unity is key for this brief treatise and fundamental for his thought in general. Physical bodies are accidentally one, since they can be divided quite easily; being continuous thus means being potentially divisible. Qualities are one in form, but are not one in the body, taking on the division of the body which possesses them; they are divided, but potentially one. Soul, by contrast, has a unity that goes beyond physical proximity, so any living thing functions as a whole and not merely as an assemblage of parts. The unity of the human soul (as well as stellar souls and the cosmic soul) is even greater as connected with the indivisible unity of Intellect itself.

1, 66–76 *Whoever catches sight . . . of [soul] itself*: These final lines reflect on the greatness of soul, of which we only have a glimpse but enough to see that it surpasses in wonder the powers of nature. Plotinus illustrates this in terms of size. The soul has no size but is nonetheless capable of being present to all kinds of things with very different sizes, even extending as a whole to the vast reaches of the cosmos. Its presence reveals at once its own singular unity, but also its ability to be divided in the different parts of the body, giving them different powers of itself while keeping all these divided powers intimately united by its own indivisibility. Plotinus uses this wonder to move to the specific topic in Chapter 2, where he uses the indivisibility of the soul to explain sensation and attack the Stoic theory as fundamentally inadequate.

1, 68–69 *Its force beyond . . . forces of nature*: I have translated *to chrēma* and *ta chrēmata* as force, which seems to capture the meaning of this elusive term in such a way as to highlight the wonder about the nature of the soul and bring out a contrast between it and other things in the sensible world.

Chapter 2

Plotinus argues that the view of soul advanced in chapter 1, as necessarily indivisible and divisible, is the only view possible in accounting for the soul's peculiar powers. Thus, if the soul were only divisible like bodies, sensation in the organism would be impossible, since sensation would occur only in the part of the organism affected, such as pain in the finger. The result would be many souls in each body and an infinite number of souls in the cosmos. He analyzes at length the alternative thesis that bodily continuity is sufficient for the nature and operation of soul, drawing out the consequences of the difference he maintains between continuity and unity. The specific case is the Stoic ruling principle (*to hēgemonoun*), which receives transmissions (*diadosei*) from the other parts of the body. As materialists, first, how can they distinguish one part of the "soul" from another? Second, what precisely is the quantitative or qualitative difference of one "part" from another? The Stoics distinguish the different senses from the ruling principle to which they report and which is the center of perception, but how do they explain how a part that does not perceive is able to transmit, merely as continuous, information to another part, the ruling principle, which is also part of the same continuous mass. He objects that if the parts, such as the organs, are themselves not adapted to sensing, there is no reason why they will transmit anything at all. Changing tack, he considers the ruling principle itself as a mass of some size, perhaps the brain, and asks what part of it is receiving the sensation, to the exclusion of the other parts, or if all the parts are receiving the sensation, then there are indeed many sensations and not just one, each claiming some relation to the sense object, as receiving its sensation first or after some other. Alternatively, each part can deceive itself into thinking it is the center of awareness. If this is the case, there is no ruling principle, but any part is equally capable of receiving the sensation. The contrary case of the soul as indivisible with no relation to division leads to a soul that would be at one point in the living thing, with the rest soulless. Thus it is necessary that soul be one and many, divided and undivided, so that it is everywhere one and the same. To deny this is to claim that the nature connecting all things does not exist. It is many because it is in many beings, giving them life, but it is also one in joining them together and leading them wisely. It is the enigmatic third kind of *Timaeus* 35a. In sum, soul is one and many, forms in bodies are many and one, but body is only many and Intellect only one.

2, 1–4 *It will be . . . way [defined] here*: This chapter indicates that the soul's nature as both divisible and indivisible is necessary from Plotinus' point of view. The discussion applies this insight in terms of the two possible cases, that soul is divisible, like bodies, or that it is only indivisible and so present to the body at a single point.

2, 4–11 *For if it . . . from one another*: Plotinus first considers the consequences of taking the soul as divisible like bodies, where each part of the body has a different soul.

Each part, such as the finger, then has its own sensation, unshared by any other part. The unity of the body thus becomes impossible; each living thing has a multitude of souls and the whole cosmos has an infinity of souls, all separate from one another. The unity of experience is precluded both on the subjective side of the individual and the objective side of the cosmos. Plotinus, as we have seen, spends IV.3–5 arguing strenuously for both of these unities, showing the centrality of this concern for the unity of soul throughout his writings. The alternative, of the soul being completely one, is not taken up until lines 35–39, while Plotinus considers briefly the Stoic account of sensation.

2, 11–19 *For the [claim of] . . . parts as well*: This section extends to 2, 35 and consists in a digression about the Stoic view, starting from the continuity, *sunecheias*, present at 1, 60–64 as the contrast between soul and body concerning divisibility and unity. Continuity is the lens Plotinus uses to analyze the Stoic theory of sensation in terms of transmission (*diadosei*) and the ruling principle (*to hēgemonoun*). Plotinus' attack is twofold, based on the continuity of parts of the body and the discontinuity of its qualities, which plays a role in his account of sensation in IV.5.2, 21–48. First, he argues that Stoic materialism entails that the soul (breath or *pneuma*) is divided, so that the ruling principle is one of these bodily parts. But if the body is one only as continuous, no bodily part is distinctive quantitatively or qualitatively from any other in such a way as to ground sensing, much less reasoning. Second, he raises the question in terms of transmission. If a sensation is a quality that is transmitted from one part to the next, the problem is whether that quality is only perceived by the ruling part or by the parts transmitting it as well. Either alternative is problematic, as the continuing analysis will indicate.

IV.7.4 discusses the nature of soul as breath (*pneuma*) in Stoic theory, with Plotinus indicating the contradictions or inconsistencies he finds in positing soul as a body in some fashion, and yet holding that this breath has intelligence and its fire is intelligence (*ennoun to pneuma kai pur noeron*, IV.7.4, 3). Breath and fire are, so to speak, refined elements, but Plotinus is not convinced that this superiority is sufficient to bring intelligence along with it. See Inwood, 1985, 27–41, for an account of the Stoic theory of rational soul, especially of the *hēgemonikon* as mind. Plotinus would not be convinced that calling it mind gives it the power to think.

2, 19–31 *And if it . . . [the affection] occurred*: The alternatives Plotinus considers are clearly indicated, by *men* at line 19, for the ruling principle alone as perceiving, and by *de* at line 31, for perception by all the parts involved in the transmission. If the ruling principle alone is what senses, and the object of sense falls upon it, its location needs to be determined. As Igal, 1985, 290n18, notes, some Stoics located the ruling principle around the heart and others in the brain, but either location needs then to be related to the distinct sense organs, if indeed these act as the origin of sensation. Plotinus continues that if sense objects fall upon other parts of the soul (such as the sense organs), since they are not what senses in the present account, they are not in a position to transmit the sensation to the ruling part, thus excluding sensation completely. If, for the sake of argument, the sensation reaches the ruling principle, the Stoics still must explain how the sensation relates to the ruling principle as itself divisible or made up of parts. His dilemma is that if it falls on one part, the other parts will not sense it, or if it falls on all the parts, there will be many sensations, not all the same. This moves the problem from the body as a whole to the ruling principle itself as made up of parts, since it too is divisible as a body. Plotinus is insistent that corporeal things simply do not have the requisite unity to explain how the sensation, as a quality, can be unified by something that itself is not unified but merely continuous.

2, 31–35 *But if not . . . as something one*: The second alternative, that any part of the body senses, is considered briefly, since the objections mentioned continue to apply in this case. He is content to list the implications: why locate the ruling principle in any particular part, why does sensation need to reach the ruling principle, and, conversely, how can the ruling principle unify sensations from the different senses. Plotinus has argued in IV.7.7 that transmission has difficulties Stoic theory cannot answer, that a pain in the toe, for example, if it needs to affect the next part and be transmitted by a number of intermediary parts to the ruling principle, ends up not being a pain in the toe but in the part next to the ruling principle. He has used the same argument in IV.5.3–5 in analyzing vision and hearing to exclude the role of the Aristotelian or Platonic medium. His consistent response is that sensation is a unity of such a type that only something already unified as a whole is capable of explaining it.

2, 35–39 *If on the . . . living thing soulless*: Plotinus leaves the digression on the Stoics and returns to consider the alternative that the soul is completely indivisible. This he argues locates the soul at a central point, but leaves the rest of the body soulless. A common illustration for this compares the soul to the pilot of a ship (Aristotle, *De Anima*, B, 1.413a9), who is able to control the ship through contact with the helm, which Plotinus examines at IV.3.21, 5–21, where he finds it indicates well the soul's separation from the body but fails to capture that the soul acts from within the body. In VI.4.7, moreover, Plotinus uses images of his own devising to illustrate different ways soul is understood to be present to body, the force in the hand present in the objects it is lifting, a small luminous mass in an opaque sphere, sunlight in the sensible world. These are like the pilot in the ship, illustrating how the activity is omnipresent in the respective objects, but remains nonetheless extrinsic to the thing. The limitations of these images is corrected in such a way that Plotinus shows that the soul's presence in the body is not at all localized, but permeates the whole body from within. Finally, all these images explain certain minimal interactions between soul and body, but they do not explain what has been central in this short treatise, the case of sensation, which is complex both for the unified qualities of the individual senses and for the unified experience that results from the combination of the different senses together, the issue examined in VI.4.6 about sensing and judging within and among individuals, the precise situation leading to these diverse images and their corrections.

2, 39–52 *It is then . . . relation to bodies*: This last section returns to a consideration of the nature of the soul, as one and many (*Parmenides* 155e5) and divisible and indivisible (*Timaeus* 35a), which Igal, 1982, 61, takes as equivalent and as central in Plotinus' understanding of the nature of soul and its relation to body. This passage begins by indicating the relation of this set of terms with soul as one and the same in many places, the topic from *Parmenides* 131b1–2 investigated in VI.4–5. Plotinus is shifting his concern from the problem of sensation in individual souls to the cosmic soul that unifies all things in the cosmos and directs them wisely. This brief excursus on the human soul and its relation to the body, especially in relation to sensation, thus takes on a deeper importance as evidence for the role of the cosmic soul in bringing all things to unity as one, continuous cosmos. Soul then must necessarily be many, the many beings of the cosmos in its rich variety and vastness, but it remains one nature, joining all things together. Plotinus specifies this in terms of the life that this multiple soul gives to all the parts of the cosmos and in terms of the wisdom manifest in the all-encompassing unity of this cosmos, themes especially examined in IV.4.30–45 above. The passage ends with the enigma from Plato's *Timaeus* of the third kind of substance, which is both indivisible and divisible, the substance of soul that Plotinus has attempted to articulate in these two chapters.

2, 48–49 *But in those . . . this [connecting power]*: The extent of the cosmic soul's reach includes even those things that do not have a life or wisdom of their own, where the unity of each of them as bodies serves as the ruling principle that imitates the cosmic soul as the ruling principle of the All, a role mentioned in II.3.13, 29; IV.4.10, 4; 16; and 42, 19. The translations of this text have not been clear. Armstrong, 1984, 19, leaves it out completely, whether by accident or design is not apparent. Igal, 1985, 291, has this unitary ruling principle imitating "intelligence," while for Brisson, 2005, there is a single principle that imitates it (*il y a un principe unique qui l'imite*). MacKenna, 1969, 259, seems to capture the sense of the text in his translation: "In the case of things not endowed with intelligence, the 'leading-principle' is their mere unity—a lower reproduction of the Soul's efficiency."

2, 52–55 *Soul is then . . . is only one*: This summation indicates briefly the thrust of Plotinus' argument. Soul is one in substance but is many in relation to bodies. The forms are many as qualities in bodies but one as the quality sensed or thought. Bodies, on the contrary, are only many, with continuity giving only a semblance of unity. Finally, Intellect is only one, with the beings within it not divided from it or from one another. Igal, 1985, 292, understands these lines as a recapitulation of the four types of substance in the treatise, while Brisson, 2005, 190n29, alludes to a dispute about their authenticity, as a gloss by Porphyry. In any case, there is nothing in them contrary to Plotinus' intent in these two chapters.

Ennead IV.2[21]

This brief note begins with the description of the intelligible world as true substance. Intellect is most excellent in contrast to souls, which are both in the intelligible world and in the sensible world. Souls in the intelligible are without bodies, but here come to be in and are divided by bodies. All beings, including souls, are together in Intellect, not divided or separated from one another. Intellect and soul are inseparable and indivisible by nature at the intelligible level, but soul can also by nature be divided, dividing first by departing from itself and then in coming to be in bodies. Departing from itself opens the soul to division, but by keeping part of itself from departing from the intelligible it is also indivisible by nature. The claims that soul is "from the indivisible and divisible in relation to bodies," from the *Timaeus*, is equivalent to the claim that soul is from Soul and remains attached to it, like lines from a center. Even the part of the soul that enters the sensible keeps the nature of the whole, so that it is also both divisible and indivisible here in relation to bodies. When the soul gives itself to the whole body, it is not divided in relation to the whole body, but is divided in the sense of being in every part.

1–12 *True substance is . . . in this way*: True substance has the Platonic meaning of indicating the difference between being and becoming (*to on kai to genomenon*), with substance or *ousia* used in reference to either, but applied in the strictest sense to the intelligible world. Plotinus then moves to the distinction between Intellect and souls, both of which are in the intelligible world, but with a similar distinction between Intellect's more absolute presence in comparison with souls, which are present without bodies in the intelligible world and come to be in bodies in the sensible world, where they are divided by those bodies. There is a nuance here slightly different from IV.1 [4], since this division is not merely about soul's presence to body but it is more explicit that souls are separate from one another and from the Soul that remains in the Intelligible. The argument then continues with a contrast between Intellect as a single whole that has neither separation nor division and souls that are together in that eternal and unchanging world in which there is no spatial extension. The manuscripts are divided between describing that world as eternal (*aiōni*) or as one (*heni*), neither of which is impossible; "eternal" does, however, receive some support as the text then describes Intellect as always inseparable and indivisible, emphasizing not its unity but its unchanging nature. Soul by contrast is only inseparable and indivisible in the Intelligible, but has a nature ripe for division, in departing from itself (*autēs to apostēnai*) and coming to be in bodies. Plotinus sees this as the claim in *Timaeus* 35a2–3, that it is "divisible in relation to bodies," repeating that this is due to its departure and subsequent division, the third kind of substance that Plato describes as between the Same and the Other, between what is undivided and what is divided as bodies. There is no mention here of the fourth kind that Plotinus inserts in IV.1, but that discussion has the additional task of countering the Stoic theory of sensation. The fourth kind introduced there is not in fact another substance, but an account of quality and thus of accidents relative, on the one hand, to bodies as divisible and, on the other hand, to living things as able to unite these qualities into unified affections for sensation and reason.

12 *How then is it "indivisible"*: This brief question turns the discussion to the continued indivisible nature of soul, both as remaining in Intellect and as present in bodies.

12–22 *Because the whole . . . in every part*: The argument here is also slightly different from the one in IV.1, 41–66, where Plotinus is more concerned with distinguishing soul's relation to bodies from that of forms as qualities of bodies. In this treatise, on the contrary, "the whole soul" (*holē*) did not depart, which is then explained rather curiously: "something of it" (*ti autēs*) did not come into the sensible world and is naturally indivisible. This refers most strictly to the hypostasis Soul, which is not the soul of any body and remains entirely in the Intelligible. This claim becomes generalized, however, in Plotinus' theory that parts of other souls, including the human soul, do not entirely descend to the sensible world. See Dillon, 2005, 339–351 for a discussion of this and its controversial status among later Neoplatonists. In the present context, this undescended soul is pressed into service to reconcile two claims, that the soul that is "from the indivisible and is divisible in relation to bodies" (*Tim* 35a1–3) is the same as the soul that "is from above and attached There but also flows out to things here." This second position is illustrated very briefly with a reference to the line from a center, the same image used in IV.1.1, 24–29 to describe the relation of the primarily indivisible substance to its content as multiple. The parallel indicates a similar unity and multiplicity in soul, with an indivisible aspect rooted in the hypostasis Soul that the many souls share in being attached to it as their center, and with a divisible aspect as they flow out to things here. The next lines elucidate how this operates in the case of a soul going out from the center. Soul comes with this part as already divided from other souls, but also with this same part it "sees" that it also keeps the nature of the whole. There is a degree of separation among souls greater than among intelligible beings, but this separation does not cut the soul off from the whole soul in its undescended aspect. The final lines confirm this by clarifying that even in relation to its division in the body, soul retains its indivisibility by being present as a whole not only to the body as a whole but also to each part of the body.

17–18 *When the soul . . . of the whole*: This text is, as Brisson, 2005, 497n8, notes, confused or corrupt; Igal, 1985, 278, also proposed some emendations. I have combined aspects of both, following Brisson in leaving *hora* as it appears, but following Igal in reading *hōs* rather than *hō* and leaving *autō tō merei*. I have attempted to show how it expresses the double purpose Plotinus has in mind in attributing to soul both divisibility and indivisibility, and how the soul itself is aware of this.

Select Bibliography

I. Ancient Authors

Boeri, Marcelo. 2003. *Aristóteles, Física Libros VII–VIII.* Tr., Intro. y Com. Buenos Aires: Editorial Biblos.

Galen. 1821–1833. *De Usu Partium Corporis Humani* (On the use of parts of the human body). Trans. & ed. by K. G. Kühn (1754–1840); for an account of the four humors: http://en.wikipedia.org/wiki/Humorism (last modified March 18, 2015).

Archer-Hind, R. D. 1888. Πλατωνος Τιμαιος *The Timaeus of Plato*, with Introduction and Notes. London: Macmillan.

Ptolemy. *Tetrabiblos*: http://en.wikipedia.org/wiki/Tetrabiblos (last modified March 4, 2015); for Ptolemaic visual: http://csep10.phys.utk.edu/astr161/lect/retrograde/aristotle.html (accessed March 25, 2015).

II. Editions and Translations of the Enneads

Armstrong, A. H. 1966–1982. *Plotinus.* Greek Text with English Translation and Introduction. (7 vols.) Cambridge, MA: Loeb.

Bréhier, E. 1924–1938. *Plotin Ennéades.* Greek Text and French Translation with Introduction and Notes. (7 vols.) Paris: Les Belles Lettres.

Brisson, Luc. 2002–2010. *Plotin Traités* 1–54. (9 vols.) Paris: GF Flammarion.

Igal, Jesús. 1982–1998. *Porfirio, Vida de Plotino, Plotino,* Enéadas *I–VI.* Madrid: Biblioteca Clásica Gredos.

MacKenna, S. 1962, *Plotinus. The Enneads.* English Translation revised by B.S. Page. London: Pantheon Books.

III. Studies on **Ennead** *IV.3–5*

Brisson, Luc. 2000. “Entre physique et métaphysique. Le terme ógkos chez Plotin, dans ses rapports avec la matière (*húlē*) et le corps (*sōma*).” Étude *sur Plotin,* ed. M. Fattal. Paris: L’Harmattan.

Brunschwig, J. 1997. “Les stoïciens.” *Philosophie grecque.* Ed. M. Canto. Paris: PUF.

Clark, G. H. 1942. “Plotinus’ Theory of Sensation.” *Philosophical Review,* 51, 357–382.

Clarke, Norris. 1952. "The Limitation of Act by Potency: Aristotelianism or Neoplatonism." *The New Scholasticism* 26, 167–194.

Cobb, H. 1936. "Consciousness and the Self in the Philosophy of Plotinus and Its Relation to Greek Thought." PhD Dissertation. Yale University.

Deck, J. N. 1967. *Nature, Contemplation and the One.* Toronto: University of Toronto Press.

Dillon, John. 2005. "Iamblichus' Criticisms of Plotinus' Doctrine of the Undescended Soul." In *Studi Sull'Anima in Plotino*, ed. Riccardo Chiardonna, Naples: Bibliopolis, 337–361.

Graeser, A. 1972. *Plotinus and the Stoics.* Leiden: E. J. Brill.

Gurtler, Gary M. 1978. "Human Consciousness and Its Intersubjective Dimension in Plotinus." PhD Dissertation. Fordham University.

———. 1988. *Plotinus: the Experience of Unity.* Bern, New York: Peter Lang Publishing Co.

———. 2002. "Providence: The Platonic Demiurge and Hellenistic Causality." In *Neoplatonism and Nature*, ed. Michael Wagner, New York: SUNY, 99–124.

———. 2003. "The Activity of Happiness in Aristotle's Ethics." *The Review of Metaphysics*, 56, 801–834.

———. 2005a. "Plotinus: Self and Consciousness." In *History of Platonism: Plato Redivivus*, ed. R. Berchman & J. Finamore. New Orleans: University Press of the South, 113–129.

———. 2005b. "Plotinus: Matter and Otherness, 'On Matter' (II 4[12])." *Epoche*, 9, 197–214.

———. 2006. "St. Paul and Plotinus: The Ontology of Evil." In *St. Paul: Between Athens and Jerusalem*, ed. J. Panteleimon Manoussakis. Athens: The American College of Greece, 57–66.

———. 2008. "Plotinus on the Soul's Omnipresence in Body." *International Journal of the Platonic Tradition*, 2, 113–127.

———. 2013. "Imitations of Beings Enter and Exit: Plotinus on Incorporeal Matter in Plato: III 6 [26] 11–15." *Philosophy Study* (ISSN 2159-5313), 3, 123–130.

Igal, Jesús. 1979. "Aristóteles y la evolución de la antropología de Plotino." *Pensamiento* 25, 315–345.

Inwood, Brad. 1985. *Ethics and Human Action in Early Stoicism*. Oxford: Clarendon Press.

Manchester, Peter. 1978. "Time and the Soul in Plotinus III, 7[45] 11." *Dionysius* 2, 101–136.

Mossé-Bastide, R.-M. 1959. *Bergson et Plotin*. Paris: Presses universitaire de France.

———. 1972. *La Pensée philosophique de Plotin*. Paris: Bordas.

Merker, A. 2003. *La visión chez Platon et Aristote*. Sankt Augustin: Academia Verlag.

Riley, Mark. 1987. "Theoretical and Practical Astrology: Ptolemy and His Colleagues." *Transactions of the American Philological Association* 117, 235–256.

Rutten, Charles. 1956. "La Doctrine des deux actes dans la philosophie de Plotin." *Revue Philosophique de la France et de l'étranger* 146, 100–106.

Schwyzer, H.-R. 1960. "'Bewusst' und 'Unbewusst' bei Plotin." In *Les Sources de Plotin*, Entretien sur l'antiquité classique, Tome V, 21–28 August 1957. Vandoeuvres-Genève: Fondation Hardt, 343–370.

Shaw, Michael. 2006. "Teleology and Nutrition in *De Anima* B.4." Paper presented at the Sixth Annual Independent Meeting of the Ancient Philosophy Society, DePaul University, Chicago, 1–20.

———. 2014. "Unqualified Generation in Aristotle's Natural Philosophy." *Proceedings of the Boston Area Colloquium in Ancient Philosophy*, Vol. 29, 77–106.

Smyth, Herbert W. 1980 [1920]. *Greek Grammar.* Cambridge, MA: Harvard University Press.

Stern-Gillet, Suzanne. 2013. "When Virtue Bids Us Abandon Life (*Ennead* VI 8 [39] 6, 14–26)." In *Plato Revived: Essays on Ancient Platonism in Honour of Dominic O'Meara*. Boston, Berlin: Walter de Gruyter, 2013.

Warren, E. 1961. "The Concept of Consciousness in the Philosophy of Plotinus." PhD Dissertation. The Johns Hopkins University.

———. 1964. "Consciousness in Plotinus." *Phronesis* 9, 83–97.

IV. General Publications

Alt, K. 1993. *Weltflucht und Weltbejahung. Zur Frage des Leib-Seele Dualismus bei Plutarch, Numenius, Plotin.* Stuttgart: Franz Steiner Verlag.

Armstrong, A. H. 1940. *The Architecture of the Intelligible Universe in the Philosophy of Plotinus.* Cambridge: Cambridge University Press.

———, ed. 1967. *The Cambridge History of Later Greek and Early Medieval Philosophy.* Cambridge: Cambridge University Press.

Arnou, R. 1968. *Le Désir de Dieu dans la philosophie de Plotin.* 2nd ed. Rome: Presses de l'Université Grégorienne.

Dillon, J. 1977/1996. *The Middle Platonists: A Study of Platonism, 80 B.C.–A.D. 220*, London: Duckworth, 1977, 1996^2.

Emilsson, E. K. 1988. *Plotinus on Sense-Perception.* Cambridge: Cambridge University Press.

———. 2007. *Plotinus on Intellect.* Oxford: The Clarendon Press.

Gatti, M. L. 1996. *Plotino e la metafisica della contemplazione*, Milan: Vita e Pensiero.

Gerson, L. P. 1994. *Plotinus*, London/New York: Routledge.

———, ed. 1996. *The Cambridge Companion to Plotinus*, Cambridge: Cambridge University Press.

———, ed. 2010. *The Cambridge History of Philosophy in Late Antiquity.* 2 vols. Cambridge: Cambridge University Press.

Gottschalk, H. B. 1980. *Heraclides of Pontus*, Oxford: Oxford University Press.

Guthrie, W. K. C. 1967–1978. *A History of Greek Philosophy*, 5 vols., Cambridge: Cambridge University Press.

Hadot, Pierre. 1993. *Plotinus on the Simplicity of Vision.* Translated by M. Chase. Chicago: Chicago University Press.

Inge, W. R. 1948. *The Philosophy of Plotinus.* 3rd ed. London: Longmans, Green.

Les Sources de Plotin, 1960. Entretiens Fondation Hardt V. Vandoeuvres-Genève.

Lloyd, Anthony C. 1990. *The Anatomy of Neoplatonism*. Oxford: Clarendon Press.

Meijer, P. A. 1992. Plotinus *on the Good or the One (Enneads VI, 9): An Analytical Commentary*, Amsterdam: J. C. Gieben.

O'Daly, G. 1973. *Plotinus' Philosophy of the Self*, Irish University Press: Shannon.

O'Meara, Dominic J., 1993. *Plotinus: an Introduction to the Enneads.* Oxford: Oxford University Press.

Pépin, J. 1958. *Mythe et allégorie: les origins grecques et les contestations judéo-chrétiennes.* Paris: Aubier.

Remes, Pauliina. 2008. *Neoplatonism.* Berkeley: University of California Press.

Rist, John M., 1967. *Plotinus: The Road to Reality.* Cambridge: Cambridge University Press.

Schniewind, Alexandrine. 2003. *L'Éthique du Sage chez Plotin.* Paris: J. Vrin.

Smith, A. 1974. *Porphyry's Place in the Neoplatonic Tradition: A Study in Post-Plotinian Neoplatonism*, The Hague: Nijhoff.

———. 1981. "Potentiality and the Problem of Plurality in the Intelligible," in *Neoplatonism and Early Christian*

Thought, eds. H. J. Blumenthal and R. A. Markus. London: Variorum, 99–107.

———. 2004. *Philosophy in Late Antiquity*. London: Routledge.

Theiler, W. 1960. "Plotin zwischen Platon und Stoa," in *Les Sources de Plotin*, Entretiens Fondation Hardt V, Vandoeuvres-Genève: Fondation Hardt, 63–103.

Wallis, R. T. 1995. *Neoplatonism*. 2nd ed. London: Duckworth.

West, M. L. 1966. *Hesiod* Theogony, *Edited with Prolegomena and Commentary*. Oxford: Clarendon Press.

Index of Ancient Authors

Index of Names and Subjects

• ALSO AVAILABLE FROM PARMENIDES PUBLISHING •

PRE-SOCRATICS

By Being, It Is: *The Thesis of Parmenides* by Néstor-Luis Cordero

Parmenides and the History of Dialectic: *Three Essays* by Scott Austin

Parmenides, Venerable and Awesome: *Proceedings of the International Symposium* edited by Néstor-Luis Cordero

The Fragments of Parmenides: *A Critical Text with Introduction and Translation, the Ancient Testimonia and a Commentary* by A. H. Coxon. Revised and Expanded Edition edited with new Translations by Richard McKirahan and a new Preface by Malcolm Schofield

The Legacy of Parmenides: *Eleatic Monism and Later Presocratic Thought* by Patricia Curd

The Route of Parmenides: *Revised and Expanded Edition, With a New Introduction, Three Supplemental Essays, and an Essay by Gregory Vlastos* by Alexander P. D. Mourelatos

To Think Like God: *Pythagoras and Parmenides. The Origins of Philosophy.* Scholarly and fully annotated edition by Arnold Hermann

The Illustrated To Think Like God: *Pythagoras and Parmenides. The Origins of Philosophy by* Arnold Hermann with over 200 full color illustrations

Presocratics and Plato: *A Festschrift in Honor of Charles Kahn* edited by Richard Patterson, Vassilis Karasmanis, and Arnold Hermann

PLATO

***A Stranger's Knowledge: Statesmanship, Philosophy, and Law in Plato's* Statesman** by Xavier Márquez

God and Forms in Plato by Richard D. Mohr

***Image and Paradigm in Plato's* Sophist** by David Ambuel

Interpreting Plato's Dialogues by J. Angelo Corlett

One Book, the Whole Universe: *Plato's* Timaeus *Today* edited by Richard D. Mohr and Barbara M. Sattler

Platonic Patterns: *A Collection of Studies* by Holger Thesleff

***Plato's Late Ontology**: A Riddle Resolved* by Kenneth M. Sayre

***Plato's* Parmenides:** *Text, Translation & Introductory Essay* by Arnold Hermann. Translation in collaboration with Sylvana Chrysakopoulou with a Foreword by Douglas Hedley

Plato's Universe by Gregory Vlastos

***The Philosopher in Plato's* Statesman** by Mitchell Miller

ARISTOTLE

Aristotle's Empiricism: Experience and Mechanics in the Fourth Century B.C. by Jean De Groot

One and Many in Aristotle's* Metaphysics—Volume I: Books Alpha-Delta* by Edward C. Halper

One and Many in Aristotle's* Metaphysics—Volume 2: The Central Books* by Edward C. Halper

Reading Aristotle:* Physics *VII.3 "What is Alteration?" *Proceedings of the International ESAP-HYELE Conference* edited by Stefano Maso, Carlo Natali, and Gerhard Seel

HELLENISTIC PHILOSOPHY

***A Life Worthy of the Gods:** The Materialist Psychology of Epicurus* by David Konstan

THE *ENNEADS* OF PLOTINUS

Translations with Introductions & Philosophical Commentaries

Series edited by John M. Dillon and Andrew Smith

Ennead IV.3–4.29: **Problems Concerning the Soul** by John M. Dillon and J. H. Blumenthal

Enneads VI.4 & VI.5: On the Presence of Being, One and the Same, Everywhere as a Whole by Eyjólfur Emilsson and Steven Strange

Ennead IV.8: On the Descent of the Soul into Bodies by Barrie Fleet

Ennead V.5: That the Intelligibles are not External to the Intellect, and on the Good by Lloyd P. Gerson

ETHICS

***Sentience and Sensibility:** A Conversation about Moral Philosophy* by Matthew R. Silliman

PHILOSOPHICAL FICTION

Pythagorean Crimes by Tefcros Michaelides

The Aristotle Quest: A Dana McCarter Trilogy. Book 1: Black Market Truth by Sharon M. Kaye

AUDIOBOOKS

The Iliad (unabridged) by Stanley Lombardo

The Odyssey (unabridged) by Stanley Lombardo

The Essential Homer by Stanley Lombardo

The Essential Iliad by Stanley Lombardo

FORTHCOMING

Plato in the Empire: Albinus, Maximus, Apuleius. *Text, Translation, and Commentary* by Ryan C. Fowler

FORTHCOMING TITLES IN THE SERIES

THE *ENNEADS* OF PLOTINUS

Translations with Introductions & Philosophical Commentaries

Series edited by John M. Dillon and Andrew Smith

Ennead I.2: On Virtues by Suzanne Stern-Gillet

Ennead I.6: On Beauty by Andrew Smith

Ennead II.4: On Matter by Anthony A. Long

Ennead II.5: On What Exists Potentially and What Actually by Cinzia Arruzza

Ennead II.9: Against the Agnostics by Sebastian Ramon Philipp Gertz

Ennead III.8: On Nature and Contemplation by George Karamanolis

Ennead IV.7: On the Immortality of the Soul by Barrie Fleet

Ennead V.1: On the Three Principial Hypostases by Eric D. Perl

Ennead V.8: On Intelligible Beauty by Andrew Smith

Ennead VI.8: On Free Will and the Will of the One by Kevin Corrigan and John D. Turner